Jesus Christ and His
REVELATION
The Centerpiece of God's Universe

COMMENTARY AND BIBLE STUDY ON
THE BOOK OF REVELATION

Ronald A. Clower

WESTBOW
P R E S S®
A DIVISION OF THOMAS NELSON
& ZONDERVAN

THE HOLY BIBLE, NEW INTERNATIONAL VERSION®, NIV® Copyright © 1973, 1978, 1984, 2011 by Biblica, Inc.® Used by permission. All rights reserved worldwide.

Scripture taken from the King James Version of the Bible.

This book is a work of non-fiction. Unless otherwise noted, the author and the publisher make no explicit guarantees as to the accuracy of the information contained in this book and in some cases, names of people and places have been altered to protect their privacy.

Literary Editor: Cheryl S. Clower
Artwork and Illustrations: Ronald A. Clower
Graphics Editor: Justin A. Clower
A Publication of CenterpieceMinistries.com

WestBow Press books may be ordered through booksellers or by contacting:

WestBow Press
A Division of Thomas Nelson & Zondervan
1663 Liberty Drive
Bloomington, IN 47403
www.westbowpress.com
1 (866) 928-1240

ISBN: 978-1-5127-7871-7 (sc)
ISBN: 978-1-5127-7870-0 (e)

Library of Congress Control Number: 2017903888

Print information available on the last page.

WestBow Press rev. date: 03/23/2017

Dedication

This book is proudly dedicated to the honor and memory of my father

John (Jack) Scott Clower, Sr.

Loving husband to our mother, Sandra for sixty-one years

Father to three boys, John Jr., Ronald, and Terry

Grandfather to six children

Great-Grandfather to five children

Our father was a selfless and generous soul, and a godly servant on many levels.
Jack Clower was a Mason and Shriner for over fifty-four years working on behalf of
Scottish Rite Hospital – Children's Healthcare of Atlanta.
Our dad was also a tireless volunteer for many other causes including:
Meals-On-Wheels, Square Foot Ministry, and various food ministries at his
home church, Inman United Methodist Church in Fayetteville, Georgia.

———————————

A portion of the proceeds from the sale of this book will go to:
Scottish Rite Hospital – Children's Healthcare of Atlanta in dad's memory.

Table of Contents

Preface

"In the beginning was the Word, and the Word was with God, and the Word was God. He [Jesus] was with God in the beginning ... The Word became flesh and made His dwelling among us. We have seen His glory, the glory of the One and only, who came from the Father, full of grace and truth" (John 1:1 – 2; 1:14). God's original desire was to live in perfect communion with mankind, the glory of His creation. In response, mankind was to worship and praise its creator and live in such a manner that glorified God's greatness. However, mankind was disobedient and that perfect communion was lost, for a time. God, gracious and loving as He is, made another way. Now, perfect communion with the Father is possible again through a personal relationship with the Son, God's only begotten Son, Jesus Christ. Hence, Jesus comforted His disciples with these simple words: "I am the way and the truth and the life. No one comes to the Father except through me" (John 14:6).

Eschatology is defined as theological doctrines associated with death, judgment, and immortality. To the layman, it is simply the study of end-time prophecies. I have read a great many publications that use these end-time prophecies as a basis for their narratives. However, all the while, I also began my own regimen of reading, researching, and studying what other theologians and authors really had to say regarding the prophecies found in the Book of Revelation.

In the Greek Dictionary of the New Testament, the word *revelation* is translated from the Greek word *apokalupsis*, which means "manifestation" or "appearing." When used as a verb, the Greek word is *apokalupto*, which means "to uncover or unveil." This word describes the progressive and immediate unveiling of the otherwise unknown and unknowable God to His church. Here, in God's last chapter of His Word, is the unveiling of His Son, Jesus Christ, in all his glory and majesty. Jesus Christ is the centerpiece of God's universe. He is the plumb line God uses to reconcile all things to Him. Jesus is our Lord and our Savior; He is our King and our Friend. The Book of Revelation is God's message to the world and His children (the church) revealing how He intends to finish out the history of mankind, as well as the fate of those who have trusted in His Son, and those who have not.

God is omniscient. Simply stated, this means that God is all-knowing (Proverbs 15:3). God is omnipotent, meaning He is all-powerful (Romans 11:36). God is also omnipresent, which simply means that God is present everywhere (Psalm 139:7 – 12). Lastly, God is sovereign. The sovereignty of God is a phrase used to express the absolute, irresistible, infinite, and unconditional exercise of God's self-will over every aspect of His creation, including the eternal destiny of mankind; and thus, nothing can interrupt it. The Book of Revelation reveals in detail the awesome prophecies describing the events leading up to and following the glorious return to earth of God's Son – our Lord and

Savior Jesus Christ – when all things in heaven, on earth, and beneath are brought under Christ's complete dominion and authority.

We will read the message of encouragement that Christ gave to His church through the visions given to the Apostle John. We will discuss the rapture of the church, when Christ calls all His children home to be with Him in heaven and how the Apostle Paul described in detail this wondrous event. We will study the dreadful Tribulation Period, the Antichrist, and the judgments levied on a rebellious and unrepentant human race. Christ will return to earth again, not as Savior, but as Warrior and Judge. We will read about His judgment, His Millennial Kingdom, the demise of Satan, and the fate of unbelievers from all ages.

The first printing of *Jesus Christ, The Centerpiece of God's Universe* in 2011 was the result of over a decade of intense study, evolving from simple journal notes into a concise verse-by-verse study of the *Revelation* of Jesus Christ. My goal was to make the study of the Book of Revelation comprehensive but not complex, thorough yet easy to follow. Bible commentary, related subject lessons, and illustrations all combine to add redundancy and visual interest to the study. In this installment, the Bible commentary remains much the same as in my original manuscript. However, new to this edition is a revised narrative, with additional details and references including new related lessons, illustrations, and frequently asked questions (FAQ) taken from the classroom; and even more, a new title. *Jesus Christ and His REVELATION* was written to appeal to all age groups, young adult through senior. Throughout the chapters reference is made to supporting verses located elsewhere in Scripture. Some of these passages are quoted in their entirety, while others are left simply in parentheses. Those references are left unquoted for the purpose of encouraging the reader to dive deeper into the Scriptures. This is why I have chosen not to include the complete Revelation Bible text in this book. Scripture segments are taken from the New International Version, unless otherwise noted. The unquoted passages can also be used, in a classroom setting, to facilitate oral class reading and participation. At the end of each chapter are "Review Questions" meant to highlight and emphasize key elements in order to build upon the reader's knowledge of the message. The "Up For Discussion" sections are optional and can be used for personal reflection or to facilitate additional classroom discussion on a deeper level. This may include relating the subject matter to current events or encouraging class members to share some of their own personal experiences.

From the moment I first affirmed my faith in Jesus Christ as a child growing up in the sixties, I have felt God's presence and knew he intended me for ministry. Over the years following the first publishing *of Jesus Christ, The Centerpiece of God's Universe,* I have had the exciting opportunity to lead many in-depth studies on the Book of Revelation at our home church, Providence United Methodist. I have also participated in and led several Disciple Bible study classes and completed leadership training in the "Alpha" program from Asbury Seminary. I currently serve as a co-facilitator in our church's adult Sunday school ministry. However, I believe my greatest calling and heartfelt commitment is to my on-line ministry and website: CenterpieceMinistries.com. It is on-line and in connection with social media, that I reach out to the world, not only to promote my books, but more importantly, to promote the gospel of Jesus Christ through the study of God's Word. The website changes monthly with new and insightful Bible commentary and guest insight. I also post my One-Year Bible Reading Calendars and every color illustration from my books for anyone to copy and use in their personal or group Bible study at no charge (copyrights apply).

I have grown closer to the Lord with every exercise, but nothing compares to the lesson I learned while working one weekend alongside the Reverend Dan McFarland on an Emmaus Walk. Throughout the weekend I was literally amazed at his knowledge of the Scriptures and how he could quote, by verse, a passage from the Bible that related to whatever it was we were discussing at the time. I asked how he had memorized the Scriptures so well. His reply was simply, "I read the Bible through every year, and I have been doing that for over thirty years." He then gave me a copy of his Bible Reading Calendar. Ever since that day in 2004, I have made it a priority in my life to spend time every day reading God's Word. I have just recently completed my twelfth year of reading the Holy Scriptures cover to cover. I thank Reverend McFarland for his gift and inspiration, and there is nothing greater that I could recommend to anyone than to spend time everyday reading and dwelling on God's Word. I have included a copy of Reverend McFarland's Bible Reading Calendar at the end of chapter 10 to encourage you to start your own tradition of reading God's Word daily. I promise you God will honor that commitment in your life. You will come to realize that the Holy Scriptures and the prophecies included, from the early chapters of Genesis to the last chapter of the Revelation, all point to our Messiah and Lord Jesus Christ.

The Book of Revelation is the unveiling of Jesus Christ, "The Centerpiece of God's Universe." Amen. Come Lord Jesus.

Introduction

The subject of this book is very important to recognize, and it is emphasized in the very first sentence of the first chapter, "The revelation of Jesus Christ ...." The Lamb is the center around which everything in this book revolves. The Lamb is the Lord Jesus Christ, and our generation has more reason to believe Jesus could return for His children (the church) during our lifetime than any generation in the almost 2,000 years of church history. This removal of the church from the earth, often referred to as the rapture, puts into motion a string of prophetic events that are foretold in this book. Our Lord Jesus Christ, referred to as the Lamb, directs all these events from heaven while using various figures, both good and evil, to accomplish His plan and purpose on earth.

There are a number of exciting and unique reasons for studying the Book of Revelation:

1) Though some prophecy is mentioned in the gospels and letters, Revelation is the only complete book of prophecy, containing both prophetic and apocalyptic (end-times) writings, to be found in the New Testament. In contrast, there are seventeen in the Old Testament.

2) A special blessing is promised to those who read this book. This book opens and closes with a blessing for those who read it and keep the message dear to their hearts.

3) Revelation is not a "sealed" book of prophecy. The Prophet Daniel was told to seal his book "until the time of the end" (Daniel 12:9) because it concerned a distant future time. We will consider Daniel's prophecy later in chapter 5. John, on the other hand, is told: "Do not seal up the words of the prophecy of this book, because the time is near" (Revelation 22:10). The Book of Revelation reveals God's ultimate and wonderful plan for the future.

4) Revelation gives clearer detail concerning biblical prophecy than any other book in the Bible. All prophecies originating elsewhere in the Scriptures find their conclusion in the Book of Revelation. For example, John describes the dreadful events of the Tribulation Period, the rise and fall of Antichrist, the glorious return of our Lord and Savior Jesus Christ, the establishment of His earthly kingdom, the demise of Satan, and the Holy City that Christ is preparing for His saints, to name just a few.

5) The Book of Revelation completes the cycle of biblical truths – Genesis gives us the beginning and Revelation gives us the end.

Contrast between the Books of Genesis and Revelation

In Genesis, we see mankind's beginning and how he communed with God in a paradise called Eden (Genesis 2:8; 3:8). Revelation details the beautiful paradise yet to come where mankind will again commune intimately with God (Revelation 21:10 – 22:5).

In Genesis, the darkness was called night and the waters called seas (Genesis 1:4; 1:10). Revelation describes the new heaven and the new earth as having no more night and no longer any sea (Revelation 21:1, 25).

Genesis shows how mankind lost a chance to eat from the tree of life (Genesis 3:22 – 23). Revelation tells us that God's children will one day eat fruit from that tree (Revelation 22:1 – 2).

Genesis introduces the serpent (Satan) as the deceiver of mankind and pronounces his fate (Genesis 3:1 – 15). Revelation details Satan's last rebellion and his final judgment (Revelation 20:10).

Genesis tells of mankind's first rebellion against God (Genesis 3 – 4). Revelation promises an end to all rebellion against God (Revelation 20:10; 21:8).

In Genesis, we see mankind's first temptation from Satan in his attempt to discredit the Word of God (Genesis 3:1 – 5). In Revelation, God gives a dire warning to all who deliberately seek to manipulate His written Word (Revelation 22:18 – 19).

In Genesis, man's sin resulted in the curse (Genesis 3:15 – 18). Revelation promises, "No longer will there be any curse" (Revelation 22:3).

Genesis chronicles the first death (Genesis 4:8). Revelation promises "There will be no more death" (Revelation 21:4).

Suggestions for Studying this Book

1) Follow the golden rule of interpretation of Bible prophecy: When the plain sense of Scripture makes common sense, then seek no other sense. Let's take every word at its usual and literal meaning unless the facts of the immediate text clearly indicate otherwise.
2) Locate the scene of activity. Keep in mind whether the scene under discussion takes place in heaven or on earth.
3) For the most part, Revelation unfolds chronologically. But rather than looking at it chronologically, let's approach this study in a logical order because some chapters represent an interlude in the chronology. These chapters will introduce elements or events that further on in the book, will be recounted with added detail. The Holy Spirit has used this method throughout the Scriptures to convey God's truths. For example, we have the giving of the Mosaic Law in Exodus and then in Deuteronomy the interpretation of the Law with greater detail added. Also, in the New Testament, we find not only one but four gospel records because it takes four to give the many sides of the glorious person of Jesus Christ.

Author and Date of Revelation

All indications point to the writing of the Book of Revelation by the Apostle John (the writer of the Gospel of John and the Epistles of John) while imprisoned on the Isle of Patmos during the reign of the Roman Emperor Domitian (A.D. 81 – 96). Evidence has been discovered confirming that Patmos and surrounding islands were used to incarcerate prisoners of Rome during that period of history. That would make the writing of Revelation in and around the traditionally accepted date of A.D. 95, near the very end of John's life.

As a result of his excessive cruelty, the Emperor Domitian was assassinated in A.D. 96 by a conspiracy led by his own wife. Subsequently, the senate later annulled his acts and this allowed John to return to Ephesus under Emperor Nerva. Tradition has it that John lived until the time of Emperor Trajan (whose reign began in A.D. 98), sixty-eight years after the resurrection of Jesus. John founded and built churches throughout Asia Minor. During his last days John appointed bishops in the new Christian community. John died a natural death and was buried in Ephesus. Polycarp and Papias were his disciples. The historian and biblical scholar Eusebius confirmed the location of the tomb of St. John by his quotation from the Epistle of Polycarp (the Bishop of the Church of Ephesus) which read: "John that rested on the bosom of our Lord … he also rests at Ephesus."

A story was told and handed down that John, as an old man in Ephesus, had to be carried to the church in the arms of his disciples. At these meetings he was accustomed to say no more than, "Little children, love one another!" After a time his disciples, wearied at always hearing the same words, asked their leader, "Master, why do you always say this?" John replied, "It is the Lord's command. And if this alone be done, it is enough!"

One final legend concerning John's death tells how Christ, along with all the other apostles, visited him and said: "Come, my beloved one, and join me and all the other brethren of thine at my table; the time has finally come to do so … the Sunday next, thou wilt come to stay henceforth with me."

As the story is told, the following Sunday, St. John preached the gospel of Jesus Christ as was his normal custom, and afterward, informed his disciples of his appointed time. St. John then entered the cave of his church whereupon an intense light shone, preventing his disciples from proceeding farther. When the light had diminished, John also had vanished. This legend was further confirmed when the opening of St. John's tomb during the reign of Constantine resulted in no body or relics found within. St. John is the only apostle and saint whose body is not claimed by anyone or anywhere.

John outlived all the other apostles; thereby making this unique revelation of Jesus Christ and the wonderful prophetic plan God has for all of His children a fitting closure for the entire volume of the sixty-six books of God's revelation to mankind.

Israel Becomes a Nation
Ezekiel Lesson

Throughout the Old Testament there are prophecies of a final return of the Jewish exiles to the Promised Land in the latter days. The prophet Ezekiel, like Daniel, was carried off to Babylon as a captive. Also, like Daniel, he was aware from the prophecies of Jeremiah that the captivity in Babylon would last seventy years. When the Lord appeared to Ezekiel in a vision, he gave him the prophecy we find in Ezekiel 4:3 – 6:

"Then lie on your left side and put the sins of the house of Israel upon yourself. You are to bear their sins for the number of days you lie on your side. I have assigned you the same number of days as the years of their sins. So for 390 days you will bear the sin of the house of Israel. After you have finished this, lie down again, this time on your right side, and bear the sin of the house of Judah. I have assigned you forty days, a day for each year."

This prophecy makes it clear that each day represents one biblical year. Ezekiel was told Israel would be punished for 390 plus forty years. In Jeremiah (25:11) the prophet writes: "This whole country will become a desolate wasteland, and these nations will serve the king of Babylon seventy years." As prophesied by Jeremiah, at the end of seventy years of captivity in Babylon, during the spring of 536 B.C. and under the decree of the Persian King Cyrus a small remnant of the house of Judah returned to Jerusalem to begin the rebuilding of the temple. However, the vast majority of Jews were content to remain in the pagan Persian Empire as colonists. From the total prophesied punishment of 430 years for Israel and Judah's sin (390 years + 40 years = 430 years), deducting the seventy years of Babylonian captivity which ended in 536 B.C., there remains a total of 360 years of further punishment beyond the year 536 B.C.

The Lord warned Israel regarding disobedience with these words: "If after all this you will not listen to me, I will punish you for your sins seven times over" (Leviticus 26:18). Remember that only a remnant returned to Jerusalem while the majority of the Jews remained in Persia. In other words, if Israel did not repent (which the majority did not), then the punishment already promised would be prolonged or multiplied seven times:

$360 \text{ years} \times 7 = 2,520 \text{ biblical years}$. Next, we convert the years to days.
God's Word is consistent; thus our prophetical chronology should use a thirty-day month:
$30 \text{ days} \times 12 \text{ months} = 360 \text{ days}$
$2,520 \text{ biblical years} \times 360 \text{ days} = 907,200 \text{ days of further punishment}$.

Next, we must convert this figure to our present day calendar by dividing 365.25 into 907,200 days. We reach a total of 2,483.8 calendar years of further punishment remaining for Israel. Now we can start our calculation from 536 B.C., keeping in mind there is only one year between 1 B.C. and A.D. 1 (because there is no year zero). This puts the end of Israel's worldwide captivity at 1948!

On May 15, 1948, the Jews proclaimed Israel as an independent state. As an old Jewish rabbi blew on the traditional shofar, the Jewish people celebrated the end of their worldwide dispersion and captivity at the exact time prophesied over twenty-five hundred years earlier by the prophet Ezekiel. This all means that despite the apparent anarchy of the events of our time, God is still in full control of worldwide events and the universe is unfolding precisely as our Lord ordained millennia ago. This revelation regarding Israel's rebirth in 1948 renews our interest in the words of our Lord Jesus Christ taken from His Olivet Discourse: "Now learn this lesson from the fig tree: As soon as its twigs get tender and its leaves come out, you know that summer is near. Even so, when you see all these things, you know that it is near, right at the door. I tell you the truth; this generation will certainly not pass away until all these things have happened" (Matthew 24:32 – 34).

The fig tree (Israel) has put forth its leaves (been reborn). It is our generation that has witnessed the miracle of Israel's rebirth from "the valley which was full of dry bones" as described by the prophet (Ezekiel 37:1). The Bible defines a generation as a hundred years (Genesis 15:13 – 16). A generation was also defined as the age of a man when his first son was born, and in the case of Abraham (and Sarah), the father of the nation of Israel, that also was a hundred years. Thus, we have more reason then any generation before to believe we are living in the "latter days" or end-times.

So what did our Lord Jesus Christ preach in his last sermon to his disciples? It was not love, or family, or the importance of the church. Jesus made preparedness the theme of that last sermon. His message tells of the wise and foolish servant. The wise one was ready for the return of the master where the foolish one was not. His message tells about the ten bridesmaids. Five were wise and ready when the groom came, and the other five were foolish and at the corner store looking for more oil. His message tells of the three servants and the bags of gold. Two of the servants put the money to work and made more money for their master while the third hid his money in a hole. The first two were ready and rewarded when the master returned. The third servant was unprepared and punished.

"Be ready" was the theme of Jesus' last sermon, and so in the words of our Lord: "Therefore keep watch, because you do not know on what day your Lord will come" (Matthew 24:42). Therefore brothers and sisters, let us join with the Apostle John in his closing prayer found in Revelation (22:20): "He who testifies to these things says, 'Yes, I am coming soon.' Amen. Come, Lord Jesus."

One Day is with the Lord as a Thousand Years

Our Lord Jesus Christ taught the apostles for three years before His crucifixion and for forty days following His resurrection. During this time, He opened the Scriptures to His disciples concerning prophecies about Himself (Luke 24:25 – 27, 45). As a result of this time of training, the Apostle Peter discussed the Lord's second coming, knowing that this event was far into the future, he wrote the following: "First of all, you must understand that in the last days scoffers will come, scoffing and following their own evil desires. They will say, "Where is this 'coming' he promised? Ever since our fathers died, everything goes on as it has since the beginning of creation" (2 Peter 3:3 – 4).

Peter then explained to the church that there was one particular fact regarding this apparent delay of the "last days" of which we should be aware: "But do not forget this one thing, dear friends: With the Lord a day is like a thousand years, and a thousand years are like a day. The Lord is not slow in keeping His promise, as some understand slowness. He is patient with you, not wanting anyone to perish, but everyone to come to repentance" (2 Peter 3:8 – 9). The "day" he spoke of referred to the days of the creation week, as a microcosm of the seven days of the great Sabbath Week of God's historic dealing with His creation – mankind. Just as the creation and replenishing of the earth took six days and then God rested on the seventh day; accordingly, there would be 6,000 years and then the great Sabbath rest of 1,000 years. This is the "millennium" as described in Hebrews (4:4, 7 – 9) and Revelation chapter 20.

The psalmist referred to the same symbolic time scale when he wrote: "For a thousand years in your sight are like a day that has just gone by, or like a watch in the night" (Psalm 90:4).

The Scriptures do not give any date for determining when the universe was originally created. However, the chronology of the Old Testament suggests that the time of the creation of man, Adam and Eve, occurred approximately 4,000 B.C. In 1650, Archbishop Ussher wrote a volume titled *The Chronology on the Old and New Testament*, wherein he calculated back from the birth of Christ, based on the dates and chronological data given in Scriptures, and arrived at the date of 4,004 B.C. as the year of Adam's creation.

Early church commentators, including Methodius, Bishop of Tyre, point out that the reason Adam died at the age of 930 years (Genesis 5:5) and did not live past 1,000 years was because God had prophesied so: "But you must not eat from the tree of the knowledge of good and evil, for when you eat of it you will surely die" (Genesis 2:17). Therefore, since a day equals 1,000 years in God's sight, Adam had to die before the day (1,000 years) was completed.

Other ancient writings include those by Rabbi Elias, who lived 200 years before Christ. He wrote, "The world endures 6,000 years: 2,000 before the law, 2,000 under the law, and 2,000 under Messiah." The Christian scholar Lartantius (A.D. 300) held a similar view. In the seventh volume of his *Book of Divine Institutions*, he wrote the following: "Because all the works of God were finished in six days, it is necessary that the world should remain in this state six ages that is 6,000 years. Because having finished the works He rested on the seventh day and blessed it; it is necessary that at the end of the 6,000th year all unrighteousness should be abolished out of the earth and justice should reign for a 1,000 years."

Considering all of the above, we might look for the beginning of the seventh day (the Millennium – the 1,000 years of peace described in Revelation 20:2 – 6) to commence at some point in our generation – 2,000 years following the birth of Christ. It is unfortunate, but perhaps providential, that changes in the calendar make it impossible to calculate with precision when the 2,000-year period will end, except to note that it could likely occur during our generation.

In regard to the foregoing interpretation, it is important to remember these are only interpretations and time will prove whether or not they are accurate. In addition, if these interpretations of the beginning of the Millennium are correct, the time of the rapture of the church still cannot be determined. The time of the rapture is known only by God.

Let us be mindful of the words of our Lord Jesus Christ: "No one knows about that day or hour, not even the angels in heaven, nor the Son, but only the Father. As it was in the days of Noah, so it will be at the coming of the Son of Man. For in the days before the flood, people were eating and drinking, marrying and giving in marriage, up to the day Noah entered the ark; and they knew nothing about what would happen until the flood came and took them all away. That is how it will be at the coming of the Son of Man. Two men will be in the field; one will be taken and the other left. Two women will be grinding with a hand mill; one will be taken and the other left. Therefore, keep watch, because you do not know on what day your Lord will come. But understand this: If the owner of the house had known at what time of night the thief was coming, he would have kept watch and would not have let his house be broken into. So you also must be ready, because the Son of Man will come at an hour when you do not expect him" (Matthew 24:36 – 44).

Chapter 1

1:1: The word *revelation* is translated from the Greek word *apokalupsis*, which means "appearing." When used as a verb, the Greek word is *apokalupto*, which means "to uncover or unveil" such as the unveiling of a piece of artwork for example. In this case, "the revelation" is the unveiling of Jesus Christ in all His glory and majesty.

In this opening verse of the first chapter, we also see the first of many angels portrayed throughout the Book of Revelation. Angels are servants sent by God to accomplish His purpose on earth.

1:2: The Apostle John is the eyewitness to the visions of the Revelation, and he will testify to them. The Word of God refers to the fact that the revelations shown to John are indeed divinely inspired. The "testimony of Jesus Christ" is the eternal gospel. We will see this phrase used later in this book.

1:3: "Blessed is the one who reads the words of this prophecy …." The word *blessing* means to declare or wish God's favor and goodness upon others. Taken from the Greek and used throughout Scripture, the word blessing is similar in meaning to the word "happy." As you know, true happiness is not found in the things of this world but in the things that come from God. Therefore, this book is a source of happiness (or blessing) to "those who hear it and take to heart what is written in it, because the time is near."

1:4: "Grace and peace," are both generated from God, not human beings. One's relationship to God determines one's possession of grace and peace. This verse shows that the Trinity shares in the dispensing of grace and peace: God the Father, God the Son, and God the Spirt. The number seven denotes perfection or completeness. The expression "seven spirits" does not mean seven Holy Spirits but the seven ministries of the Holy Spirit as referred to by the prophet in Isaiah 11:2. They are as follows:

1) The Spirit of the Lord.
2) The Spirit of wisdom.
3) The Spirit of understanding.
4) The Spirit of counsel.
5) The Spirit of power.
6) The Spirit of knowledge.
7) The Spirit of the fear of the Lord, which according to Proverbs 1:7 "is the beginning of knowledge."

1:5 – 6: These verses describe six of the seven titles given to our Lord Jesus Christ describing His works – past, present, and future:

1) The "faithful witness." We cannot always trust in man, but the witness of Jesus Christ for the Word of God is trustworthy and true.
2) The "firstborn from the dead." Jesus is the first and only one to return from the dead in a glorified body. All believers likewise will follow Him in resurrection one day.
3) The "ruler of the kings of the earth" refers to His ultimate kingship and rule during the Millennium (Revelation 20).
4) "Him who loves us" refers to His present works and should melt our fears of the Book of Revelation. His love for us endures forever (Psalm 136)!
5) "Him who … freed us from our sins by his blood." The blood is important. The Scriptures tell us that there is no forgiveness without the shedding of blood (Hebrews 9:22). Christ shed His blood and died for the sins of all mankind, once and for all.
6) He has "made us to be a kingdom and priests to serve his God and Father." This refers to our future position to rule alongside our Lord during the Millennium.

1:7 – 8: These verses describe the seventh title of Jesus Christ: "I am the Alpha and the Omega … the Almighty." To Him is all glory and dominion forever! The Prophet Daniel was given a similar vision (Daniel 7:13 – 14). Here we see the first of many descriptions of Jesus Christ in the glory and majesty befitting His person and nature. In our Lord's first coming, He was despised and rejected by men. In His second coming, our Lord will be worshipped by those who have trusted in Him and feared by those who had rejected Him, for He will come "with power and great glory" (Luke 21:27). Recall the angelic messenger's proclamation: "This same Jesus, who has been taken from you into heaven, will come back in the same way you have seen him go into heaven" (Acts 1:11). This can only mean that Jesus will return visibly to the earth. Jesus Himself told His disciples: "They will see the Son of Man coming on the clouds of the sky, with power and great glory" (Matthew 24:30).

Do not lose sight of the fact that Revelation presents Jesus Christ in His glory as Judge of all the earth.

The subject of this book is the person of Jesus Christ. If the Book of Revelation teaches us nothing else, it teaches us that Jesus Christ is coming again, not as Savior but as Judge, and the basis of His judgment will be whether or not people have put their faith and trust in Him as Lord and Savior. For a list of scriptural references for Christ's return, see the illustration entitled, "Two Phases of the Second Coming of Christ," at the end of chapter 5.

1:9: John is going through suffering as a member of the early church that was persecuted miserably by the emperors of Rome, who had already claimed the lives of James, Peter, and Paul and probably most of the other apostles. The "kingdom" here is the spiritual kingdom that Jesus set up on the day of Pentecost. It is in operation today and can be entered into only by being born again (John 3:3 – 7). The "patient endurance" is seen in our faithfully enduring the trials of this fallen world until Christ comes at the end of the age.

There are at least seven reasons why early Christians were persecuted by Rome:

1) They were revolutionary in their faith; their focus was evangelical and mission-based.
2) They required complete obedience to Jesus Christ as their Lord and King, not to Caesar.

3) They refused to bow down before idols.
4) They were looked upon as cannibals because they met in secret, and it was heard that they "ate flesh and drank blood" during their worship service (referring of course to the sacrament of communion, which is the Lord's Supper).
5) They offended those who made their living fabricating and selling idols.
6) They usually recruited from the poor and slaves and were therefore looked down upon.
7) They refused emperor worship. Domitian, for example, would sign his decree as "Lord and God."

1:10: "On the Lord's Day I was in the Spirit." The Holy Spirit was moving upon John and giving him a vivid vision. The Lord's Day is a reference to Sunday, the day our Lord Jesus Christ rose from the grave. This is the reason Christians worship on Sunday. The reference to "a loud voice like a trumpet" is similar to that described in verse 15 below.

1:11: John is told by our Lord Jesus Christ to write what he sees and send it to the "seven churches." Obviously, these were literal churches with which the apostle was familiar. However, some prophecy scholars suggest that, according to history, these seven churches parallel seven periods or stages of evolution of the church.

1:12: The "seven golden lampstands" are a fitting symbol. While in this world, Jesus said, "I am the light of the world" (John 8:12); however, He told His disciples, "You are the light of the world" (Matthew 5:14) speaking forward to the age of the church. The lampstands are defined in verse 20 as seven churches. Jesus is the head of the church made up of individual believers. He is walking in the midst of the churches, both then and now. He is also judging the churches – He pours His Holy Spirit (fuel) into them and He wants them to give out the Word of God (light) to the world.

Ten Characteristics of the Glorified Christ

1) Verse 13: "Someone 'like a son of man'" indicates that He was human in appearance.
2) "Dressed in a robe reaching down to his feet." This was typical of the robe of the high priests as they ministered in the Holy Place in the temple. Two of the duties of the high priest were to tend to the lampstand in the temple and to intercede for the people before God. Jesus Christ is now our High Priest.
3) "With a golden sash around his chest" refers to a symbol of strength and authority in the ancient world and is again reminiscent of the garment of the high priest.
4) Verse 14: "His head and hair were white like wool, as white as snow." The whiteness mentioned here, and elsewhere in Scripture, speaks of the righteousness of God.
5) "His eyes were like blazing fire." These eyes speak of judgment and indicate that He is eyewitness to the deceitful irrelevance of the apostate (false) churches.
6) Verse 15: "His feet were like bronze glowing in a furnace." Bronze speaks to us of judgment as well and reminds us of the bronze altar of the tabernacle where sin was judged.
7) "His voice was like the sound of rushing waters." Like Niagara Falls, in that day all other voices will be stilled by the deafening and overpowering voice of the Son of God. This is the voice that called the universe into existence, the voice that will call His children up and out of this world to be with Him at the coming of the rapture, and the same voice that will one

day speak destruction upon all wickedness and rebellion. In chapter 4, we will see another reference to His voice as the trumpet.

8) Verse 16: "In his right hand he held seven stars." As before, our Lord gives us the meaning of the seven stars in verse 20. They are defined as the seven angels of the seven churches. The word *angel* is translated from the Greek word *aggello*, which means "a messenger." I believe the word "angel" here refers not to angelic beings, but to the messengers divinely appointed by God to lead the local congregations. In other words, the spiritual leader or pastor of those churches.

9) "Out of his mouth came a sharp double-edged sword." This refers to the spoken word of Christ, which will go forth as a sharp sword against which there will be no defense on the Day of Judgment – the day Christ returns to earth as the Warrior King. Other references to the sword representing the Word of God are found in Ephesians 6:17 and Hebrews 4:12.

10) "His face was like the sun shining in all its brilliance." This speaks of the divine nature of Christ and reminds us of the event that took place on the Mount of Transfiguration, found in Matthew 17:2 and Luke 9:29.

1:17: John does what everyone will do someday when brought into the presence of the glorified Christ – he "fell at his feet as though dead." The effect of the vision upon John was paralyzing. Since the apostle reacted like that, we can be sure that when we come into the presence of the Lord Jesus, we are going to approach Him in like-manner.

But look at what our Lord and Savior Jesus Christ does here. This is one of the most tender and most precious scenes in the entire Bible. Jesus reaches down and touches John and says, "Do not be afraid." In the words of the late J. Vernon McGee, "This is a beautiful picture of Deity reaching down to humanity."

1:17 – 18: The greatest cure for one's natural fear is the personal presence of Jesus Christ. Our Lord gives us four reasons why we should not fear:

1) "I am the First and the Last" speaks of Christ as our Creator and our eternal King.
2) "I am the Living One: I was dead" speaks of Christ's sacrificial death for our sins and His resurrection.
3) "I am alive for ever and ever!" This assures us Christ "died for sins once and for all" (1 Peter 3:18). He will not die again!
4) "And I hold the keys of death and Hades." These keys were purchased with His own blood, for according to the writer of Hebrews, "By his death he might destroy him who holds the power of death – that is, the devil – and free those who all their lives were held in slavery by their fear of death" (Hebrews 2:14 – 15).

The writer of Hebrews further tells us: "Jesus Christ is the same yesterday and today and forever" (Hebrews 13:8).

John saw Jesus as no one else has ever seen Him before – unveiled in all His power and glory and majesty. This is how we will all see Him one day. As the song, by contemporary Christian artist MercyMe, goes, "I can only imagine …."

1:19: Here Christ is giving John a basic three-part outline for the revelation. The vision of Christ and His introduction recorded in verses 12 – 20 make up the "what you have seen." The "what is now" is represented by Christ's specific address to each of the seven churches recorded in chapters 2 and 3, as we will look at next. The balance of the Book of Revelation will cover the "what will take place later."

1:20: Here is our first example of rule number three for studying the Book of Revelation as we recall earlier from the introduction section. In verse 12 we have the mention of the seven lampstands and in verse 16 the mention of the seven stars. Here in this final verse, our Lord is giving us the meaning of the two symbols in order to assist us, as we look closer at the churches in the following two chapters. This method will be used elsewhere throughout this book.

Let us pray that the Holy Spirit will guide us in truth as we study God's revelation
to the Apostle John and to the world of His wonderful Son Jesus Christ.
All glory and praise to God.

Review Questions

1) The word revelation means _____ or_____.

2) The number seven denotes _____.

3) The subject of the Book of Revelation is _____.

4) The seven golden lampstands are representative of _____.

5) The seven stars represent _____.

6) What did John do when he was brought before the glorified Christ? _____
_____.

7) Give the four reasons why Jesus said we should not be afraid in His presence. _____
_____
_____.

Up For Discussion

"I was in the Spirit on the Lord's day,
and heard behind me a great voice, as of a trumpet."
(Revelation 1:10 KJV)

We have just looked at the ten characteristics of the glorified Christ. What John saw was a vision of Christ as He appears today after His resurrection and ascension to heaven in all His majesty. In contrast to the meek and humble Servant that we see depicted in the gospel accounts, what is your initial reaction or impression?

Chapter 2

The church is the body of Christ, Jesus Christ is its head, and it is of divine origin (Ephesians 1:22 – 23). The purpose of the church is to worship God, to pray, and to edify fellow believers. The mission of the church is to evangelize the world. Unfortunately, there are things that divide the church, such as heresy, false doctrine, and discord. So why did our Lord choose these seven churches and not the ones at Rome, Antioch, or Jerusalem? Seven is God's number for completeness, and these seven churches represent the complete message Jesus wants to give to the church. Though these are seven literal churches of the time, some scholars have theorized that they may also represent seven periods or stages of church evolution throughout the church age. Regardless, Jesus is saying something to them and certainly to us today as well, and that is why Christ ends each message with: "He who has an ear let him hear."

The speaker in this vision, of course, is Jesus Christ, described by John as walking in the midst of the seven golden lampstands. This indicates that Christ and His power have always been available to the church. He is thus fulfilling His words to the apostles: "Therefore, go and make disciples of all nations, baptizing them in the name of the Father and of the Son and of the Holy Spirit, and teaching them to obey everything I have commanded you. And surely I am with you always, to the very end of the age" (Matthew 28:19).

See the illustration entitled, "The Seven Churches of the Revelation," at the end of chapter 3 for a summarized comparison of Christ's complete message to the church.

Church of Ephesus – the Apostolic Church, A.D. 30 – 100

2:1 – 3: Jesus has seven words of commendation:

1) Their good works. In James (2:26) we read: "As the body without the spirit is dead, so faith without deeds is dead." Calvin said, "Faith alone saves, but the faith that saves is not alone." We serve others through our "deeds" out of our love for Christ.
2) Their labor refers simply to their hard physical work.
3) Their perseverance or patience is one of the fruits of the Spirit (Galatians 5:22).
4) They did not tolerate wicked men.
5) They tested those claiming to be an apostle. Were they eyewitness to the resurrected Christ?

6) They persevered for the name of Jesus Christ. They preached Christ and defended the gospel during a time of relentless persecution by Rome.

7) They had not grown weary. You may get weary *in* the work of Christ, but it is tragic if you get weary *of* the work of Christ.

2:4: "You have forsaken your first love." Even though the Ephesians received much commendation from the Lord, they had somehow let go of the most important thing of all – their sacred romance with Jesus Christ. That romance was kindled over the years of close and intimate fellowship while the apostles were present with them. As these apostles, one by one, suffered and died as martyrs, that romance with Christ subsequently began to diminish.

2:5: Christ's counsel to them was to "Repent …." Some believers do not view an absence of intimate love for Jesus Christ as a sin, but simply something they lack. If God's absolute priority for all followers of Christ is love – for Him first and others second – then the absence of such love is sinful. We need to pray incessantly to love Jesus more than anything else. The phrase "remove your lampstand" does not mean they would lose their place in heaven, but that they (or we) would lose a position of godly influence on earth. In other words, we lose our light in the world.

2:6: "You hate the practices of the Nicolaitans." Nicolaitans is a compound word. *Nikao* means "to conquer," and *laos* means "the people." We get our word laity from that. In the early days of the church the followers of the Nicolaitans held two serious heretical views: First, they practiced sensuality by completely separating one's spiritual and physical natures, thus giving them license to sin. Secondly, they tried to establish an ecclesiastical order. Laypeople were given no voice in church affairs but were required to obey blindly the decrees of the church leaders.

2:7: "The tree of life." The tree of life was called accordingly because the eating of its fruit resulted in eternal life (Genesis 3:22); however, it is now reserved for the righteous in heaven, as we will see later in chapter 22.

Church of Smyrna – the Persecuted Church, A.D. 100 – 312

It is interesting to note here that there was not one word of condemnation from our Lord to this church.

2:8 – 9: "I know your afflictions and your poverty." This was a severely persecuted church.

Because of the intense hatred of Christians, when a man took a stand for Jesus Christ, not only did his life become in danger of persecution, but his employment suffered economically as well.

"Yet you are rich!" This illustrates a divine principle: Regardless of one's economic state, knowing Jesus Christ brings spiritual wealth in this life and in the life to come.

I know those who "are a synagogue of Satan." The remnant of Israel, which was being saved, had left the synagogue by this time. They had given up the Law as a means of salvation and sanctification, and thus began the church. Those who continued in the synagogue were now considered in a false religion. In fact, those Jews may have also identified the Christians to the government and greatly heightened the persecution against them. In Matthew (23:14 KJV), Jesus referred to the Scribes and Pharisees as "hypocrites" and promised them "the greater damnation." The Apostle Paul made it clear, "For not all who are descended from Israel are Israel" (Romans 9:6); in others words, they were no longer true Jews. Paul considered the true Israelite to be one who turned to Christ.

2:10: Christ's counsel was "Do not be afraid …." We do not know for certain what Christ meant by the phrase, "you will suffer persecution for ten days." It may possibly be a reference to the ten emperors of Rome that persecuted Christians. They include Nero, Domitian, Trajan, Marcus Aurelius, Severus, Maximinius, Decius, Valerian, Aurelian, and Diocletian. Each of these Roman emperors put Christians at the top of their hate list.

Christ further counseled them to: "Be faithful, even to the point of death and I will give you the crown of life." They were martyrs for Christ. Crowns are a heavenly reward and our Lord has a special crown for those who suffer. We will discuss heavenly rewards later in chapter 19.

How were the believers in Smyrna as well as us today, in light of the 9/11 tragedy and worldwide terrorism, able to be faithful through such terrible suffering? Those who are faithful in the midst of intense suffering learn to lean on the awesome power and grace of the indwelling Holy Spirit to allow their fiery trials to purify rather than destroy them. The Apostle Peter wrote: "These [trials] have come so that your faith – of greater worth than gold, which perishes even though refined by fire – may be proved genuine and may result in praise, glory, and honor when Jesus Christ is revealed" (1 Peter 1:7).

Christ wanted the believers in Smyrna to be aware, but He did not want them to be afraid. I believe that much of the Book of Revelation was written to believers for the same reason.

2:11: "He who overcomes will not be hurt at all by the second death." The first death is physical death. The second death is spiritual death and results in eternal punishment and separation from God. Hades is the present abode of the unbelieving dead. The lake of fire is their eventual fate. We will discuss this in further detail later in chapter 20.

Church of Pergamum – the Indulged Church, A.D. 312 – 606 (freedom of one's desire)

2:12 – 13: "I know where you live – where Satan has his throne." Satan has a kingdom, and Babylon has from earliest times been considered the capital of his kingdom. Idolatry and sexual immorality gained its start in Babylon through Nimrod, grandson of Ham (Genesis 10) and his mother, inspired by Satan. However, when Babylon's glory began to decline and it was left desolate, Satan looked for another location. He selected Pergamum because of its strongly idolatrous religions instituted by the local Roman government. Pergamum was the uncontested center of pagan worship in Asia Minor. Keep in mind that Satan's primary goal is to keep people blinded to truth while providing something that momentarily seems to satisfy their spiritual hunger. Pergamum delivered.

The reason our Lord said that Satan's throne was in Pergamum was likely because of the many heathen temples located there. They included the temple of Athena, the great temples of Caesar Augustus and Hadrian, the great altar to Zeus, the temple of Dionysius, and the temple of Asklepios. Some scholars believe that the great altar of Zeus represented Satan's throne, where others strongly feel it was the combination of all of these heathen temples that made up Satan's throne.

"Yet you remain true to my name. You did not renounce your faith in me." Because the organized church in Pergamum held fast to Christ's name, it did not teach anything but the personal deity of Jesus Christ for over 1,000 years.

2:14: "You have people there who hold to the teaching of Balaam." In Numbers chapter 22 we read about Balak, the king of Moab. He was afraid of the children of Israel as they were coming through his land. He hired Balaam to use his gift of prophecy against Israel, and Balaam sought every means at his disposal to do so. However, his efforts continuously failed when he encountered Israel's God. In desperation, he gave Balak the suggestion of enticing the Israelites into making an unholy alliance with the Moabites through intermarriage with them (Numbers 25:1 – 3, 31:16). Therefore, the basic concept of Balaam's teaching is this: If you can't curse them, try to seduce them. In other words, some in the church of Pergamum were being enticed into sin by others among them. It is unclear as to whether or not the seducers were truly saved; however, Christ commanded the church in verse 16 to "repent" or be judged by the Word of God.

2:15: "Teaching of the Nicolaitans." Refer back to verse 6 for this explanation.

2:16: Christ's counsel was to "Repent." Recall from chapter 1 that we defined "the sword of my mouth" as the spoken Word of Christ for which there is no defense on the Day of Judgment. Understand that Christ has only to speak and His will is accomplished.

2:17: The hidden manna:

Manna was the heavenly food sent by God to the children of Israel in the desert. It also represents the spiritual food provided by God in His Word. The words of our Lord Jesus tell us, "I am the bread of life. He who comes to me will never go hungry, and he who believes in me will never be thirsty" (John 6:35). No matter what life's dilemma, if God's children will only look to Him, their needs will be supplied. Jesus Christ came to earth as the "manna" provided by the Father to bring salvation and eternal life. Today His Holy Spirit falls like manna from heaven to all who hunger, all who believe, and all who "overcome" the world. It is "hidden" only to those who choose not to believe in Jesus Christ and reject the precious gift of salvation offered by the Father. Recalling the reaction and words of our Lord Jesus upon His triumphal entry into Jerusalem beginning the final week before His death, the gospel writer wrote: "As he approached Jerusalem and saw the city, he wept over it and said, 'If you, even you, had only known on this day what would bring you peace – but now it is hidden from your eyes'" (Luke 19:41 – 42). Because of their rejection of Jesus Christ as Messiah, God has, for a time, hardened the hearts of the Jewish people and thus "hidden" from them the true Prince of Peace.

The white stone:

In ancient times a white stone meant acquittal when used by jurors publishing their vote in a court case. Hence the white stone stands as a beautiful symbol of the eternal acquittal we gain through faith in Jesus Christ – not because we are innocent but because our Lord and Savior Jesus Christ paid our sin debt with His blood shed on a Roman cross. As for the new name on the stone, it could be Christ's name; or as some suggest, we may all be given a new name, just as Abram was given the name

Abraham, Simon was called Peter, and Saul became Paul. Considering the multiple duplications of names used in this world, Christ may likely desires that each of His children have their own special and unique name going into eternity.

Church of Thyatira – the Pagan Church, A.D. 606 – 1520 (the Dark Ages)

2:18: Recall from chapter 1 the ten characteristics of Christ John envisioned. Both "eyes like blazing fire" and "feet like burnished bronze" represent judgment and are likened or compared to the bronze altar of the tabernacle where sin was judged.

2:19: Our Lord's commendation:

1) Their deeds remind us that works are the credentials of real believers.
2) Their love is representative as one of the fruits of the Spirit (Galatians 5:22).
3) Their faith is what drives the two above.
4) Their ministry of service.
5) Their perseverance or patience is also one of the fruits of the Spirit.
6) "Now doing more than you did at first." In this church, works increased rather than diminished.

2:20 – 22: "You tolerate that woman Jezebel, who calls herself a prophetess." Thyatira was one of the most thriving commercial centers in all Asia. Her city boasted of the finest wool and linen workers, dyers, leather workers, potters, tanners, bakers, slave traders, and bronze smiths. Almost every commentary you read speaks about the powerful trade guilds that ran the city like the modern day mob. They were morally corrupt because they involved their members in all sorts of idolatrous practices. Not only did unethical deals and practices prevail, but sexual immorality ran rampant. Jezebel could have been an actual woman, but I think Christ was more likely drawing a parallel between women of Thyatira who were successful and held positions of authority in the church and the brazen wife of King Ahab.

Whenever a woman is used symbolically to convey a religious teaching, she always represents a false religion. The worship of Baal reached its heights during the days of King Ahab and Jezebel (1 Kings 16:31 – 33). The "Jezebel" mentioned here was obviously a very powerful woman (or influence) that did everything she could to infiltrate the church. The text tells us here that the teaching of the false prophetess Jezebel took two forms, both of which are contrary to God:

1) "By her teaching she misleads my servants into sexual immorality." This false teaching emphasized self-indulgence above all and is a reference to their idolatry.
2) "The eating of food sacrificed to idols" was a practice which demonstrated union of the church (its members) with the world (unbelievers).

2:23: Our Lord has patiently dealt with this false system of religion, but there has been no real change; therefore, she will suffer judgment. The "children" mentioned here are those who were brought up under this system. The meaning of "dead" refers to the second death we saw earlier (v.11) and refers to eternal punishment and separation from God.

11

2:24: "Satan's so-called deep secrets" may refer to a Gnostic sect at the time known as the Ophites who worshiped the serpent, who we know from the Garden of Eden as the devil. They mocked the writings of the Apostle Paul and boasted of a higher spiritual perception.

2:25: "Until I come" is a reference to the rapture of the church. We will discuss this in detail later in chapter 4. Christ is telling the church, both then and today, that He is coming back for her; thus, the church should stand firm in their faith in the Lord Jesus Christ.

2:26 – 27: "I will give authority over the nations." The Apostle Paul wrote likewise: "Do you not know that the saints will judge the world?" (1 Corinthians 6:2). This is a reference to the millennial reign of Christ in which believers will share.

2:28 – 29: The morning star:

This beautiful title is clearly understood in light of our Lord's word in Revelation 22:16 (KJV), where Christ explains that He is the "the bright and morning star." The children of Jezebel will not hear, but the true children of the Lord Jesus Christ will hear. This promise is clearly the promise of Christ to come and abide with all those who "overcome" the world.

Chapters 2 and 3 combined make up Christ's complete message to the churches of all ages. Review questions for this section are included at the end of chapter 3.

FAQ: Women and False Religion

In chapter 2 (v.20 – 22), our Lord Jesus Christ in His discourse concerning the church at Thyatira, compares the successful women of high position in that city with Jezebel, the wife and driving force behind the wicked rule of King Ahab of Israel during the time of the divided kingdom. These women infiltrated the church and as the Bible text reads, "mislead my servants into sexual immorality and the eating of food sacrificed to idols." In other words, they corrupted the church!

In my text, I mention that whenever a woman is used symbolically to convey a religious teaching, she always represents a false teaching. The absoluteness of that statement would naturally raise questions, and in classroom discussion, I have found it oftentimes does.

There is a simple answer, but let's first take a quick look at some background:

1) In chapter 14, I give a brief history of Babylon, the place where idolatry began. It was here that Semiramis, wife (some scholars say mother) of Nimrod was queen of Babel, which later became Babylon. She devised a story (a lie) in which she stepped fully grown out of an egg in the Euphrates River, thus beginning a whole system of idolatry. The worship of Semiramis introduced the female deity of false religion and identifies Babylon as the birthplace of all false religion.

2) The goddess Asherah was believed to be the wife of Baal, the chief male deity of the Canaanites. The Lord commanded the Israelites through Moses to drive out the Canaanites and cut down their Asherah poles, and "Do not worship any other god, for the Lord, whose name is Jealous, is a jealous God" (Exodus 34:10 – 14).

3) Throughout the time of the divided kingdom, the wicked kings would allow the worship of Asherah and the erecting of Asherah poles. In turn, when a righteous king came into power, he would command that these poles be cut down as he sought to bring the people back to the Lord. Even the Prophet Elijah challenged "the four hundred prophets of Asherah" on Mount Carmel (1 Kings 18:19).

4) As with Ahab and Jezebel, other wicked kings had women as the driving force behind their reign. One such example was Ahaziah, King of Judah. After his death, his mother, Athaliah, "proceeded to destroy the whole royal family" of the house of Judah. She went on to assume power and ruled the land for six years. She was killed in a coup led by Jehoiada the priest and Joash, the only remaining son of Ahaziah, was crowned king (2 Kings 11).

Throughout the Bible we are commanded to worship the one true God. The New Testament introduces and teaches the concept of the Trinity – God in three persons – God the Father, God the Son, and God the Spirit. Later in our study of the Book of Revelation, we will witness as the Apostle John bows twice at the feet of an angel sent by Christ, and is twice told, "Do not do it!" The consistent pattern in the Word of God is that we worship God only, and to worship anyone or anything else is, in the Christian faith, a false religion.

The simple answer is: There is no female deity in the Godhead.

Chapter 3

Church of Sardis – the Dead Church, A.D. 1520 – 1790 (the Protestant Reformation)

The Protestant Reformation developed as the result of continued emphasis by the Church of Rome on pagan doctrines rather than adherence to scriptural principles. The basic emphasis of the Reformation church was originally Martin Luther's watchword, taken from Romans (1:17): "the righteous will live by faith."

3:1: "I know your deeds," is Christ's commendation. If we look at the church of Sardis as a historical stage of the church, this may well refer to the early stages of the Reformation when Martin Luther and others chose to defy Roman authority, even at the risk of their own lives. The Reformation recovered the doctrine of justification by faith, and this faith produced works.

"But you are dead," is Christ's condemnation. The tragedy of the Reformation churches that earned them condemnation by the Lord for being "dead" was formalism – they appeared alive on the outside but were spiritually dead on the inside. The result was twofold:

1) They became state churches. The danger of this is that the church then includes the entire population, thus eliminating the need for personal acceptance of Jesus Christ and an emphasis on the individual's relationship to God. Another danger is the tendency to please the government rather than God.
2) The Reformation churches did not sufficiently change many of the customs and teachings of the Church of Rome. Ritual and formality, characteristic of pagan forms of worship, are not conducive to genuine worship, for they appeal to the sensuous human nature. The Bible teaches that God must be worshiped in spirit and in truth. Ritual and ceremonies that come from paganism are not inspired by the Holy Spirit and do not convey truth.

As for the church of Sardis at the time of John's writing, how can anything that carries the name of Jesus Christ be dead? Above all things, Christ is life! The city of Sardis was best known for a necropolis called the "cemetery of the thousand hills" about seven miles from town. Sardis was built on a small, elevated plateau that looked out onto a distant horizon of burial mounts. The people of Sardis became fixated with death and thoughts of death over-shadowed thoughts of life. Sardis also tried to rely on their past achievements and fame. Unfortunately, these same factors contributed to the deadness that invaded the church there; consequently, a lifeless church is made up of lifeless Christians.

3:2 – 3: Christ's counsel was to "wake up! Strengthen what remains … I will come like a thief." Twice in their history the enemies of Sardis invaded them because they felt secure. Christ's warning was to "wake up" and "strengthen" what little faith you still have. Today, just as in Sardis, Christ's imminent return is what we should anticipate. Sardis didn't know when the enemy was coming, and we don't know when Christ is coming. Considering that the rapture could take place at any moment, the church is to be alert! Remember that preparedness was the theme of Christ's last sermon.

"I have not found your deeds complete in the sight of my God." The church had lost their authority and stopped proclaiming the Word of God.

3:4: "Yet you have a few people in Sardis who have not soiled their clothes." As in all church ages, the Reformation had individuals who were faithful to the Lord and had not conformed to the attitude and conduct of the world around them. They chose to live separate and godly lives.

3:5 – 6: "He who overcomes will, like them, be dressed in white." This refers to the righteousness of Christ with which we are clothed when we are reconciled to God through faith in His Son, Jesus Christ as explained by the Apostle Paul (2 Corinthians 5:21).

"I will never blot out his name from the book of life, but will acknowledge his name before my Father and his angels." This indicates the security with which a believer is held against the Day of Judgment in contrast to non-believers as we will study later in chapter 20 (v.11 – 15). The book of life is not a roll of those who are saved but rather a list of those for whom Christ died – all mankind. The way to guarantee that your name will never be blotted out of the book of life is to receive Jesus Christ as your Lord and Savior. The adverb "never" suggests that once you are truly saved through faith in Jesus Christ, then your salvation is secured for eternity. These words of our Lord give us comfort: "I give them eternal life, and they shall never perish; no one can snatch them out of my hand" (John 10:28). Dr. Charles Stanley stated in one of his sermons, "If God is big enough to save you, than He is big enough to keep you." I strongly agree with Dr. Stanley.

Church of Philadelphia – the Missionary Church, A.D. 1750 up to the Rapture (The Church Christ Loved)

The word *Philadelphia* literally means "brotherly love." Philadelphia was marked by vitality of life. In this church age, God worked in a thrilling manner that produced revivals in Europe and the British Isles, spreading even to America. These revivals in turn produced what is known today as the modern missionary movement. Just as with the church in Smyrna, our Lord did not have a single word of condemnation for this church. It is interesting to note that these are the only two cities of the seven that have had a continuous existence. Their lampstands have been moved, but there are a few Christians still remaining there. They do not come out in the open because Christians are persecuted even today in modern Turkey.

3:7: Christ's nature is revealed:

1) He is holy. He was holy at His birth, He lived a sinless life, He was holy at His death, and He is holy today.

2) He is true, which means "genuine." Our Lord told His disciples: "I am the way, the truth, and the life. No one comes to the Father except through me." (John 14:6).
3) "Him who holds the key of David." Here our Lord is quoting the Prophet Isaiah (22:22). These are the keys to the kingdom over which He will reign from the throne of David during the Millennium.
4) "What he opens no one can shut, and what he shuts no one can open." The Lord Jesus Christ controls the doors of opportunity for preaching the gospel and no one can close them unless Christ so wills it. In the next verse this point is emphasized by their deeds.

3:8: Christ's commendations:

1) "Your deeds" refers to their missionary works.
2) "Little strength" means that they were characterized by small congregations.
3) "Kept my word." They obeyed the Word of God and faithfully continued to sow seeds even though the harvest seemed dreadfully lean and distant.
4) "Not denied my name." They refused to deny the name of the Lord during this time in history portraying the greatest increase of false Christs and false religions.

3:9 – 10: Christ promises the church in Philadelphia two things:

1) Vindication: Christ promised that all false religions (including the synagogue of Satan we looked at back in chapter 2) would someday be subdued before them and that the very people who sneered at them would one day acknowledge how much Christ loved the church.
2) Preservation: "I will keep you from the hour of trial that is going to come upon the whole world to test those who live on the earth." The world has never known a universal period of tribulation. This is an obvious reference to the seven-year Tribulation Period that we will cover in our study of chapters 6 through 18. This promise to the church in Philadelphia is a promise to all who make up the body of Christ by their trust and faith in our Lord and Savior; the church will be removed before that Tribulation Period begins. These words from our Lord represent one of several passages in Scripture that support our belief in a pre-tribulation rapture.

3:11: "I am coming soon." Our Lord's promise is made on the basis that the church of Philadelphia will be in existence at His coming. The church of Philadelphia is characterized by a spirit of revival that promotes evangelism, a return to the Word of God, and a great emphasis on the second coming of Christ.

3:12 – 13: Christ's challenge to overcome:

1) "I will make a pillar in the temple of my God." A pillar is symbolic of strength and stability; thus, Christians have stability in this life and a hope for eternity to come, only in Christ Jesus.
2) "I will write on him the name of my God and the name of the city of my God …." True believers are identified with Christ by the seal of the name of God (Ephesians 1:13), which entitles them entrance into the Holy City of the New Jerusalem described later in chapters 21 and 22.

3) "I will also write on him my new name." Believers of the church of Philadelphia will also have the name of Christ, which "will be on their foreheads" and entitles them to be "his servants … they will see his face" as also described later in chapter 22 (v.3 – 4).

Church of Laodicea – the Apostate (False) Church, A.D. 1900 – the Midpoint of The Tribulation Period

3:14: Christ's description of Himself:

1) *Amen* is a Hebrew word that means "true" and carries with it the meaning of finality. In this sense, Christ is the final truth. The Apostle Paul confirmed this truth in 2 Corinthians 1:20.
2) "The faithful and true witness." The Lord Jesus is Truth and the faithful witness of truth. His Word can be accepted as absolute authority for He is God.
3) "The ruler of God's creation." All things were created through Christ's power as the apostle wrote: "Through him all things were made; without him nothing was made that has been made" (John 1:3).

This is the only church whose conduct was so reprehensible that even Christ, who knew all about her, could not find one thing on which to commend her.

3:15 – 16: Christ's condemnation was "you are lukewarm."

1) Lukewarm means dishonest or deceptive. This church claimed to represent Jesus Christ, but instead deceived many because they never acknowledged the power of the gospel of Christ. They never witnessed the conversion of a soul from darkness to light.
2) Lukewarm also shows indifference. We are called to faith-centered works, but the church in Laodicea was more focused on work-centered faith. They were more absorbed in social action than gospel action and spent more time planning than praying. They attempted to maintain a middle-of-the-road position. They were not against God, but they were not excited about God either. Consequently, they were sickening to the Lord.

My friends, there is nothing lukewarm about Christ!
We all need to get excited and get committed for Jesus.

3:17: Laodicea was a rich city. Wealth by itself is not the issue. We serve a God of infinite wealth who can distribute the riches of this world any way He sees fit. However, the problem is the deceitfulness of wealth and unfortunately, as was the case here, material abundance is not conducive to spiritual vitality. From a spiritual standpoint, this church was the worst of the seven. In it was no study of God's Word, no love of Christ, and no witnessing of His saving grace; yet it is blind to its own true condition. This wealthy church did not grasp the principle Jesus taught us: "From everyone who has been given much, much will be demanded" (Luke 12:48).

Notice back in chapter 2 (v.9) how Christ's address to the church at Smyrna stands in stark contrast to Laodicea: "I know your afflictions and your poverty – yet you are rich!"

A true test of any works claiming to be performed in the name of Jesus Christ is: Does it glorify Jesus Christ or does it glorify humanity – man?

3:18 – 19: Christ's counsel to the church in Laodicea:

1) "Buy from me gold refined in the fire, so you can become rich." Here gold refers to something of great worth or value – our salvation. Salvation is not purchased through human efforts but has been purchased for us by the precious blood of Christ.

2) "White clothes to wear." As mentioned before, this denotes the righteousness required to come into God's presence. We have that righteousness because of our faith in Christ's sacrificial death. Ironically, Laodicea was famous all over the world for its black wool fabric. Christ suggested they trade their fashions for holiness.

3) "Salve to put on your eyes, so you can see." This is an indication of a human being's need for spiritual illumination. We must be indwelled by the Holy Spirit in order to understand the ways of God.

4) "So be earnest, and repent." This lukewarm, indifferent, and materialistic church was challenged by our Lord, on the basis of His love for them (even in their lost state), to repent and turn to Him.

3:20: "Here I am! I stand at the door and knock. If anyone hears my voice and opens the door, I will come in and eat with him, and he with me." The door is one's heart. This verse refers to fellowship and a personal relationship with Jesus Christ. You are incomplete until you have fellowship with God through His Son Jesus Christ (1 John 1:3), which is only possible by inviting Him into your heart.

3:21 – 22: Here is simply a promise that we will one day rule and reign alongside Christ when He returns to establish His earthy kingdom. This ultimate victory for all Christians, not seen in this life but in the life to come, is a challenge to faithfulness.

The overcomers are those who put their faith, their trust, and their hope in Jesus Christ. Jesus Christ is the head of the church and He never takes His eyes off of her.

Review Questions

1) Define the church. _____

_____

_____

2) The purpose of the church is _____.

3) The mission of the church is _____.

4) The speaker in the vision is _____.

5) Which churches did Christ have no rebuke for? _____

_____.

6) Which church did Christ have no praise for? _____.

7) The overcomers are those who _____.

Up For Discussion

"He that hath an ear, let him hear what the Spirit saith unto the churches."
(Revelation 2:7, 11, 17, 29, 3:6, 13, 22 KJV)

Our Lord Jesus Christ is even today walking amongst the churches of the world, including your own. His power is always available to inspire and motivate the ministry of His church. Using the chart "The Seven Churches of the Revelation" as a guideline, discuss how your home church might stand up to the teachings and values as established by Christ.

What would Christ's praise be for your church? Would it be your ministry to the local community, to charities throughout our country, or to the needy worldwide? Would it be your love for one another? Or would it be your love for His Word and the teaching of it?

What would Christ's rebuke be? Are there divisions in your church? Is there gossip? Is blatant sin such as adultery, substance addiction, or abuse being addressed or overlooked? Is the Word of God being taught? Do your pastor and church leaders believe the entire Bible to be the inspired and infallible Word of God?

What would Christ's counsel to your church be? Would it be to simply continue in the good work that you are doing? Or is your church able to do more?

The Seven Churches of the Revelation
Christ's Complete Message to the Church Then & to Us Today

	Ephesus Apostolic Church Rev. 2:1-7	Smyrna Persecuted Church Rev. 2:8-11	Pergamum Indulged Church Rev. 2:12-17	Thyatira The Pagan Church Rev. 2:18-29	Sardis The Dead Church Rev. 3:1-6	Philadelphia Missionary Church Rev. 3:7-13	Laodicea Lukewarm Church Rev. 3:14-22
	A.D. 30-100	A.D. 100-312	A.D. 312-606	A.D. 606-1520 Dark Ages	A.D. 1520-1790 Reformation	A.D. 1750- The Rapture	A.D. 1900- Tribulation Midpoint
Christ's Praise	Good deeds, hard works, perseverance, and hated the Nicolaitans.	Poverty, but rich in faith, suffer persecution.	Remained true to my name, did not deny your faith.	Good deeds, love, faith, service, and perseverance.	Good deeds and a reputation for being alive.	Mission deeds, little strength, kept my word, have not denied my name.	None
Christ's Rebuke	You have forsaken your first love.	None	You have false teachers of Balaam, and Nicolaitans.	You allow Jezebel to teach sexual immorality and idolatry.	You are dead, and your deeds are incomplete.	None	You are lukewarm, wretched, pitiful, poor, blind, & naked.
Christ's Counsel	Remember from where you have fallen and repent.	Do not be afraid, and be faithful	Repent	Hold on to what you have until I come.	Wake up! Strengthen what remains. Remember, obey and repent.	Hold on to what you have.	Buy gold tried by fire, white clothes, anoint your eyes, and repent.
Christ's Challenge	Will give to eat from the tree of life.	Will not be hurt by the second death.	Will give hidden manna, and a white stone with a new name.	Will give authority over the nations and the morning star.	Will walk with me dressed in white, names remain in the book of life.	Will make them pillars, will write on them name of God & My new name.	Will give right to sit with me on my throne.

The Seven Churches of the Revelation
Viewed as Seven Stages of Evolution of the
Church through the Church Age

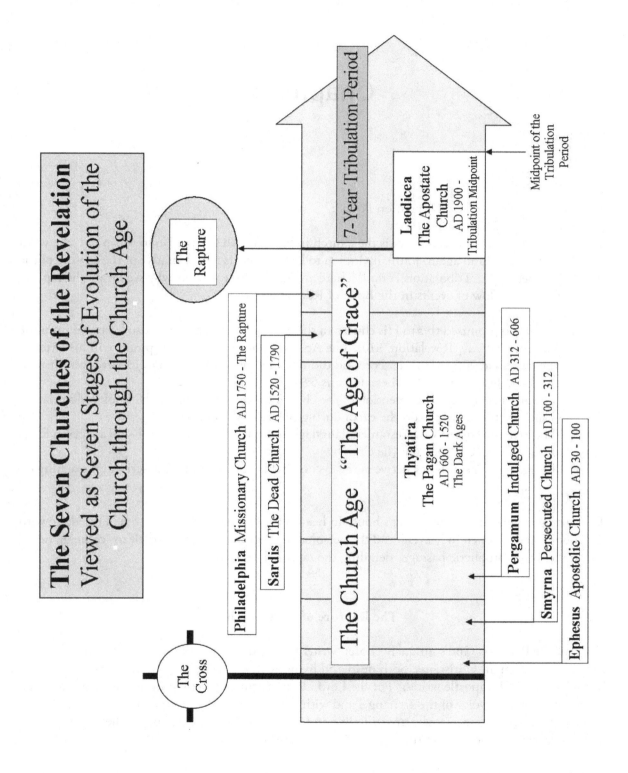

The Cross

The Rapture

7-Year Tribulation Period

Midpoint of the Tribulation Period

The Church Age "The Age of Grace"

Philadelphia Missionary Church AD 1750 - The Rapture

Sardis The Dead Church AD 1520 - 1790

Thyatira
The Pagan Church
AD 606 - 1520
The Dark Ages

Pergamum Indulged Church AD 312 - 606

Smyrna Persecuted Church AD 100 - 312

Ephesus Apostolic Church AD 30 - 100

Laodicea
The Apostate
Church
AD 1900 -
Tribulation Midpoint

Chapter 4

4:1: The rapture before the Tribulation Period:

The unspoken theme of this chapter is the church in heaven with Christ. Up to this point, the word church occurs again and again. John's invitation to heaven here is representative of the rapture of the church just before the Tribulation Period. There are at least four reasons why we locate the rapture at this spot in the flow of events in the Book of Revelation:

1) Our Lord promised this to His church in the previous chapter: "I will also keep you from the hour of trial …" (Revelation 3:10). The Apostle Paul reinforced this promise in his letter to the church at Thessalonica: "For God did not appoint us to wrath but to salvation through our Lord Jesus Christ" (1 Thessalonians 5:9).
2) The absence of any other mention of the church in the remainder of the Book of Revelation indicates it is no longer on the earth during the Tribulation Period.
3) The extensive use of Old Testament language and symbols in chapters 4 – 18 suggest a focus on the nation of Israel, not the church.
4) There is much similarity between the events of this passage and other scriptural teaching on the rapture.

The calling of John up to the Father's house in heaven likely represents the church. This along with the "door standing open in heaven" and the personal invitation of Christ Himself to "come up here," all parallel other prophetic passages detailing the rapture of the church.

The Rapture of the Church

The Apostle Paul was God's uniquely chosen writer to reveal to His church the wonderful details of the rapture, when all Christians, both dead and living, will be "caught up" (raptured) to heaven to be with Christ. The apostle writes: "For the Lord Himself will come down from heaven, with a loud command, with the voice of the archangel and with the trumpet call of God, and the dead in Christ will rise first. After that, we who are still alive and are left will be caught up together with them in the clouds to meet the Lord in the air" (1 Thessalonians 4:16 – 17).

As Christians, we trust that when a believer dies their soul or spirit leaves the body and goes immediately to heaven to be with the Lord; this is according to the Apostle Paul: "We are confident, I say, and would prefer to be away from the body and at home with the Lord" (2 Corinthians 5:8).

The apostle also explained that when the rapture occurs, "God will bring with Jesus those who have fallen asleep in him" (1 Thessalonians 4:14). The purpose is that He is going to resurrect the body, and the soul is going to re-enter the body permanently in resurrection. Living Christians are instantly changed as Paul foretold: "Listen, I tell you a mystery: We will not all sleep, but we will all be changed – in a flash, in the twinkling of an eye, at the last trumpet. For the trumpet will sound, the dead will be raised imperishable, and we will be changed. For the perishable must clothe itself with the imperishable and the mortal with immortality" (1 Corinthians 15:51 – 53). The King James Version says: "For this corruptible must put on incorruption, and this mortal must put on immortality." In other words, we will each receive a new glorified body, such as that of our Risen Lord. We need a new body, thus imperishable and incorruptible means holy or pure, without and never again to have a sin nature. This will enable us to stand (and bow) in the presence of our Lord Jesus Christ; that we may rejoice in Him throughout eternity to come. Furthermore, with our new glorified bodies, our sanctification becomes complete; and we are, in the words of the writer of Hebrews, "made perfect" (Hebrews 12:23).

There is only one second coming of Christ, but it occurs in two phases. The first phase is called the *rapture* and occurs prior to the Tribulation Period when Christ comes down to the clouds to remove His church (all believers) from the world before the Tribulation Period. The second phase is called the *revelation* and occurs at the end of the Tribulation Period when Christ returns to earth to put an end to all wickedness and rebellion and establishes His millennial kingdom. This fact cannot be questioned as Jesus Himself foretold that His return would come "immediately after the distress of those days" (Matthew 24:29).

Seven Characteristics of the Throne of God

The remainder of chapter 4 gives us seven distinct characteristics of the throne of God:

1) 4:2 – 3: The Trinity: We know that God the Father is there and, as taught in Scripture, God the Son is "seated at the right hand of God." This verse indicates that the Holy Spirit is present as well; and as in chapter 1, is still moving upon John and guiding him into new truths. We also know from several passages of Scripture that God the Father cannot be seen (John 1:18; 6:46; 1 Timothy 6:16). John could distinguish no form of a person so he simply describes the splendor of the One seated on the throne like brilliant gems, "appearance of jasper and carnelian." Jasper is later described in chapter 21 (v.11) as clear crystal and is probably the most brilliant of all precious jewels, the diamond. The other stone, carnelian, is blood red and may well be the ruby. Thus the two together might symbolically represent the idea of glory and sacrifice. John's next description is that "a rainbow, resembling an emerald, encircled the throne." John's vision here is consistent with that of the Prophet Ezekiel (1:26 – 28). The throne of God is beyond anything we can imagine; yet the writer of Hebrews tells us that because of our great High Priest Jesus we can approach it with confidence (Hebrews 4:14 – 16).

2) 4:4: The twenty-four elders: Elders are representatives. We know that Israel had elders and that elders were appointed in the early church to help govern and represent the entire church (Titus 1:5). These twenty-four elders likely represent the church in its totality in heaven. The fact that they were "dressed in white and had crowns of gold on their heads," further

reinforces what we have already read: that white represents the righteousness of God through faith and that crowns are a heavenly reward for the believer. It is my opinion that all twelve apostles (and in some manner including Paul) are here, as well as those representing the redeemed from the nation of Israel. Our Lord confirmed to His disciples at the last supper that they would, "sit on thrones, judging the twelve tribes of Israel" (Luke 22:30).

3) 4:5a: The signs of judgment: Three things are mentioned here: "Lightning, rumblings, and peals of thunder," all proceeding from the throne of God. Lightning and thunder have long been associated with the concept of judgment; thus we can conclude that they are a prelude to the judgment about to fall upon the earth as described in chapters 6 – 19.

4) 4:5b: The seven spirits of God: These were described in chapter 1 (v.4) as mentioned by the Prophet Isaiah: The Spirit of the Lord, of wisdom, of understanding, of counsel, of power, of knowledge, and of reverence of the Lord.

5) 4:6a: The Sea of glass: This may represent stability because a glassy sea is a calm sea, untroubled by winds and storms. Two suggestions for this sea might be: First, the church at rest and in heaven, no longer a victim of the storms of life. Secondly, the Word of God symbolized by the Lord's holiness and purity. This imagery is also similar to that found in Ezekiel (1:22, 25 – 28).

6) 4:6b – 8a: The four living creatures: These four living creatures are the seraphim described by the Prophet Isaiah in his vision of the throne of God (Isaiah 6:1 – 3). The fact that they are "covered with eyes, in front and in back" speaks of knowledge or awareness. Because of their nature, it may well be they are leaders of the realm they depict. Some scholars identify each with one of the four gospels, while still others see each as representing specific characteristics of God. Let's look at each representation:

A lion is the leader of the kingdom of wild animals. The Gospel of Matthew presents the Lord Jesus as the King. The lion represents majesty and omnipotence – God is all-powerful.

A calf or ox is the leader of the domestic animals. The Gospel of Mark presents Christ as the Servant. The ox speaks of strength and might.

A man is the leader of the angelic hosts responsible for the human race. The Gospel of Luke presents the Lord Jesus as the Son of Man, and His humanity is emphasized. The man characterizes knowledge.

A flying eagle is the leader of the kingdom of fowls of the air. The Gospel of John communicates the deity of Christ. The eagle represents the sovereignty and supremacy of God.

7) 4:8b – 11: The heavenly worship of Christ: As mighty as these celestial beings of the heavenly order are, none of them could have qualified to redeem the human race from their sin. They are unworthy and that is why they fall down and lay their crowns before the throne. However, the blood of God's own Son could – and did! This act of worship seems to be their expression of devotion and adoration to the Lord Jesus Christ for redeeming from the earth what they could not redeem. The song they sing is also a song of glory and honor to God because He is the Creator of all things. The apostle tells us: "Through him all things were made; without him nothing was made that has been made" (John 1:3). This is another acknowledgement that the Lord Jesus Christ is the one being worshiped.

How much more should our hearts rejoice as we worship Him?
We are the recipients of His redemption!

Review Questions

1) The theme of this chapter is _____.

2) The rapture of the church occurs before _____.

3) The two phases of the "second coming" are _____

_____.

4) We can approach the throne of God because of _____.

5) The twenty-four elders are representatives of _____.

6) The four living creatures are _____.

7) To whom is the heavenly worship directed? _____.

Up For Discussion

"After this I looked, and behold, a door was opened in heaven:
and the first voice which I heard was as it were of a trumpet talking with me;
which said, 'Come up hither ....'"
(Revelation 4:1 KJV)

Skip to the end of chapter 5 and to the illustration entitled "Two Phases of the Second Coming of Christ." Using the illustration, review on your own or as a class by taking turns reading aloud the Scripture verses – alternating between rapture passages and revelation passages. Compare them in class discussion as you go. Notate below any newfound revelations from your readings.

A Rapture Analogy
Sodom and Gomorrah

Then the Lord said, "The outcry against Sodom and Gomorrah is so great and their sin so grievous that I will go down and see if what they have done is as bad as the outcry that has reached me. If not, I will know" (Genesis 18:20 – 21).

Here is the story of the three visitors that came to see Abraham. The "Lord" referred to in these verses, as in other accounts throughout the Old Testament, is believed by most biblical scholars to have been the pre-incarnate Christ, while the other two visitors with Him were angels. Before leaving, the Lord told Abraham He was going down to Sodom and Gomorrah to investigate the wickedness that had come up to Him. The first thing that came to Abraham's mind was his nephew Lot and his relationship with God. Abraham began to plead to the Lord for the righteous with the following question: "Will the Judge of all the earth do right?" My friends, God's Word, the Scriptures testify to the fact that whatever God does is right! Abraham began to plead with the Lord. He started at fifty, then he went to forty-five, then to forty, then to thirty, then to twenty, and finally Abraham pleaded down to ten, and the Lord agreed if even ten righteous were found there then He would not destroy the cities and all their dwellings. As it turned out, there was only one righteous man there – Lot – and God told Lot (along with his family) to get out before He destroyed them.

The same is true today. The Tribulation Period described in the Book of Revelation cannot begin as long as the church (the righteous) remains in the world. Why? The reason is that Jesus Christ bore our judgment on Calvary's cross once and for all; therefore, we are not destined to some future time of wrath. The Tribulation Period is God's judgment that is coming upon the rest of the world – the unrighteous, wicked, rebellious, and unbelieving. This is the reason the church cannot go through the Tribulation Period. Sodom and Gomorrah is an illustration of the world today. The Lord is returning soon, and that is in keeping with the story we have here in Genesis.

Words Not Found in the Bible

It is in chapter 4 of the Revelation, when we discuss the rapture of the church before the Tribulation Period that Bible skeptics question this teaching and point to the fact that the word *rapture* is not found in the Bible. We do not have to see a specific word in the Bible in order for the concept it describes to be true. Let's take a look at just a few words, common to our faith, that do not appear in the Bible.

1) Rapture: This term defines the concept of a person or group of people caught up or taken to heaven to be with God without experiencing death. The Apostle Paul explained the wonderful details of the rapture, when all Christians, both dead and living, will be "caught up" (raptured) to heaven to be with Christ. The apostle writes: "For the Lord Himself will come down from heaven, with a loud command, with the voice of the archangel and with the trumpet call of God, and the dead in Christ will rise first. After that, we who are still alive and are left will be caught up together with them in the clouds to meet the Lord in the air" (1 Thessalonians 4:16 – 17). Moreover, this concept is not exclusive to the New Testament. We read all the way back in Genesis (5:24) that the patriarch Enoch, "walked with God; then he was no more, because God took him away." Yet again, as the Prophet Elijah and Elisha were "walking along and talking together, suddenly a chariot of fire and horses of fire appeared and separated the two of them, and Elijah went up to heaven in a whirlwind" (2 Kings 2:11). As you can see, the concept of rapture is not new, and definitely seems to be an important part of God's future plan for His children.

2) Trinity: Refers to the concepts of God in three person – God the Father, God the Son, and God the Spirit. No true Christian disputes this doctrine.

3) Divinity: Means to have divine quality or God-like character.

4) Incarnate or incarnation: God (the Word) coming into the world in the flesh. The Apostle John describes this concept: "In the beginning was the Word, and the Word was with God, and the Word was God. The Word became flesh and made his dwelling among us. We have seen his glory, the glory of the One and only, who came from the Father, full of grace and truth" (John 1:1 and 14). Regrettably, this term has also come to be used by Bible commentators of the Book of Revelation to describe the embodiment and deceitful resurrection of the end-time dictator of the world – Antichrist – by Satan at the mid-point of the seven-year Tribulation Period.

5) Monotheism: The teaching that there is only one God.

6) Sacrament: One of the ceremonial observances of the Christian church, i.e. Baptism and Communion (the Lord's Supper).

The above mentioned is a list of the more obvious examples. In addition, the word *Bible* itself is only mentioned in the title of God's Word; and, the word *Christian* is only mentioned twice throughout the entire New Testament. When people question or challenge these words, they are attempting to rob you of the hope and joy that is yours through our faith in Jesus Christ. I call them "joy robbers." Don't let a joy robber distract you from studying God's Word and from the faith we hold so dear.

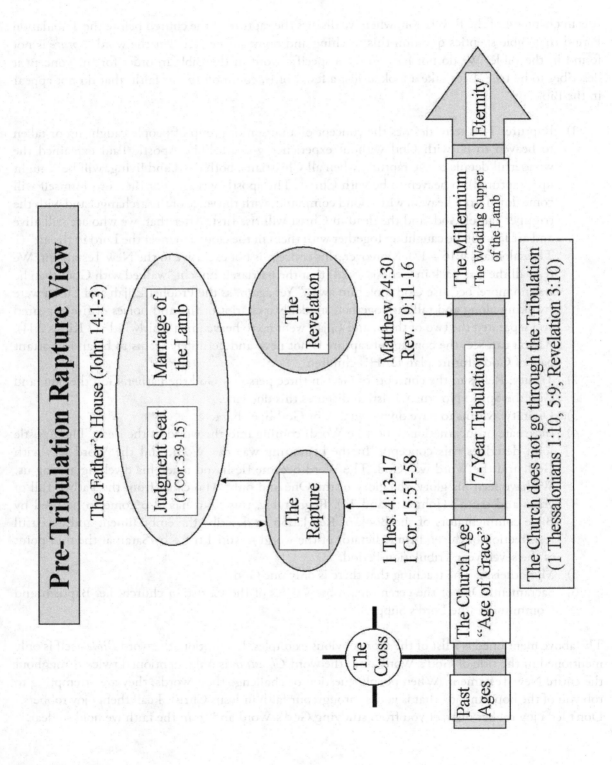

Pre-Tribulation Rapture View

The Father's House (John 14:1-3)

Marriage of
the Lamb

Judgment Seat
(1 Cor. 3:9-15)

The
Revelation

The
Rapture

Matthew 24:30
Rev. 19:11-16

1 Thes. 4:13-17
1 Cor. 15:51-58

The Millennium
The Wedding Supper
of the Lamb

Eternity

7-Year Tribulation

The Church Age
"Age of Grace"

The
Cross

Past
Ages

The Church does not go through the Tribulation
(1 Thessalonians 1:10, 5:9; Revelation 3:10)

Chapter 5

Whenever a chapter in the Bible opens with the word "and" or "then," we know it should be joined to the proceeding chapter. Therefore, we continue the scene of the church in heaven with Christ. The throne was the center of chapter 4. The Lion and the Lamb, both of which represent Christ, are the center of chapter 5. John has seen the throne of God, and now his attention focuses on an object in the hand of God.

5:1 – 4: "A scroll with writing on both sides and sealed with seven seals."

John weeps because he knows that this scroll contains God's final plan for the redemption of the earth, and as long as the scroll is left sealed, Satan will continue his destructive influence in the world. Jesus Himself referred to Satan as "the prince of this world" (John 12:31). The scroll is being handed to the Lord Jesus because this earth belongs to Him. He created it, and He redeemed it. Many, including myself, identify this scroll as the "Book of Judgment" and believe it to be the same scroll as the one from Daniel's vision (Daniel 12:4), whereby the prophet was commanded to "seal the words of the scroll until the time of the end." This book of judgment could also be likened to the "flying scroll" from the vision given to the Prophet Zechariah (5:1 – 3). The Prophet Isaiah, as well, had a vision of judgment which became to him as "nothing but words sealed in a scroll" (Isaiah 29:11). Either way, as we will see, the opening of this scroll and its seals will bring a series of judgments upon the earth leading to its eventual redemption.

Who has the right to bring judgment upon a wicked and rebellious world and to establish eternal justice and righteousness? The words of our Lord Jesus Christ tell us: "Moreover, the Father judges no one, but has entrusted all judgment to the Son" (John 5:22).

Five Characteristics of the Lord Jesus Christ

5:5 – 6: As John looks on, he sees a Lamb that appears as if it has already been sacrificed. This vision gives us five characteristics of the Lord Jesus Christ:

1) "The Lion of the tribe of Judah." This identifies Christ with the tribe of Judah of the people of Israel. Before his death, Jacob blessed his sons, and to Judah he said, "You are a lion's cub …

The scepter will not depart from Judah, nor the ruler's staff from between his feet, until he comes to whom it belongs and the obedience of the nations is his" (Genesis 49:9 – 11).

2) "The Root of David." This refers to Jesus' incarnation – His birth with His roots in the family of David. God told David: "I will raise up your offspring to succeed you, who will come from your own body … Your house and your kingdom will endure forever before me; your throne will be established forever" (2 Samuel 7:12 – 16).

3) "A Lamb, looking as if it has been slain … standing in the center of the throne." "Slain" refers to the redemptive and substitutionary death of Christ, where "standing" speaks of His resurrection. He is no longer seated at the right hand of God. He is standing, and He is coming to judge this earth.

4) "He had seven horns." A horn in Scripture indicates a power or authority and the number seven indicates completeness. The Lamb's power and authority to redeem on earth came through His willingness to be slain. When Christ came the first time as a Lamb, though He displayed certain powers, He did not manifest all of His power. When He comes the next time as a Lion, at the Revelation, it will be in the manifestation of His complete omnipotence – His all-consuming power.

5) "Seven eyes, which are the seven spirits of God sent out into all the earth." These eyes speak of the knowledge and wisdom of our Lord. Here again, seven is God's number for completeness. Therefore, when Christ comes to judge the world at the end of the Tribulation Period, it will be as the perfect judge, who has all power and complete knowledge about mankind.

The Lord Jesus Christ is a Lion and a Lamb:

1) The lion refers to His second coming where the lamb referred to His first coming.
2) The lion is symbolic of His majesty where the lamb symbolized His meekness.
3) As a lion, He is sovereign, where as a lamb He is our Savior.
4) As a lamb, He was judged by the world. As a lion, He will return to judge the world.
5) The lion represents the government of God, and the lamb represents the grace of God.

5:7 – 8: The moment Christ takes the seven-sealed scroll, the four living creatures and the twenty-four elders fall down before Him. They are described as having two things in their hands:

1) "Harps," which represent the music and praise of heaven.
2) "Golden bowls filled with prayers of the saints." Who are the "saints"? All believers in the Lord Jesus Christ are saints. These are unanswered prayers that will be answered at the return and revelation of Jesus Christ. All Christians have prayed as our Lord taught us: "Your kingdom come, your will be done on earth as it is in heaven" (Matthew 6:10). This will not be accomplished until Christ returns to earth to set up His millennial rule. This is another indication that all prayer is answered, though we may not receive the answer in our lifetime.

5:9 – 10: This is a song of praise, and it indicates that our Lord Jesus Christ is worthy of our praise and worship for three reasons:

1) "Because you were slain." This is a reference to Christ's sacrificial death on Calvary's cross to pay our sin debt.
2) "With your blood you purchased men for God from every tribe and language and people and nation." The precious blood of Jesus was shed for all men. This assures us that millions

of people in the world who do not have the Bible in their mother tongue will hear about our Lord and Savior Jesus Christ (as we will see in chapter 7).

3) "You have made them to be a kingdom and priests to serve our God, and they will reign on the earth." This refers to those who put their trust and faith in Jesus during this coming time of judgment and who we will call "Tribulation Saints." The church will not reign on earth but from an exalted position above the earth.

5:11: "The voice of many angels, numbering thousands upon thousands, and ten thousand times ten thousand." This verse gives us a rare glimpse of the enormity of those in heaven, both angelic and human. The church is now in heaven and joining in the singing of praise. When questioned by the Sadducees, our Lord replied that at the resurrection (rapture) we "will be like the angels" (Matthew 22:30).

5:12: The angels in heaven, who know Him best, proclaim Jesus worthy to receive seven things: Power, wealth, wisdom, strength, honor, glory, and blessing. We should accept the angel's description here; and as such, direct all of our praise and worship at the Lamb, Jesus Christ – for He is worthy.

5:13 – 14: Here we see others who join in the glorious song of praise to our Lord. This passage of Scripture should be viewed alongside that which the Apostle Paul wrote: "Therefore God exalted him to the highest place and gave him the name that is above every name, that at the name of Jesus every knee should bow, in heaven and on earth and under the earth, and every tongue confess that Jesus Christ is Lord, to the glory of God the Father" (Philippians 2:9 – 11). Apparently, even all the animals on earth and fish in the sea are going to join in this "singing" of praise to our Lord.

What John saw was heaven in complete joyful jubilation of the Lord Jesus Christ, the Son of God. All of heaven breaks loose in praise. He is the one who paid the price for man's redemption. He is the only one worthy to break the seals and judge mankind. He, and only He, is worthy of our praise and worship.

Worthy is the Lamb.

Ronald A. Clower

Review Questions

1) The Lion and the Lamb both represent _____.

2) We suggest in our study that the scroll is the _____.

3) A horn in Scripture is symbolic of _____.

4) Eyes in Scripture are symbolic of _____.

5) Harps in Scripture are symbolic of _____.

6) Incense in Scripture is symbolic of _____.

7) Name the seven things Jesus is worthy to receive. _____
_____.

Up For Discussion

"And every creature which is in heaven, and on the earth, and under the earth,
and such as are in the sea, and all that are in them, heard I saying,
Blessing, and honour, and glory, and power, be unto him …."
(Revelation 5:13 KJV)

Does it seem odd that all creation would sing out praises to our Lord?

Recall the story of Jesus' triumphal entry into Jerusalem the Sunday before His death, and how the crowd was joyfully singing praises to God in loud voices for all the miracles they had witnessed. They sang, "Blessed is he who comes in the name of the Lord," and "Hosanna in the highest!" Remember that some of the Pharisees told Jesus to rebuke his disciples. But Jesus' reply was, "If they keep quiet, the stones will cry out," (Luke 19:40).

Discuss how nature reveals the majesty of God.

Discuss how nature reveals the curse of mankind.

32

Two Phases of the Second Coming of Christ

| The Rapture | | The Seven-Year Tribulation Period | The Revelation |

Rapture Passages

Matthew 24:36-41, John 14:1-3
1 Corinthians 1:7-8, 15:51-53
Philippians 3:20-21, 4:5
Colossians 3:4
1 Thessalonians 1:10, 2:19
4:13-18, 5:9, 5:23
2 Thessalonians 2:1
1 Timothy 6:14
2 Timothy 4:1, 4:8
Hebrews 9:28, James 5:7-9
1 Peter 1:7, 1:13, 4:12-13, 5:4
1 John 2:28-3:2, Jude 21
Revelation 2:25, 3:10

Titus 2:13

Revelation Passages

Isaiah 9:6-7, 66:15-16
Daniel 2:44-45, 7:13-14, 12:1-3
Zechariah 12:10, 14:1-9
Matthew 13:41, 24:27-31
Matthew 26:64
Mark 13:24-27, 14:62
Luke 21:25-28
Acts 1:9-11, 3:19-21
1 Thessalonians 3:13
2 Thessalonians 1:6-10, 2:8
2 Peter 3:3-14, Jude 14-15
Revelation 1:7, 19:11-16
Revelation 22:7, 22:12, 22:20

Contrasting Events of the Second Coming

The Rapture

1– Christ comes down to clouds to take all Christians to Heaven.
2– Judgment Seat in Heaven.
3– Rapture is imminent. It could happen at any moment.
4– For believers only.
5– Before the "Day of the Lord."
6– No mention of Satan.
7– Only Christians will see Him.
8– The Tribulation Period begins.

The Revelation

1– Christ returns to earth to judge & set up His earthly Kingdom.
2– Judgment of the nations on earth.
3– Christ's return cannot occur for at least 7 years.
4– Affects all of humanity.
5– After the Tribulation Period.
6– Satan bound for a 1,000 years.
7– Every eye on earth will see Him.
8– The Millennial Kingdom begins.

Chapter 6

The Tribulation Period

As we come to chapter 6, the scene shifts back to earth. Now that the church is out of the world and in heaven, what then is to happen to the earth?

The Tribulation Period is one of the most significant periods of God's dealing with mankind and certainly occupies a most prominent place in His prophetic plan. Read Daniel 9:24 – 27. The actual event that triggers the Tribulation Period is found in Daniel 9:27 when Antichrist, "the ruler who will come," makes a covenant (peace treaty) with Israel for seven years. Chapter 6 introduces the seal judgments, which make up the first quarter of the seven-year Tribulation Period. As John beholds the Lord Jesus Christ, represented by a Lamb, breaking the first seal, we encounter the first of a long series of events that begin in heaven and are brought to completion on earth. God will use this time, through a progressive series of judgments, to force all people remaining on earth after the rapture to make a choice:

1) Either repent of their sinful lifestyle and be saved by receiving God's Son, Jesus Christ as their Lord and Savior; or
2) Continue to reject Him and suffer eternal punishment and separation from God.

Each of these judgments is a symbolic announcement in heaven of an event that actually takes place on earth. This seven-year period of future world history, graphically described in chapters 6 – 18, will be the darkest time the world has ever known. The good news is: If you have put your trust and faith in Jesus Christ as your Lord and Savior, then you and I are not destined to some future time of judgment. Our sin debt was paid for eternity on the cross by the atoning death of Jesus Christ. The Apostle Paul tells us that the Lord Jesus "rescues us from the coming wrath" (1 Thessalonians 1:10).

The Four Horsemen of the Apocalypse

6:1: At first glance this opening verse gives the impression that a command was given to John to "Come!" However, since the order is issued from heaven and carried out on earth, a more appropriate translation would be "Watch!" The KJV uses the phrase "Come and see." John heard and then he saw, and his vision began with that of four horsemen.

6:2: The first seal – the rider on the white horse:

The rider on the white horse symbolizes the end-times Antichrist and his kingdom. We will take a closer look at this person, Antichrist, in chapter 13. The purpose of this rider is clearly stated: "A conqueror bent on conquest." One interesting characteristic of his coming is that he has a bow in his hand, symbolic of warfare, but no arrows, indicating that he will conquer by diplomacy rather than by war. Amidst widespread chaos throughout the world resulting from the rapture, Antichrist will come onto the scene as a great diplomat and problem solver, ushering in a false peace. The crown on his head indicates his rise to a worldwide position of power and authority. However, the peace that he brings is only temporary.

6:3 – 4: The second seal – the rider on the red horse:

The red horse is symbolic of war; thus this rider has the ability to "take peace from the earth and to make men slay each other." This is also evident by the fact that a great sword is given to him. As Antichrist rises politically to international acceptance, some disenchanted nations will choose to revolt, thus beginning a world war. Their attempt will ultimately be unsuccessful, evident from the opening of the third seal. This will be a widespread and bloody war.

6:5 – 6: The third seal – the rider on the black horse:

The black horse is symbolic of famine. Black is used to depict famine in other passages of Scripture (Lamentations 4:8 – 9), and famine often follows war as it did after World War I. Inflation also tends to grip the world right after a world war. The "pair of scales" in the hands of this rider indicates the scarcity of food. "A quart of wheat for a day's wages and three quarts of barley for a day's wages" suggests that a person will have to work for a whole day just to earn enough money to survive. The rider is instructed not to "damage the oil and the wine," which are traditionally foods of the rich. Thus this famine will take its heaviest toll on the common people.

6:7 – 8: The fourth seal – the rider on the pale horse:

The pale horse is literally corpse-like; his name is "Death," and he represents plague and pestilence. The death rate of the first twenty-one months of the Tribulation Period will be tremendously high as a result of war, famine, and inflation. In fact, one-fourth of the entire world's population will die. The fact that "Hades" follows the pale horse and its rider indicates that these are unsaved dead. Hades is the place reserved for the wicked, rebellious, and unbelieving of all generations while they await their final judgment as we will study later in chapters 9 and 20.

6:9 – 11: The fifth seal – the Old Testament and martyred Tribulation Saints:

These are individuals who had not received Christ during the age of grace (church age). These Old Testament Saints have the "righteousness that comes by faith" (Romans 4:13). The Tribulation Saints will receive Christ as a result of the faithful witnesses depicted in chapter 7. These Tribulation Saints died "because of the word of God and the testimony they had maintained." We know that they are believers because each one is clothed in "a white robe." Recall from chapter 3 (v.5), the phrase "dressed in white" is symbolic of the righteousness of Christ with which we are clothed when we accept God's

Son, Jesus Christ as our Lord and Savior. Without a doubt, the Tribulation Period will be the greatest period of Christian persecution the world has ever known.

6:12 – 14: The sixth seal – catastrophe on earth, "the Wrath of the Lamb!"

When the sixth seal is opened, the entire earth is violently shaken by a giant earthquake, the likes of which the world has never seen. As persecution of God's people by Antichrist begins, the Lord shows His displeasure. This judgment describes a physical shaking of the whole earth caused by earthquakes and volcanic eruptions. Such things have happened before. As the result of a volcanic eruption, ash has often blotted out the sun for hundreds of miles and caused the moon to appear red.

"Stars in the sky fell to earth" suggests that meteors will shower down from the sky.

"The sky receded like a scroll, rolling up, and every mountain and island was removed from its place." All we can conclude is that this catastrophe will bring about widespread changes to the physical earth. The earthquakes that we see today in Haiti and elsewhere throughout the world are not a fulfillment – they merely demonstrate that these things can happen just as God's Word says it will.

6:15 – 17: "Every free man hid in caves and among the rocks of the mountains." Great fear will grip human hearts. Because of their stubborn and rebellious ways, instead of turning to God in their hour of peril, they will hide in the rocks and dens of the earth. You need to understand that when you live a life in rejection of God, your heart becomes hard and fixed against God, just as Pharaoh's did during the time of the Exodus.

It seems evident from these verses that the world will know this is a judgment from the Lord Jesus Christ, for they refer to Him as "him who sits on the throne" and "the Lamb."

Let's take to heart the words of King David:
"Be wise now therefore, O ye kings, be instructed, ye judges of the earth.
Serve the Lord with fear, and rejoice with trembling.
Kiss the Son, lest he be angry, and ye perish from the way,
when his wrath is kindled but a little.
Blessed are all they that put their trust in him."
(Psalm 2:10 – 12 KJV)

Review Questions

1) The event that triggers the Tribulation Period is _____

_____ .

2) The rider on the white horse symbolizes _____ .

3) The rider on the red horse symbolizes _____ .

4) The rider on the black horse symbolizes _____ .

5) The judgment resulting from the rider on the pale horse is _____

_____ .

6) White robes are symbolic of _____ .

7) Another name for the catastrophe on earth caused by the opening of the sixth seal is _____

_____ .

Up For Discussion

In a short paragraph of commentary written by the late J. Vernon McGee, he stated the following: "But what about 'the wrath of the Lamb?' Wrath is strange and foreign even to the person of God, is it not? You see God loves the good, but God hates the evil. God does not hate as you and I hate. He is not vindictive. God is righteous. God is holy. And He hates that which is contrary to Himself." The Apostle Paul tells us, "The wrath of God is being revealed from heaven against all the godlessness and wickedness of men who suppress the truth by their wickedness" (Romans 1:18).

Look at the world we live in today. Christianity seems to be under constant attack by our mainstream secular press. Does the world or our nation "reveal" the wrath of God, or the judgment of God, as the Apostle Paul suggests above? Give some examples. One example might be the continued loss of religious freedoms for Christians in order to accommodate the needs of nonbelievers in an ever-growing "politically correct" society.

Using the illustration "Daniel's Seventy Sevens," review on your own or begin classroom discussion by reading the Daniel passage in the top title block. Continue reading and discussing each block of the chart moving from left to right. For a complete analysis, see chapter 9 of my book, *Captivity to Eternity, DANIEL, God's Faithful Servant*.

Do more: Compare and contrast the six seal judgments with Christ's Olivet Discourse found in chapter 24 of Matthew.

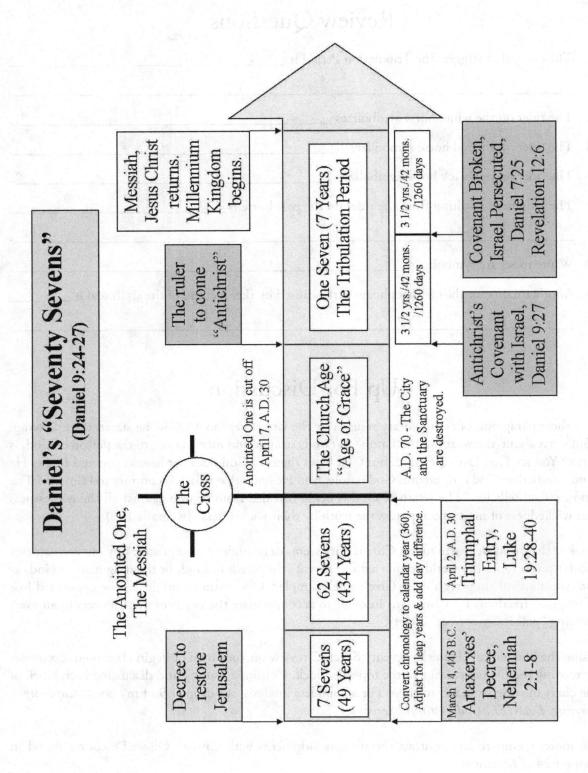

Daniel's "Seventy Sevens"
(Daniel 9:24-27)

The Anointed One,
The Messiah

The Cross

Messiah, Jesus Christ returns. Millennium Kingdom begins.

The ruler to come "Antichrist"

One Seven (7 Years) The Tribulation Period

3 1/2 yrs./42 mons. /1260 days

3 1/2 yrs./42 mons. /1260 days

Covenant Broken, Israel Persecuted, Daniel 7:25 Revelation 12:6

Antichrist's Covenant with Israel, Daniel 9:27

Anointed One is cut off April 7, A.D. 30

The Church Age "Age of Grace"

A.D. 70 - The City and the Sanctuary are destroyed.

62 Sevens (434 Years)

April 2, A.D. 30 Triumphal Entry, Luke 19:28-40

Decree to restore Jerusalem

7 Sevens (49 Years)

Convert chronology to calendar year (360). Adjust for leap years & add day difference.

March 14, 445 B.C. Artaxerxes' Decree, Nehemiah 2:1-8

Chapter 7

This chapter represents an interlude between the sixth and seventh seal. The reason is to explain what will happen to those people who turn to God and receive Christ as their Savior during the seven-year Tribulation Period. These are those we refer to as Tribulation Saints.

144,000 Sealed Witnesses

7:1 – 3: The work of angels in the Book of Revelation reveals they are the special ministers of God. In this chapter we find that they supervise the administration of two things:

1) Verse 1: They control the winds of wrath (forces of nature) from the four corners of the earth. In other words, they halt God's judgment for a time. The four corners of the earth refer to the north, south, east, and west – meaning the entire earth.
2) Verse 2 – 3: They seal the servants of God – the 144,000 tribulation witnesses. This corresponds with the breaking of the fifth seal. Once the sealing angel had finished his work, then the destroying angels were allowed to continue their execution of judgment, as we saw with the breaking of the sixth seal, "the Wrath of the Lamb."

7:4 – 8: The Bible is much easily understood if we simply accept God's Word at face value and do not try to force upon it any meaning other than that which it naturally conveys. Twelve thousand Jews will be sealed from each of the twelve tribes of Israel, totaling 144,000. Notice the tribe of Joseph is represented twice – Joseph and his son Manasseh. The tribes of Dan and Ephraim were likely omitted because of their worship of idols (Judges 18:30 and Hosea 4:17). In some manner, these servants will have the seal of God on their forehead. We do not know of what this seal will consist, but the text suggests that it will be visible and for the purpose of protecting the 144,000 witnesses from any judgments to come. The Holy Spirit will undoubtedly be present to empower the ministry of the 144,000. Concerning the Day of the Lord and this time of tribulation, the Prophet Joel foretold that the outpouring of the Holy Spirit would be much the same as was experienced on the day of Pentecost (Read Joel 2:28 – 32).

A Great Multitude in Heaven

7:9 – 10: The phrase "after this" (after the sealing of the witnesses) simply means next in order as John's vision again shifts to heaven. Foremost in the mind of God is the salvation of souls and the apostle makes it clear that the Lord "is patient with you, not wanting anyone to perish, but everyone to come to repentance" (2 Peter 3:9). This "great multitude that no one could count" refers to people from every nation, language, and tribe of the world who will receive the gospel of Jesus Christ as a result of the ministry of the 144,000 witnesses. In fact, it is believed by most scholars of prophecy that more people will turn to Christ as Lord and Savior during the time of the Tribulation than have been saved during the entire church age. In other words, the 144,000 witnesses of the Tribulation Period will do in seven years what the church has not done in nearly 2,000 years. The fact that this multitude stands before the throne and before the Lamb confirms they are redeemed from the earth, and their song indicates they are the recipients of personal salvation. The "white robes," mentioned here again, represent the "righteousness of Christ" (Corinthians 5:21) and the palm branches (the Greek word *phoinix*, meaning palm trees) are both signs of victory and represent our victory in Christ.

7:11 – 12: We have heard time and again in church: "I tell you that in the same way there will be more rejoicing in heaven over one sinner who repents than over ninety-nine righteous who do not need to repent" (Luke 15:7). The angels continue their song of praise to God and the Lamb that they began back in chapter 5 while looking on and rejoicing over those who have been redeemed from the earth.

7:13 – 14: The identity of this multitude is clearly spelled out. They are "out of the great tribulation." This explains why John cannot identify any of them. The fact that these are believers is unquestionable because they have "washed their robes and made them white in the blood of the Lamb."

The Prophet Isaiah wrote the following: "How then can we be saved? All of us have become like one who is unclean, and all our righteous acts are like filthy rags; we all shrivel up like a leaf, and like the wind our sins sweep us away" (Isaiah 64:5 – 6). Here in verse 14, John gives us a beautiful picture of our personal acceptance of salvation. When someone is willing to come to God by the blood of His Son, acknowledging personal sin, then his or her filthy rags are cleansed by the blood of the Lamb, Jesus Christ, and that person is made righteous and white as snow.

7:15 – 17: Eternal rewards for this multitude:

1) "They are before the throne of God and serve him day and night in his temple." We now know for sure this is not the church, for the church is never identified with the temple. As we will see later, the eternal home of the church is the New Jerusalem and there is no temple there. However, there will be a temple on the New Earth.
2) "He who sits on the throne will spread his tent over them." This symbolizes God's eternal protection over this redeemed multitude.
3) Their every need will be supplied. They will evidently experience hunger and thirst during the Tribulation Period and will undergo extreme exposure to the elements, but their faith in the Savior will guarantee them entry into Christ's earthly kingdom where they will never suffer hardship again.

4) "God will wipe away every tear from their eyes." It is possible to believe that this may also relate to God's omnipotent ability, toward His children, to remove or clear our memories of unpleasant experiences in life, including loved-ones eternally lost (Psalm 34:16, Isaiah 65:17).

The most important decision we will ever make in this life is whether we will accept or reject God's wonderful gift of salvation and eternal life through His Son Jesus Christ. This multitude is permitted to stand before the throne of God because they voluntarily "washed their robes and made them white in the blood of the Lamb."

Review Questions

1) Those who turn to God and receive His Son Jesus Christ as Lord and Savior during the Tribulation Period are referred to as _____.

2) The angels holding back the four winds is a reference to the holding back of _____

_____.

3) The tribes of Dan and Ephraim were most likely not included with the 144,000 witnesses because of _____.

4) The purpose of sealing the 144,000 witnesses was to _____

_____.

5) The ministry of the 144,000 witnesses will be empowered by _____.

6) The "great multitude" is made up of _____

_____

_____.

7) They washed their robes and made them white in _____.

Up For Discussion

"And I saw another angel ascending from the east, having the seal of the living God, and
he cried with a loud voice to the four angels … Hurt not the earth, neither the sea,
nor the trees, till we have sealed the servants of our God in their foreheads."
(Revelation 7:2 – 3 KJV)

The 144,000 Jewish witnesses are given the seal of God on their foreheads for the distinct purpose of protecting them from harm as they witness to the gospel of Jesus Christ throughout the entire world and to all people during the seven-year Tribulation Period. They are protected against any harm resulting from God's judgments that are coming upon the earth and from those on the earth who are in direct rebellion against God and His children.

The Apostle Paul tells us, "Now it is God who makes both us and you stand firm in Christ. He anointed us, set his seal of ownership on us, and put his Spirit in our hearts as a deposit, guaranteeing what is to come" (2 Corinthians 1:21 – 22).

I strongly believe every person has a divine purpose in life. Could it be that once an individual turns their life over to Christ through faith, that God then places this seal that the apostle mentioned on their forehead in order to protect them, physically and spiritually, until their divine purpose is fulfilled on earth?

Chapter 8

As we come to this section containing symbols, let us keep in mind that a symbol is a representation of a fact. When symbols are used in Scripture, the clues to their meaning are given as well. Scripture will supply the explanation. The Apostle Peter wrote: "Knowing this first that no prophecy of the scripture is of any private interpretation" (2 Peter 1:20). The Book of Revelation is the last book in the Bible because a working knowledge of the sixty-five books preceding it is the basis for an understanding of its vivid language. The symbols are going to be given to us, but we need to understand the symbols stand for awesome realities to come.

8:1 – 2: "When he opened the seventh seal, there was silence in heaven." The "he," of course, is the Lord Jesus Christ. The significance of the "silence in heaven" is twofold:

1) It is entirely opposite the usual sound patterns of heaven as seen in earlier chapters, sounds of great joy, praise, and worship.
2) It is a result of the revelation by Jesus Christ to the heavenly hosts concerning what is about to fall upon the earth. It is the calm before the storm.

The opening of the seventh seal introduces the seven trumpet judgments – judgments that are a direct action from the Lord Jesus Christ. The Lord directs all actions from heaven. Do not lose sight of the fact that Revelation presents the Lord Jesus Christ in His glory as the Judge of all the earth. These judgments are so terrible the angels stand breathless in wonder. Each of the seven angels is given a trumpet that will be blown in proper sequence, introducing a form of future judgment.

The late J. Vernon McGee wrote the following: "As the trumpets of Israel were used at the battle of Jericho, so will the walls of this world's opposition to God crumble and fall during the Great Tribulation." What remarkable insight; and as such, an appropriate Old Testament analogy for the condition of the world today.

8:3: The "golden altar" is the place where prayer is offered. Incense is likened to prayer and is a type of prayer. The psalmist wrote: "May my prayer be set before you like incense; may the lifting up of my hands be like the evening sacrifice" (Psalm 141:2).

8:4 – 6: "The smoke of the incense, together with the prayers of the saints" is a beautiful symbol which expresses the fact that God always hears our prayers and that now those prayers are going to be answered by the Lord Jesus Christ. Remember back in chapter 6 (v.10) we saw the saints under the altar, and they sang, "How long, Sovereign Lord, holy and true, until you judge the inhabitants of the earth and avenge our blood?" Their song of prayer is symbolized here by the incense that ascends before God. The censer "filled with fire from the altar and hurled to earth" is also a symbol. It represents the answer to those prayers, and it comes in the form of the next set of judgments upon the earth, the trumpet judgments. The people on earth, who have rejected Christ's sacrificial death as payment for their sins, must now bear the judgment themselves.

There are "peals of thunder" and "rumblings" which denote the approach of the coming storm of God's judgment. There are "flashes of lightning" which normally accompany thunder and an "earthquake" on the earth – all introducing the fact that the seven angels are about to sound their trumpets.

The Trumpet Judgments

One way to determine whether the trumpet judgments are literal or symbolic might be to study them in connection with the plagues of Egypt as found in chapters 7 – 11 of Exodus. There we see Moses performing the symbolic act of waving his staff over the waters of Egypt, which then literally turns the water into blood. Here we see an angel performing the symbolic act of blowing a trumpet and thus initiating a form of judgment upon the earth. It is interesting to note that five of the plagues of Egypt are repeated here in the Book of Revelation.

8:7: The first trumpet:

Hail and fire are literal judgments that fall on one-third of the earth's surface, burning up all the vegetation it rains down upon. The first global judgment was the flood; now it is going to be fire. This should not strike us as strange for such things have happened before: "Then the Lord rained down burning sulfur on Sodom and Gomorrah – from the Lord out of heaven" (Genesis 19:24). Here, the hail parallels the seventh plague of Egypt (Exodus 9:18 – 26), and nearly every advocate of the Bible, to my knowledge, believes the plagues of Egypt to be true and literal.

I am not certain what is meant by the phrase "mixed with blood," but the words of the prophet tell us the following concerning the dreadful Day of the Lord: "I will show wonders in the heavens and on the earth, blood and fire and billows of smoke" (Joel 2:30). At any given time, there could be hundreds of thousands of people traveling in planes around the globe. Let me suggest this "blood" may be the result of this judgment of hail and fire as it passes through our atmosphere destroying both the planes and their occupants. In addition, multitudes of the earth's fowl are killed by this shower of judgment. Their combined blood becomes mingled with the hail and fire as it all falls to earth. On the other hand, the blood may be symbolic and represent the immense suffering of mankind as a result of these judgments from God.

8:8 – 9: The second trumpet:

John says he sees "something like a huge mountain, all ablaze thrown into the sea," which might likely be a giant burning meteorite; but we do not know for certain. Whatever this mass is, it turns one-third of the sea to blood, it kills one-third of the creatures living in the sea, and it destroys one-third of the ships – that fact John makes very clear.

8:10 – 11: The third trumpet:

The "great star" is literal and is most likely a meteor containing poison that contaminates one-third of the earth's fresh water supply. When this meteorite strikes, it will embitter great rivers, and those dependent on them will die. Its name is *Wormwood*, for God created all the stars and named them (Job 9:9). Wormwood is a name used as a metaphor in the Old Testament in the following ways:

1) The idolatry of Israel (Deuteronomy 29:18 KJV).
2) As calamity and sorrow (Jeremiah 9:15, 23:15; Lamentations 3:15, 19 KJV).
3) As false judgment (Amos 5:7 KJV).

8:12: The fourth trumpet:

This judgment deals with the luminous bodies as they affect the earth. The same God that created the light in the first chapter of Genesis is also able to diminish it by one-third. This corresponds to the ninth plague of Egypt (Exodus 10:21 – 23). Jesus warned His disciples concerning His coming and the end of the age: "Immediately after the distress of those days, the sun will be darkened, and the moon will not give its light; the stars will fall from the sky, and the heavenly bodies will be shaken" (Matthew 24:29). In like manner, Jesus foretold: "There will be signs in the sun, moon, and stars. On the earth, nations will be in anguish and perplexity at the roaring and tossing of the sea. Men will faint from terror, apprehensive of what is coming on the earth, for the heavenly bodies will be shaken" (Luke 21:25 – 26).

8:13: Is this literally an "eagle" (NIV) speaking, or is this an angelic being of the heavenly order, as the King James Version states, making this loud proclamation? It is most likely an angel; however, if God made the donkey of the Moabite prophet Balaam speak (Numbers 22:28 – 30), then I believe God will have no problem enabling an eagle to speak as well. This verse introduces the three woes of the Book of Revelation. They inform us that as horrific as the first four trumpet judgments were; they will be surpassed in misery by those to follow. The rebellion of human beings against God strangely gets progressively worse. The first and second woes of the Tribulation Period are actually the fifth and sixth trumpet judgments, beginning our study in the next chapter. The third woe coincides with the seventh trumpet judgment at the mid-point of the Tribulation Period.

It is interesting to note that in Matthew 24:27 – 28 (KJV) our Lord used the eagle to speak of His coming – referring to the carnage following the great battle of Armageddon.

Review Questions

1) All judgments are the direct action from _____.

2) The incense is symbolic of _____.

3) The censer filled with fire from the altar and hurled to earth is symbolic of _____

_____.

4) The first trumpet judgment of hail and fire does what? _____

_____.

5) The second trumpet judgment of a huge mass all ablaze falling into the sea causes what?

_____

_____.

6) The third trumpet judgment of a giant poisonous meteorite striking the earth results in what?

_____.

7) The fourth trumpet judgment did what? _____

_____.

Up For Discussion

"And I saw the seven angels which stood before God,
and to them were given seven trumpets."
(Revelation 8:2 KJV)

As John's vision in heaven continued from the previous chapter, we interpreted the different elements in verses 3 – 6 symbolically and pointed to the Psalms for reference. However, when John's vision shifted back to earth, we took a more literal interpretation of the judgments described in verses 7 – 13.

Recall the first rule of interpretation from our introduction: When the plain sense of Scripture makes common sense, seek no other sense; therefore, take every word at its usual and literal meaning unless the facts of the immediate text clearly indicate otherwise. Thus far in our study, do you feel that our commentary is proper, and likewise, giving you a clearer understanding of the Book of Revelation? Can you point to anything specifically that stands out as a new-found "revelation" in this study of God's Word? How might our analysis contrast with other interpretations you may have read or studied prior?

Chapter 9

We are moving into a section of our study that is very strange and wild, and admittedly difficult to interpret. However, let us continue with our rule of following the literal line even though the figures presented are the most vivid and wild. If another interpretation is in order, then John will supply the explanation.

The Fifth and Sixth Trumpet Judgments

9:1: The fifth trumpet: "The first woe."

The use of the word "star" in this verse is obviously intended figuratively rather than literally, for the "star" is referred to as "he" (v.2), hence clearly having personality. A "key to the shaft of the Abyss" is given to this being. I have studied this passage extensively and still cannot be certain as to the identity of this being; there seems to be two possible explanations adopted by most scholars:

1) Some indicate that at this point in the tribulation, an angel is given this "key." This would coincide with Revelation 20:1, where we find that at the end of the Tribulation an angel comes down from heaven "having the key to the Abyss and holding in his hand a great chain." In other words, this angel retains the key during the Tribulation Period and is given the enormous responsibility of controlling the awful demonic forces to be released from the "shaft of the Abyss." His location in heaven indicates that he is a good angel, for fallen angels do not reside in heaven.

2) Others identify this star as Satan because of the phrase "star that had fallen from the sky." They reference the words of the Prophet Isaiah: "How you have fallen from heaven, O morning star, son of the dawn! You have been cast down to earth, you who once laid low the nations!" (Isaiah 14:12). In our New Testament, the Lord Jesus stated likewise: "I saw Satan fall like lightning from heaven" (Luke 10:18).

Though both explanations seem to be quite extreme to one another, I tend to lean towards the first interpretation for the following three reasons:

1) The events of the Book of Revelation are unfolding chronologically (for the most part). As such, Satan cannot be the "star" that falls from heaven at this point in the Tribulation Period

because we will see later that it is at the mid-point of the Tribulation Period where "the great dragon (Satan) was hurled down …" (12:9).

2) Recall from chapter 1 (v.18) that Jesus holds "the keys to death and Hades" and that they were purchased with His precious blood. Assuming Hades and the Abyss to be closely related, then I do not believe our Lord would entrust the key to Satan.

3) In the above mentioned reference to Revelation 20:1, I must give emphasis to the word "having." This angel already has the key. If Satan had the key, then I do not believe he would voluntarily turn it over to a good angel so that the angel could, in turn, imprison him with it. Whoever this being is, he is given a key which denotes power and authority – and this is given from the Lord Jesus Christ.

The Abyss represents the extreme remote opposite of heaven. Originally, the term referred to a "deep" mass of water and was associated with the water in the creation story (Genesis 1:2). In the New Testament, its meaning has been broadened to refer to the literal place of confinement for evil spirits (fallen angels/demons) until their day of judgment (Luke 8:30 – 31, 2 Peter 2:4, and Jude 6). Furthermore, the term Abyss has become synonymous with hell or *Hades* (the Greek word translated from the Old Testament Hebrew word *Sheol*) and defined as the present abode of all wicked/unsaved spirits. Our Lord taught that, in Hades, there exists a great chasm or gulf which separates the place of torment from the place of comfort (Luke 16:19 – 31). In His parable, Jesus explained, "In hell, where he (the rich man) was in torment, he looked up and saw Abraham far away," again illustrating the "deep" remoteness of the abyss of hell. Though its precise meaning is uncertain, there are other scholars that believe the Abyss to be simply the great chasm, that is, the deep shaft leading downwards to Hades as mentioned here in verse 1. See Hades Illustration at the end of this chapter.

9:2 – 10: When the Abyss was opened, smoke rose from it until the air was filled with a smog-like condition worse than any metropolitan area today has ever experienced. Out of this smog came locust-like scorpion creatures that have no counterpart in all history. They are called locusts but are in some way likened to a horse. They have faces like men, hair like women, teeth as lions, and breastplates of iron. Their wings are as "the thundering of many horses and chariots rushing into battle," and they possess stingers in their tails as do scorpions. These "locusts" are to be interpreted spiritually, for they depict a demonic creature (from the spiritual realm) able to inflict physical torture on unrepentant mankind, though they are beyond our human comprehension.

Unlike any kind of locust that has existed before, they are not going to harm the vegetation. They wore crowns, which indicate a power or authority, and the power given to them is to harm human beings, "those people who do not have the seal of God on their forehead." They do not have the authority to kill them. They will only torment them, and for only five months. This torment is described as "the sting of a scorpion when it strikes a man." The pain will be so intense, producing unimaginable agony and suffering, that "men will seek death, but will not find it; they will long to die, but death will elude them." The power of God over the spirit world will protect believers from these demonic creatures. Just as God protected the children of Israel in the land of Goshen from the plagues of Egypt, so He will also protect His children (Tribulation Saints) during the Tribulation Period. Our Lord Jesus tells us: "He who stands firm to the end will be saved" (Matthew 24:13). So far, martyrdom (6:9) is the only means by which Christians will die during this period.

9:11 – 12: The leading demonic angel of these evil spirits from out of the pit of the Abyss is, in the Hebrew *Abaddon* which means "destruction," and in the Greek *Apollyon* which means "the destroyer." He is a very powerful fallen angel – a demon that assists Satan in his evil spirit kingdom. He may well be comparable in Satan's kingdom to the archangel Michael in God's heavenly host.

9:13 – 15: The sixth trumpet: "The second woe."

The sixth trumpet judgment reveals another army of demonic creatures to be unleashed on unrepentant mankind. This time the judgment is far more severe because these demonic spirits are not only able to inflict pain on people but also physical death.

At the blowing of the sixth trumpet, John heard the voice of the Lord, "coming from the horns of the golden altar before God," and He said, "Release the four angels who are bound at the great river Euphrates." The fact these angels were "bound" indicates that they are evil; in other words, they are fallen angels – demons. Apparently, they are intent on bringing havoc onto mankind but have been bound by God until their purposed time had arrived. Now they will be "released to kill a third of mankind." The very hour is even marked out.

No doubt the "great river Euphrates" is the most prominent river referenced in the Bible, and the importance of its surrounding area in Scripture cannot be overlooked. This river formed one of the boundaries of the Garden of Eden, and was also a boundary for Israel. The sin of man began here. The first murder was committed here. Here is where the flood began and spread over the entire world. The tower of Babel was erected here. It was to this area that the Israelites were exiled during the Babylonian captivity. The Euphrates River and its surrounding area have been used throughout Scripture as a symbol of Israel's enemies. Lastly, it is here, according to chapter 18 of our study, that the ancient city of Babylon will be rebuilt and become headquarters of the commercial and governmental activities of the world under the rule of the end-times Antichrist. In Zechariah (5:5 – 11), the prophet locates Babylon as the last stand of false religion.

9:16 – 19: A demonic army of two hundred million would be a dreadful host to confront mankind. These four demonic angels seem to be the leaders of these evil spirits, riding on horse-like creatures, having heads of lions, and emitting fire, smoke, and sulfur. They have tails "like snakes, having heads with which they inflict injury." Their power comes from their mouths and their tails. These horsemen are not to be taken as human but literally as demonic evil spirits. I believe what we have here is a blanket invasion of the earth by the demonic world, which is a further result of opening the door to the shaft of the Abyss (Luke 8:30 – 31). The underworld is now bringing war onto mankind, and these creatures from the Abyss are unnatural, terrifying, and very literal.

At this point, another one-third of the world's unrepentant population is killed. Remember that one-fourth of the world's population has already been slain as a result of the fourth seal judgment.

9:20 – 21: It seems as if the purpose of this judgment, like the preceding one, is to rid the earth of those who will never trust in the Lord Jesus Christ and receive God's gift of salvation through faith in His Son as their Savior. Over one-half of the population of the earth will be destroyed during the Tribulation Period. No wonder our Lord Jesus told His disciples: "If those days had not been cut short, no one would survive …" (Matthew 24:22).

Instead of turning to God during the Tribulation Period, mankind will turn in rebellion away from God to indulge the pleasures of the flesh, and in so doing, condemn their depraved and wicked souls for eternity. These are the same sins that keep people from coming to God today:

1) Idolatry. Human beings will never be truly happy unless they have communion with God. Since the days of Nimrod, Satan has used idolatry to deceive and lead men away from a relationship with the one true God in heaven.

2) Murder. Wherever the influence of the gospel is unknown, human life is cheap; thus, violence and murder will become common practice during the Tribulation Period.

3) Magic arts. The King James Version uses the term *sorceries*. The Greek word is *pharmakeia*, from which we get our English word pharmacy. Pharmacy means drugs, which suggests there will be widespread use of drugs for any and all purposes, most specifically evil. In fact, the use of drugs most likely will not be controlled and may even play a large role in the apostate religion of the times. As a result, drug addiction will flourish. Sorceries are also a linked reference to witchcraft and the occult, all of which are contrary to God and His Word.

4) Sexual Immorality. Even during the Tribulation Period, when the world is in a state of chaos, sexual promiscuity will continue to thrive worldwide as a destructive force spreading disease, corrupting souls, and destroying lives.

5) Theft. This larceny substantiates the lawlessness that will abound during the Tribulation Period. Godless thugs of every level of society will openly rob, cheat, and steal monetary funds and other material possessions by any means possible.

The Tribulation Period will be a time when people give in to the fulfillment of the desires and lust of the flesh. Unrepentant mankind will turn further and further from God and will resort to anything and everything that will deaden the pain and lift them out of the trouble of that time. Understand this: The moment that you reject the gospel and shut your heart to God, you are wide open for the big lie when it comes. The Apostle Paul, when writing about the man of lawlessness (the end-times Antichrist), wrote: "For this reason God sends them a powerful delusion so that they will believe the lie and so that all will be condemned who have not believed the truth but have delighted in wickedness" (2 Thessalonians 2:11 – 12). Someone once said that those who stand for nothing will fall for anything. Anyone today who is not standing for the Word of God is easy prey for all the deceivers and cults in the world.

Therefore it will be during the Tribulation Period, just as it is today,
"Be not deceived; God is not mocked: for whatsoever a
man soweth, that shall he also reap."
(Galatians 6:7 KJV)

Review Questions

1) We reasoned that the "star" of verse 1 is _____

   _____ .

2) In the New Testament, the term Abyss has become synonymous with _____ and is defined as _____ .

3) The fifth trumpet (the first woe) consists of a swarm of locust-like scorpion creatures that have the power to _____ .

4) The demonic leading angel of the Abyss is _____ .

5) The four angels at the river Euphrates are bound because _____

   _____ .

6) What prominent ancient city was located on the shores of this river? _____ .

7) The sixth trumpet (the second woe) was made up of an army of evil-spirit horses and riders that did what? _____ .

Up For Discussion

*"And they had hair as the hair of women, and their teeth were as the teeth of lions.
And they had breastplates, as it were breastplates of iron; and the sound of their
wings was as the sound of chariots of many horses running into battle."*
(Revelation 9:8 – 9 KJV)

Many sincere people attempt to read the Book of Revelation, but end up concluding that it is much too difficult to understand or impossible to interpret. Their problem is simply that they do not believe what they are reading. If you simply read it and trust it as God's Word, then it becomes very clear.

Why is it, for example, when we read Scripture that we have no problem believing some visions, such as those the Apostle John (4:2 – 11) and the Prophet Isaiah (Isaiah 6:1 – 3) saw of God's throne in heaven, but here in the Revelation, have difficulty believing John's vision and description of demons? Isn't our entire Bible the infallible Word of God?

Review the "Hades Illustration," either on your own or aloud in class. Discuss each block, going from left to right, and read the Scripture references associated with each.

Hades Illustration
Before and After the Cross

HEAVEN "Paradise"

"Today you will be with Me in Paradise." Luke 23:43

"We are confident, I say, and would prefer to be away from the body and at home with the Lord."
2 Corinthians 5:8

Ephesians 4:8-10

The Cross

Matthew 12:40

Empty

Righteous Side

Great Chasm or Gulf

"Comfort" "Abraham's Bosom"

Wicked Side

"Hell" "Torment" "Fire"

Luke 16:22-26

Sheol: In the Old Testament, this was the place made up of two compartments where the souls and spirits of the dead went before Christ's death.

*Abyss [shaft of] or Bottomless Pit

Unrighteous

"Darkness" "Weeping and Gnashing of Teeth"

Great Chasm or Gulf

Hades: In the New Testament, Christ emptied the "righteous" side. Today, only the "wicked" side remains and still receives the souls and spirits of the unrighteous.
Matthew 8:12, 25:30

*Luke 8:31; *Revelation 9:1, 20:1-3

Chapter 10

Chapter 10 and the first fourteen verses of chapter 11 represent another interlude in our study; in other words, an intermission or pause in the Revelation chronology. This time it occurs between the sixth and seventh trumpets. Recall that chapter 7 was an interlude between the sixth and seventh seal judgments. In these verses we will be introduced to three distinctively divine servants of the Tribulation.

The Mighty Angel

10:1: Who is this mighty angel? The identity of this "mighty angel" has been debated, and I have found many who believe him to be the Lord Jesus Christ. It is true that in the Old Testament the pre-incarnate Christ, on occasions, was referred to as the "Angel of the Lord" (Genesis 22:9 – 18 NKJV). However, the Lord Jesus Christ does not appear in the Book of Revelation, or elsewhere in the New Testament as an angel. An angel is a created being and our Lord Jesus Christ is the Creator (John 1:3). Ever since Jesus took on flesh, died for the sins of all mankind, was crucified, rose from the dead, and ascended into heaven; He has always appeared as the Son of God in all His deity. More importantly, in the Book of Revelation, Jesus is revealed as the glorified Christ. Let's remember that this book is the unveiling of Jesus Christ (1:1). This is not the first time we have been introduced to a mighty angel, for in chapter 5 (v.2) we saw the same term used; in fact here John says, "Another mighty angel." Angels do, however, play a prominent role in the Book of Revelation, always in a position of service. They do not create things but fulfill the administration of God in human affairs.

Do not be deceived by the glorious description of this angel. Although this angel possesses some God-like characteristics, he is not God. "Robed in a cloud" suggests an attire characteristic of the glory associated with the second coming of Christ. A "rainbow above his head" would be his cap and is a reminder of God's covenant with man. The phrase "his face was like the sun" reminds us of Moses' face, and how it shone after he had been in the presence of God (Exodus 34:29). This angel's face is shining because he has just come from the presence of Christ. Lastly, "his legs were like fiery pillars" indicates that he has come to make an awesome and grave announcement of coming judgment.

The Little Scroll

10:2 – 3: Back in chapter 5 (v.1), I suggested that the seven-sealed scroll likely represents the "Book of Judgment" for the earth. Here, I believe that the "little scroll" in the hand of this mighty angel and the seven-seal scroll from chapter 5 are one and the same. The scroll contains the judgments of the Tribulation Period through which the Lord Jesus is coming to power. The book is now open, and the judgments are in force. The scroll was originally in the hand of God the Father. He gave it to His Son, the Lord Jesus Christ who, as we saw, was the only one worthy to open it. Here the text reads, "Little scroll, which lay open in his hand." This verse reinforces the fact that Jesus has removed the seals. The Lord then handed the opened scroll to the mighty angel, who brings it to earth to give finally to John.

The mighty angel stands with "his right foot in the sea and his left foot on the land," indicating that he has authority for claiming both the sea and the earth for Christ. Now with the scroll opened in hand, the mighty angel in "a loud voice like the roar of a lion" claims all for Christ. The kingdom of this world will become the kingdom of the Lord Jesus Christ through judgment. As Creator and Redeemer, the world belongs to Him.

The "seven thunders" here are the voices of God. In the Psalm 29, "The voice of the Lord" occurs seven times. The psalmist spoke of thunder as being the voice of the Lord, the God of glory. Here is God's endorsement of this mighty angel's claim.

10:4: John was preparing to write down what these thunder voices said since apparently what he heard was literally spoken words. However, he was forbidden to do so. John then heard the voice of the Lord Jesus from heaven saying, "Seal up what the seven thunders have said and do not write it down." This is the only proclamation in the entire Book of Revelation that is sealed up. Although Jesus Christ is being revealed in this book, there are still some things that God is not telling us.

10:5 – 6: The fact that this angel is raising his right hand towards heaven and swearing "by him who lives for ever and ever, who created the heavens and all that is in them, the earth and all that is in it, and the sea and all that is in it" indicates that this mighty angel is not the Lord Jesus Christ. He is making an oath by the only sure guarantee; that is, Christ Himself. Jesus Christ is the eternal God and the Creator. The apostle wrote: "Through him all things were made; without him nothing was made that has been made" (John 1:3). The Apostle Paul wrote in even greater detail about our Creator Jesus Christ (Read Colossians 1:16).

"There will be no more delay!" We (humanity) have been living in the time of God's delay for centuries. Now this angel warns those who have rejected Him that God is about to conclude His patience in the face of their rebellion. The angel is also informing God's saints on earth that it will not be long until Christ returns.

10:7: What is this "mystery of God"? The word *mystery* appears several times in the Bible, meaning that God is going to disclose a truth only possible to know through His Word. Human wisdom has never comprehended nor will ever be able to understand these truths apart from the Word of God. The mystery referred to here can only mean salvation through Jesus Christ. One of the characteristics of salvation involves the mystery of how a holy God could love sinful human beings so much as to send His only Son into the world to die for their sins. Paul wrote extensively about this same mystery in his letters to the early church. He revealed two truths. First, Paul proclaimed the gospel, which was given directly to him by our Lord Jesus Christ. Secondly, Paul taught that the Gentiles, as well as the remnant of Israel, would share in the glorious riches and inheritance of the kingdom of God. Take a look at a few related verses: Romans 16:25 – 26; Ephesians 3:6; Colossians 1:26 – 28; Colossians 2:2 – 3. Though Paul was writing concerning the church, these same truths will continue into and as the text here states, "will be accomplished" during the Tribulation Period. God's gift of salvation will be available through and up to the last day of the dreadful Tribulation Period to all who turn to Christ in faith as their Lord and Savior.

10:8: Then the voice of the Lord Jesus Christ commands John to take the opened scroll from the hand of the mighty angel. Keep in mind that the scene is now on earth.

10:9 – 10: The meaning of the phrase "take it and eat it" is a symbolic reference to "eating the Word of God." In other words, before someone can be a spokesman for God, he must first mentally feed on or digest the Word of God and receive it in faith. The prophet used this same analogy in Jeremiah (15:16) when he spoke to God and said, "When your words came I ate them; they were my joy and my heart's delight, for I bear your name, O Lord God Almighty." The Prophet Ezekiel, as well, used the analogy of eating the scroll before speaking to the house of Israel (Ezekiel 3:1 – 4). In the wonderful Psalm 119 which glorifies the Word of God, the psalmist wrote in verse 103: "How sweet your words are to my taste, sweeter than honey to my mouth!" The sweetness comes to John in the predictions concerning our blessed Lord's return – the future is sweet. The bitterness comes to John in being confronted by the fact that judgment is pronounced and coming upon the wicked and rebellious world during this dreadful time of God's wrath.

10:11: After John had eaten the scroll, the mighty angel says to him, "You must prophesy again about many peoples, nations, languages and kings." Through the written Word of God, which includes John's gospel, John's letters, and John's Book of Revelation (the revelation of Jesus Christ), this command to the apostle is being fulfilled today, for many "peoples, nations, languages and kings" are studying the Word of God. After all, the Bible is the number one best-selling book of all time! There is much prophecy to follow; and the entire world needs to be warned that judgment is coming.

The gospel of Jesus Christ is much like the little scroll:
It is sweet to those who hear it and respond, thus being guaranteed
eternal salvation as the free gift of God.
However, it is bitter to those who reject it, for them it guarantees
judgment and eternal separation from God.

Review Questions

1) In the Old Testament the pre-incarnate Christ was referred to as _____.

2) In the New Testament Christ has always appeared as _____.

3) Angels always play a prominent role in the position of _____.

4) The seven thunders are symbolic of _____.

5) The mystery of God refers to _____
_____.

6) The meaning of the phrase "take it and eat it," regarding the scroll, is symbolic of _____
_____.

7) How is the gospel of Jesus Christ like the little scroll? _____
_____.

Up For Discussion

"Till I come, give attendance to reading, to exhortation, to doctrine."
"Meditate upon these things; give thyself wholly to them;
that thy profiting may appear to all."
(1 Timothy 4:13, 15 KJV)

A one-year Bible Reading Calendar is included in the remaining pages of this chapter. Are you currently engaged in a tradition of daily Scripture reading? If so, how has it impacted your life and your daily Christian walk? Why is it important for believers to read and study God's Word daily?

Do more: Make a commitment to read God's Word daily:

1. Purchase a Study Bible with Commentary in a version you are comfortable reading.
2. Purchase a complete Bible Commentary that is easy for you to read and understand.
3. Purchase a Bible Dictionary – some are even illustrated.
4. Purchase a complete Concordance – those in your Bible are usually abbreviated.
5. Lastly, copy and share our Bible Reading Calendar with others and make it your ministry!

Bible Reading Calendar

JANUARY

Date	Morning	Evening	Date	Morning	Evening
1	Gen. 1, 2	Matt. 1	17	Gen. 41	Matt. 13:1-32
2	Gen. 3, 4, 5	Matt. 2	18	Gen. 42, 43	Matt. 13:33-58
3	Gen. 6, 7, 8	Matt. 3	19	Gen. 44, 45	Matt. 14:1-21
4	Gen. 9, 10, 11	Matt. 4	20	Gen. 46, 47, 48	Matt. 14:22-36
5	Gen. 12, 13, 14	Matt. 5:1-26	21	Gen. 49, 50	Matt. 15:1-20
6	Gen. 15, 16, 17	Matt. 5:27-48	22	Exod. 1, 2, 3	Matt. 15:21-39
7	Gen. 18, 19	Matt. 6	23	Exod. 4, 5, 6	Matt. 16
8	Gen. 20, 21, 22	Matt. 7	24	Exod. 7, 8	Matt. 17
9	Gen. 23, 24	Matt. 8	25	Exod. 9, 10	Matt. 18:1-20
10	Gen. 25, 26	Matt. 9:1-17	26	Exod. 11, 12	Matt. 18:21-35
11	Gen. 27, 28	Matt. 9:18-38	27	Exod. 13, 14, 15	Matt. 19:1-15
12	Gen. 29, 30	Matt. 10:1-23	28	Exod. 16, 17, 18	Matt. 19:16-30
13	Gen. 31, 32	Matt. 10:24-42	29	Exod. 19, 20, 21	Matt. 20:1-16
14	Gen. 33, 34, 35	Matt. 11	30	Exod. 22, 23, 24	Matt. 20:17-34
15	Gen. 36, 37	Matt. 12:1-21	31	Exod. 25, 26	Matt. 21:1-22
16	Gen. 38, 39, 40	Matt. 12:22-50			

FEBRUARY

Date	Morning	Evening	Date	Morning	Evening
1	Exod. 27, 28	Matt. 21:23-46	17	Lev. 24, 25	Mark 1:23-45
2	Exod. 29, 30	Matt. 22:1-22	18	Lev. 26, 27	Mark 2
3	Exod. 31, 32, 33	Matt. 22:23-46	19	Num. 1, 2	Mark 3:1-21
4	Exod. 34, 35, 36	Matt. 23:1-22	20	Num. 3, 4	Mark 3:22-35
5	Exod. 37, 38	Matt. 23:23-39	21	Num. 5, 6	Mark 4:1-20
6	Exod. 39, 40	Matt. 24:1-22	22	Num. 7	Mark 4:21-41
7	Lev. 1, 2, 3	Matt. 24:23-51	23	Num. 8, 9, 10	Mark 5:1-20
8	Lev. 4, 5, 6	Matt. 25:1-30	24	Num. 11, 12, 13	Mark 5:21-43
9	Lev. 7, 8, 9	Matt. 25:31-46	25	Num. 14, 15	Mark 6:1-32
10	Lev. 10, 11, 12	Matt. 26:1-19	26	Num. 16, 17	Mark 6:33-56
11	Lev. 13	Matt. 26:20-54	27	Num. 18, 19, 20	Mark 7:1-13
12	Lev. 14, 15	Matt. 26:55-75	28	Num. 21, 22	Mark 7:14-37
13	Lev. 16, 17	Matt. 27:1-31	29	Num. 23, 24, 25	Mark 8:1-21
14	Lev. 18, 19	Matt. 27:32-66			
15	Lev. 20, 21	Matt. 28			
16	Lev. 22, 23	Mark 1:1-22			

Divide chapters for February 29 and read them
February 28 and March 1
when February has only 28 days.

MARCH

Date	Morning	Evening	Date	Morning	Evening
1	Num. 26, 27	Mark 8:22-38	17	Deut. 29, 30	Mark 16
2	Num. 28, 29	Mark 9:1-29	18	Deut. 31, 32	Luke 1:1-23
3	Num. 30, 31	Mark 9:30-50	19	Deut. 33, 34	Luke 1:24-56
4	Num. 32, 33	Mark 10:1-31	20	Joshua 1, 2, 3	Luke 1:57-80
5	Num. 34, 35, 36	Mark 10:32-52	21	Joshua 4, 5, 6	Luke 2:1-24
6	Deut. 1, 2	Mark 11:1-19	22	Joshua 7, 8	Luke 2:25-52
7	Deut. 3, 4	Mark 11:20-33	23	Joshua 9, 10	Luke 3
8	Deut. 5, 6, 7	Mark 12:1-27	24	Joshua 11, 12, 13	Luke 4:1-32
9	Deut. 8, 9, 10	Mark 12:28-44	25	Joshua 14, 15	Luke 4:33-44
10	Deut. 11, 12, 13	Mark 13:1-13	26	Joshua 16, 17, 18	Luke 5:1-16
11	Deut. 14, 15, 16	Mark 13:14-37	27	Joshua 19, 20	Luke 5:17-39
12	Deut. 17, 18, 19	Mark 14:1-25	28	Joshua 21, 22	Luke 6:1-26
13	Deut. 20, 21, 22	Mark 14:26-50	29	Joshua 23, 24	Luke 6:27-49
14	Deut. 23, 24, 25	Mark 14:51-72	30	Judges 1, 2	Luke 7:1-30
15	Deut. 26, 27	Mark 15:1-26	31	Judges 3, 4, 5	Luke 7:31-50
16	Deut. 28	Mark 15:27-47			

"Till I come, give attendance to reading, to exhortation, to doctrine."
1 Timothy 4:13

APRIL

Date	Morning	Evening	Date	Morning	Evening
1	Judges 6, 7	Luke 8:1-21	17	I Sam. 22, 23, 24	Luke 16:1-18
2	Judges 8, 9	Luke 8:22-56	18	I Sam. 25, 26	Luke 16:19-31
3	Judges 10, 11	Luke 9:1-36	19	I Sam. 27, 28, 29	Luke 17:1-19
4	Judges 12, 13, 14	Luke 9:37-62	20	I Sam. 30, 31	Luke 17:20-37
5	Judges 15, 16, 17	Luke 10:1-24	21	II Sam. 1, 2, 3	Luke 18:1-17
6	Judges 18, 19	Luke 10:25-42	22	II Sam. 4, 5, 6	Luke 18:18-43
7	Judges 20, 21	Luke 11:1-28	23	II Sam. 7, 8, 9	Luke 19:1-28
8	Ruth 1, 2, 3, 4	Luke 11:29-54	24	II Sam. 10, 11, 12	Luke 19:29-48
9	I Sam. 1, 2, 3	Luke 12:1-34	25	II Sam. 13, 14	Luke 20:1-26
10	I Sam. 4, 5, 6	Luke 12:35-59	26	II Sam. 15, 16	Luke 20:27-47
11	I Sam. 7, 8, 9	Luke 13:1-21	27	II Sam. 17, 18	Luke 21:1-19
12	I Sam. 10, 11, 12	Luke 13:22-35	28	II Sam. 19, 20	Luke 21:20-38
13	I Sam. 13, 14	Luke 14:1-24	29	II Sam. 21, 22	Luke 22:1-30
14	I Sam. 15, 16	Luke 14:25-35	30	II Sam. 23, 24	Luke 22:31-53
15	I Sam. 17, 18	Luke 15:1-10			
16	I Sam. 19, 20, 21	Luke 15:11-32			

MAY

Date	Morning	Evening	Date	Morning	Evening
1	I Kings 1, 2	Luke 22:54-71	17	II Kings 18, 19	John 6:22-44
2	I Kings 3, 4, 5	Luke 23:1-26	18	II Kings 20, 21, 22	John 6:45-71
3	I Kings 6, 7	Luke 23:27-38	19	II Kings 23, 24, 25	John 7:1-31
4	I Kings 8, 9	Luke 23:39-56	20	I Chron. 1, 2	John 7:32-53
5	I Kings 10, 11	Luke 24:1-35	21	I Chron. 3, 4, 5	John 8:1-20
6	I Kings 12, 13	Luke 24:36-53	22	I Chron. 6, 7	John 8:21-36
7	I Kings 14, 15	John 1:1-28	23	I Chron. 8, 9, 10	John 8:37-59
8	I Kings 16, 17, 18	John 1:29-51	24	I Chron. 11, 12, 13	John 9:1-23
9	I Kings 19, 20	John 2	25	I Chron. 14, 15, 16	John 9:24-41
10	I Kings 21, 22	John 3:1-21	26	I Chron. 17, 18, 19	John 10:1-21
11	II Kings 1, 2, 3	John 3:22-36	27	I Chron. 20, 21, 22	John 10:22-42
12	II Kings 4, 5	John 4:1-30	28	I Chron. 23, 24, 25	John 11:1-17
13	II Kings 6, 7, 8	John 4:31-54	29	I Chron. 26, 27	John 11:18-46
14	II Kings 9, 10, 11	John 5:1-24	30	I Chron. 28, 29	John 11:47-57
15	II Kings 12, 13, 14	John 5:25-47	31	II Chr. 1, 2, 3	John 12:1-19
16	II Kings 15, 16, 17	John 6:1-21			

JUNE

Date	Morning	Evening	Date	Morning	Evening
1	II Chr. 4, 5, 6	John 12:20-50	17	Neh. 4, 5, 6	Acts 2:14-47
2	II Chr. 7, 8, 9	John 13:1-17	18	Neh. 7, 8	Acts 3
3	II Chr. 10, 11, 12	John 13:18-38	19	Neh. 9, 10, 11	Acts 4:1-22
4	II Chr. 13-16	John 14	20	Neh. 12, 13	Acts 4:23-37
5	II Chr. 17, 18, 19	John 15	21	Esther 1, 2, 3	Acts 5:1-16
6	II Chr. 20, 21, 22	John 16:1-15	22	Esther 4, 5, 6	Acts 5:17-42
7	II Chr. 23, 24, 25	John 16:16-33	23	Esther 7-10	Acts 6
8	II Chr. 26, 27, 28	John 17	24	Job 1, 2, 3	Acts 7:1-19
9	II Chr. 29, 30, 31	John 18:1-23	25	Job 4, 5, 6	Acts 7:20-43
10	II Chr. 32, 33, 34	John 18:24-40	26	Job 7, 8, 9	Acts 7:44-60
11	II Chr. 35, 36	John 19:1-22	27	Job 10, 11, 12	Acts 8:1-25
12	Ezra 1, 2	John 19:23-42	28	Job 13, 14, 15	Acts 8:26-40
13	Ezra 3, 4, 5	John 20	29	Job 16, 17, 18	Acts 9:1-22
14	Ezra 6, 7, 8	John 21	30	Job 19, 20	Acts 9:23-43
15	Ezra 9, 10	Acts 1			
16	Neh. 1, 2, 3	Acts 2:1-13			

**Rules for Bible Study: 1. Read it through daily. Pray for discernment.
3. Mark your Bible. 4. Work it out daily in your life. 5. Copy and pass it on to others.**

JULY

Date	Morning	Evening	Date	Morning	Evening
1	Job 21, 22	Acts 10:1-23	17	Psalm 22, 23, 24	Acts 20:1-16
2	Job 23, 24, 25	Acts 10:24-48	18	Psalm 25, 26, 27	Acts 20:17-38
3	Job 26, 27, 28	Acts 11	19	Psalm 28, 29, 30	Acts 21:1-14
4	Job 29, 30	Acts 12	20	Psalm 31, 32, 33	Acts 21:15-40
5	Job 31, 32	Acts 13:1-23	21	Psalm 34, 35	Acts 22
6	Job 33, 34	Acts 13:24-52	22	Psalm 36, 37	Acts 23:1-11
7	Job 35, 36, 37	Acts 14	23	Psalm 38, 39, 40	Acts 23:12-35
8	Job 38, 39	Acts 15:1-21	24	Psalm 41, 42, 43	Acts 24
9	Job 40, 41, 42	Acts 15:22-41	25	Psalm 44, 45, 46	Acts 25
10	Psalm 1, 2, 3	Acts 16:1-15	26	Psalm 47, 48, 49	Acts 26
11	Psalm 4, 5, 6	Acts 16:16-40	27	Psalm 50, 51, 52	Acts 27:1-25
12	Psalm 7, 8, 9	Acts 17:1-15	28	Psalm 53, 54, 55	Acts 27:26-44
13	Psalm 10, 11, 12	Acts 17:16-34	29	Psalm 56, 57, 58	Acts 28:1-15
14	Psalm 13, 14, 15, 16	Acts 18	30	Psalm 59, 60, 61	Acts 28:16-31
15	Psalm 17, 18	Acts 19:1-20	31	Psalm 62, 63, 64	Rom. 1
16	Psalm 19, 20, 21	Acts 19:21-41			

AUGUST

Date	Morning	Evening	Date	Morning	Evening
1	Psalm 65, 66, 67	Rom. 2	17	Psalm 107, 108	Rom. 15:21-33
2	Psalm 68, 69	Rom. 3	18	Psalm 109, 110, 111	Rom. 16
3	Psalm 70, 71, 72	Rom. 4	19	Psalm 112-115	I Cor. 1
4	Psalm 73, 74	Rom. 5	20	Psalm 116-118	I Cor. 2
5	Psalm 75, 76, 77	Rom. 6	21	Psalm 119:1-48	I Cor. 3
6	Psalm 78	Rom. 7	22	Psalm 119:49-104	I Cor. 4
7	Psalm 79, 80, 81	Rom. 8:1-18	23	Psalm 119:105-176	I Cor. 5
8	Psalm 82, 83, 84	Rom. 8:19-39	24	Psalm 120-123	I Cor. 6
9	Psalm 85, 86, 87	Rom. 9	25	Psalm 124-127	I Cor. 7:1-24
10	Psalm 88, 89	Rom. 10	26	Psalm 128-131	I Cor. 7:25-40
11	Psalm 90, 91, 92	Rom. 11:1-21	27	Psalm 132-135	I Cor. 8
12	Psalm 93, 94, 95	Rom. 11:22-36	28	Psalm 136-138	I Cor. 9
13	Psalm 96, 97, 98	Rom. 12	29	Psalm 139-141	I Cor. 10:1-13
14	Psalm 99-102	Rom. 13	30	Psalm 142-144	I Cor. 10:14-33
15	Psalm 103, 104	Rom. 14	31	Psalm 145-147	I Cor. 11:1-15
16	Psalm 105, 106	Rom. 15:1-20			

SEPTEMBER

Date	Morning	Evening	Date	Morning	Evening
1	Psalm 148-150	I Cor. 11:16-34	17	Eccles. 1, 2, 3	II Cor. 9
2	Proverbs 1, 2	I Cor. 12	18	Eccles. 4, 5, 6	II Cor. 10
3	Proverbs 3, 4	I Cor. 13	19	Eccles. 7, 8, 9	II Cor. 11:1-15
4	Proverbs 5, 6	I Cor. 14:1-20	20	Eccles. 10, 11, 12	II Cor. 11:16-33
5	Proverbs 7, 8	I Cor. 14:21-40	21	Songs 1, 2, 3	II Cor. 12
6	Proverbs 9, 10	I Cor. 15:1-32	22	Songs 4, 5	II Cor. 13
7	Proverbs 11, 12	I Cor. 15:33-58	23	Songs 6, 7, 8	Gal. 1
8	Proverbs 13, 14	I Cor. 16	24	Isaiah 1, 2, 3	Gal. 2
9	Proverbs 15, 16	II Cor. 1	25	Isaiah 4, 5, 6	Gal. 3
10	Proverbs 17, 18	II Cor. 2	26	Isaiah 7, 8, 9	Gal. 4
11	Proverbs 19, 20	II Cor. 3	27	Isaiah 10, 11, 12	Gal. 5
12	Proverbs 21, 22	II Cor. 4	28	Isaiah 13, 14, 15	Gal. 6
13	Proverbs 23, 24	II Cor. 5	29	Isaiah 16, 17, 18	Eph. 1
14	Proverbs 25, 26, 27	II Cor. 6	30	Isaiah 19, 20, 21	Eph. 2
15	Proverbs 28, 29	II Cor. 7			
16	Proverbs 30, 31	II Cor. 8			

OCTOBER

Date	Morning		Evening		Date	Morning		Evening	
1	Isaiah	22, 23	Eph.	3	17	Isaiah	62, 63, 64	I Thess.	5
2	Isaiah	24, 25, 26	Eph.	4	18	Isaiah	65, 66	II Thess.	1
3	Isaiah	27, 28	Eph.	5	19	Jer.	1, 2	II Thess.	2
4	Isaiah	29, 30	Eph.	6	20	Jer.	3, 4	II Thess.	3
5	Isaiah	31, 32, 33	Phil.	1	21	Jer.	5, 6	I Tim.	1
6	Isaiah	34, 35, 36	Phil.	2	22	Jer.	7, 8	I Tim.	2
7	Isaiah	37, 38	Phil.	3	23	Jer.	9, 10	I Tim.	3
8	Isaiah	39, 40	Phil.	4	24	Jer.	11, 12, 13	I Tim.	4
9	Isaiah	41, 42	Col.	1	25	Jer.	14, 15, 16	I Tim.	5
10	Isaiah	43, 44	Col.	2	26	Jer.	17, 18, 19	I Tim.	6
11	Isaiah	45, 46, 47	Col.	3	27	Jer.	20, 21, 22	II Tim.	1
12	Isaiah	48, 49	Col.	4	28	Jer.	23, 24	II Tim.	2
13	Isaiah	50, 51, 52	I Thess.	1	29	Jer.	25, 26	II Tim.	3
14	Isaiah	53, 54, 55	I Thess.	2	30	Jer.	27, 28	II Tim.	4
15	Isaiah	56, 57, 58	I Thess.	3	31	Jer.	29, 30	Titus	1
16	Isaiah	59, 60, 61	I Thess.	4					

NOVEMBER

Date	Morning		Evening		Date	Morning		Evening	
1	Jer.	31, 32	Titus	2	17	Ezek.	16	Hebrews	12
2	Jer.	33, 34, 35	Titus	3	18	Ezek.	17, 18, 19	Hebrews	13
3	Jer.	36, 37	Philemon		19	Ezek.	20, 21	James	1
4	Jer.	38, 39	Hebrews	1	20	Ezek.	22, 23	James	2
5	Jer.	40, 41, 42	Hebrews	2	21	Ezek.	24, 25, 26	James	3
6	Jer.	43, 44, 45	Hebrews	3	22	Ezek.	27, 28	James	4
7	Jer.	46, 47, 48	Hebrews	4	23	Ezek.	29, 30, 31	James	5
8	Jer.	49, 50	Hebrews	5	24	Ezek.	32, 33	I Peter	1
9	Jer.	51, 52	Hebrews	6	25	Ezek.	34, 35	I Peter	2
10	Lam.	1, 2	Hebrews	7	26	Ezek.	36, 37	I Peter	3
11	Lam.	3, 4, 5	Hebrews	8	27	Ezek.	38, 39	I Peter	4
12	Ezek.	1, 2, 3	Hebrews	9	28	Ezek.	40	I Peter	5
13	Ezek.	4, 5, 6	Hebrews	10:1-23	29	Ezek.	41, 42	II Peter	1
14	Ezek.	7, 8, 9	Hebrews	10:24-39	30	Ezek.	43, 44	II Peter	2
15	Ezek.	10, 11, 12	Hebrews	11:1-19					
16	Ezek.	13, 14, 15	Hebrews	11:20-40					

DECEMBER

Date	Morning		Evening		Date	Morning		Evening	
1	Ezek.	45, 46	II Peter	3	17	Obadiah		Rev.	8
2	Ezek.	47, 48	I John	1	18	Jonah		Rev.	9
3	Dan.	1, 2	I John	2	19	Micah	1, 2, 3	Rev.	10
4	Dan.	3, 4	I John	3	20	Micah	4, 5	Rev.	11
5	Dan.	5, 6	I John	4	21	Micah	6, 7	Rev.	12
6	Dan.	7, 8	I John	5	22	Nahum		Rev.	13
7	Dan.	9, 10	II John		23	Habakkuk		Rev.	14
8	Dan.	11, 12	III John		24	Zephaniah		Rev.	15
9	Hosea	1-4	Jude		25	Haggai		Rev.	16
10	Hosea	5-8	Rev.	1	26	Zech.	1, 2, 3	Rev.	17
11	Hosea	9, 10, 11	Rev.	2	27	Zech.	4, 5, 6	Rev.	18
12	Hosea	12, 13, 14	Rev.	3	28	Zech.	7, 8, 9	Rev.	19
13	Joel		Rev.	4	29	Zech.	10, 11, 12	Rev.	20
14	Amos	1, 2, 3	Rev.	5	30	Zech.	13, 14	Rev.	21
15	Amos	4, 5, 6	Rev.	6	31	Malachi		Rev.	22
16	Amos	7, 8, 9	Rev.	7					

Chapter 11

The first fourteen verses of this chapter continue the interlude between the sixth and seventh trumpet. These verses reflect back to the beginning of the Tribulation Period in order to acquaint us with the Tribulation Temple and to introduce God's two witnesses.

These verses have to do with the spiritual life of Israel as we find the nation of Israel reverting back to the Old Testament form of worship. They rebuild the temple, likely as a result of the covenant confirmed with Antichrist (Daniel 9:27) and apart from the Messiah, since they believe He has not yet come. Believers in the Lord Jesus Christ are not taught to build a temple; on the contrary, we are taught that God does not live in temples made with hands, but that the Holy Spirit uses the believer's body as a tabernacle or dwelling place (1 Corinthians 6:19 – 20). The fact that Israel rebuilds the temple demonstrates that she has not received the Lord Jesus Christ as Messiah, but rather has turned to Antichrist and his false prophet (details in chapter 13) because of the initial peace they bring to their nation and the world. It is worth noting that the longer Antichrist and his false prophet can keep the Jews deceived and focused on them, the more souls they will win over, and the less souls that will recognize and turn to the true Messiah, which is the Lord Jesus Christ.

11:1 – 2: The Apostle John is now told: "Go and measure the temple of God and the altar, and count the worshipers there. But exclude the outer court; do not measure it, because it has been given to the Gentiles. They will trample on the holy city for 42 months (3½ years)." With the discovery in recent years of the western gate precisely opposite the eastern gate, we have more reason now to believe the original location of the temple is north of the present day Dome of the Rock. That would place the Dome of the Rock in the middle of the "Court of the Gentiles," thus fulfilling this prophecy (see end-of-chapter illustration entitled "The Temple Mount"). Though the Temple Mount is in Israeli hands, the politics of the area forbid the Jews from actual entry onto the mount. Regardless, the likely site for the rebuilding of the temple is known and available. A fund has been created and a temple priesthood of Jews from the tribe of Levi is currently in training to conduct worship based on Old Testament ritual. In light of the evidence, it seems the path is being cleared for the remarkable events described here by the Revelator John.

The fact that John is told to measure the temple suggests he may find it sadly lacking as compared to Solomon's temple, which was inspired by God. The word *measure* refers to the fact that God is about to deal with the nation of Israel (Jeremiah 31:38 – 39; Zechariah 2). The word *rod* speaks of chastisement and judgment (Psalm 2:9 KJV), but it also speaks of comfort (Psalm 23:4). Israel will be severely judged for her rejection of the Lord Jesus Christ as Messiah in spite of the 144,000 witnesses of chapter 7 and the testimony of the two witnesses of this chapter. However, the remnant of Israel that does turn to Christ will be comforted with everlasting peace and eternal life from our Savior.

The Two Witnesses

11:3 – 6: "I will give power to my two witnesses, and they will prophesy for 1,260 days (3½ years), clothed in sackcloth." During the first half of the Tribulation Period, God will establish two divine witnesses in Jerusalem. Sackcloth is the usual attire of the Old Testament prophets and reminds us of Elijah and John the Baptist. The two olive trees immediately suggest the vision in Zechariah 4. Those two were Joshua and Zerubbabel, both anointed and enabled by the Holy Spirit to stand against insurmountable difficulties. Throughout history, it has been the responsibility of the nation of Israel to declare and proclaim to the world the one true Living God. The "lampstand" is symbolic and represents an individual who brings God's light (truth) to the world, as is was with our Lord Jesus Christ. The "olive trees" provide the oil (fuel) for the lamp, which symbolizes the work of the Holy Spirit through that individual. The Holy Spirit will be present during the Tribulation Period as well. These two witnesses will be endowed with supernatural powers, similar to prophets from the Old Testament, and for the following three purposes:

1) They will "prophesy," which means they will preach concerning things to come.
2) They will "witness," meaning they will demonstrate God's power in contrast to that of Antichrist (the beast).
3) They will also "testify," which comes from the word *testimony* in verse 7, meaning they will preach the gospel of Jesus Christ.

These two witnesses are lights before the powers of darkness. They are immortal and immune to all attacks until their mission is completed. They are yet another illustration that God is so keenly interested in the souls of His children that He will even send two supernatural witnesses to convince lost humanity. Scripture has always required two or more witnesses to bear testimony to anything before it is to be heard (Matthew 18:16). Is it possible that all believers are immortal as well until their God-given purpose is fulfilled on earth; and only then will God call each home to heaven to be with Him?

We can only offer a suggestion as to the identity of these two witnesses. The prophet predicted that Elijah would come before "the great and dreadful day of the Lord" (Malachi 4:5 – 6). Furthermore, we find that the use of fire in the Old Testament was given to Elijah, who called down fire to consume the altar in the days of King Ahab and Jezebel (2 Kings 18:20 – 40). He also withheld rain from the earth for three years. There are three reasons why some scholars suggest that Moses may be the second witness:

1) When the Lord Jesus was transfigured before His Jewish witnesses – Peter, James, and John – two representatives of the Old Testament were brought before their view: Moses and Elijah (Matthew 17:1 – 4).

2) Moses manifested power to bring plagues onto the earth and to turn water into blood during the days of Pharaoh.

3) Moses remains even today an important part of Jewish family tradition.

It seems logical that Moses and Elijah combined would represent the entire Old Testament to the Jewish nation.

Another possibility to consider would be the only two Old Testament patriarchs that did not taste death but were raptured (taken up) to heaven. The first one being Enoch who was taken directly to heaven by God (Genesis 5:24); and the second one, again, being Elijah who was carried bodily to heaven in a whirlwind (2 Kings 2:11). Whether or not we choose to accept the writings from *The Lost Books of the Bible*, it is interesting to read the following from the Gospel of Nicodemus 20:4: "Here we [Enoch and Elijah] have up to now been and have not tasted death, but are now about to return at the coming of Antichrist, being armed with divine signs and miracles, to engage with him in battle, and to be slain by him at Jerusalem, and to be taken up alive again into the clouds, after three days and a half." The descriptive language in this passage is clearly specific, and leaves no doubt as to its relevance to what we read here in these verses of chapter 11. This scenario would liken Enoch as a representative to the Gentile nations and Elijah as a representative to the Jewish nation in the kingdom of God that will be established on earth at Christ's return.

Still, others suggest that John the Baptist might be the second witness. He was the forerunner to Christ at His first coming. He was similar to Elijah in manner and message. Both knew what it was like to oppose the forces of darkness and to stand alone for God against impossible odds. John the Baptist would be the witness of the New Testament, where Elijah would be the witness of the Old Testament.

11:7 – 8: "The beast" is an expression used here for the first time. The fact that he will come up out of the Abyss is a reference to the death and apparent resurrection of Antichrist, as we will study in more detail in chapter 13. The beast or Antichrist, the man of sin, will hate the two witnesses, make war against them, and eventually kill them, only after they "have finished their testimony."

These men are not even given a decent burial. This demonstrates an extremely cruel and barbaric-like culture in existence during this time. The Holy City, Jerusalem, "where also their Lord was crucified" will be so immoral and corrupt spiritually that she will be called Sodom and Egypt. Jerusalem was called Sodom by the Prophet Isaiah (Isaiah 1:10); Sodom being symbolic of immorality and rebellion against God. In contrast, Egypt is symbolic of materialism and the love for "worldly" wealth.

11:9 – 10: After Christ was crucified, even Pilate permitted His disciples to take down the body and give Him a respectable burial according to Jewish custom, but not so with the two witnesses. With our modern television media via satellite and 24-hour cable news networks, ours is the first generation that will literally see the fulfillment of this prophecy by allowing the entire "inhabitants of the earth" to witness such a gruesome spectacle.

Not content to just look on them, we see that people throughout the world will enjoy a Christmas-like celebration, giving and receiving gifts because these preachers of righteousness are now dead. This is Satan's Xmas. The world will celebrate what Antichrist has done instead of the coming of Christ to

Bethlehem. Their treatment of these two men demonstrates the worst humiliation imaginable by a depraved and godless society.

11:11 – 12: After three and a half days these men receive "a breath of life from God." In the Greek, the scriptural word for resurrection used here is the verb *histemi* which means "to make to stand." The Lord again uses the phrase "Come up here." These are the same words Jesus used back in chapter 4 which we said represented the resurrection and rapture of the church. A cloud will receive them out of sight as their enemies, with the help of modern television, look on. The cloud of glory is associated with both the ascension and return of Christ. It is no wonder "terror struck those who saw them." The resurrection of these men will be the final confirmation that they were men of God, and another illustration that God does not forget His children.

11:13 – 14: This judgment, an earthquake that collapses a tenth of the city and kills seven thousand, is a result of the shocking treatment of the two faithful witnesses of God by the inhabitants of the city of Jerusalem. This event apparently triggers a revival, for the passage reads, "and the survivors were terrified and gave glory to the God of heaven." Though they did acknowledge God, it does not necessarily mean that they repented and turned to Christ.

The Seventh Trumpet Judgment

11:15: The seventh trumpet: "The third woe."

The blowing of the seventh trumpet does not initiate anything on the earth. It may be much like the breaking of the seventh seal in that it merely introduces the next series of judgments, the seven bowls, which we will study starting in chapter 15. This coincides with the tossing of Satan from heaven and confining him to earth, as we will see in chapter 12. Satan's banishment to earth and assault during the second half of the Tribulation Period will be, without a doubt "the third woe."

It may be noteworthy that the following verses are inserted here for the encouragement of the saints remaining on earth (those who are sealed). These verses give us a glimpse of the eternity ahead when all rebellion to God is finally crushed and Christ reigns victorious.

Following the blowing of the seventh trumpet, John hears "great voices," evidently angelic voices in chorus. This is in contrast to the breaking of the seventh seal when there was silence in heaven. It is a time of joy, for God's entire created heavenly host can now anticipate the coming end and termination of all wickedness. They announce two things:

1) "The kingdom of the world has become the kingdom of our Lord and of his Christ." This is a view of the kingdom of Antichrist at the time of the Revelation (14:1) when Christ returns to earth to defeat Antichrist and overthrow his one-world empire, and to establish His earthly Millennial Kingdom.

2) "And he will reign for ever and ever." This indicates that once Christ comes to earth, there will be no interruption of His government despite the rebellion that will break out when Satan is "released from his prison" (Revelation 20:7). Our glorified Lord will extinguish it so fast it will not interfere with His kingdom.

11:16 – 18: The twenty-four elders fall on their faces before God and worship Him, announcing His eternity with the words, "The One who is and who was." This is a song of thanksgiving, indicating that they anticipate in heaven the final stage of God's activity on the earth, as they rejoice over the eventual consummation of His kingdom. They make three predictions on the basis of Christ's return:

1) "The nations were angry; and your wrath has come." Because of their stubborn rebellion against God, mankind will be angry and will resent the Lord's coming. The hearts of unrepentant men will be hardened all the way up to the end of the Tribulation Period.

2) "The time has come for judging the dead, rewarding your servants the prophets, and your saints …." This is a clear reference to the resurrection of the Old Testament Saints and the slain Tribulation Saints. These are the saints under the altar mentioned earlier (6:9). They are included in the first resurrection. This does not refer to unbelievers, who will be resurrected (the final resurrection) and judged at the end of the Millennium (Revelation 20:11 – 15). The resurrection of these Old Testament Saints is also promised in Psalm 50:1 – 6 and Daniel 12:1 – 2.

3) "And for destroying those who destroy the earth." Here, the word *destroy* is translated from the Greek word *diaphtheiro*, which means those who "ruin" or "corrupt," and refers to both man and Satan. The New Testament teaches that those who die without receiving Christ as their Savior, will go in soul and spirit to the "place of torment" (as did the rich man in Luke 16) to await the judgment of the Great White Throne, as we will study later in chapter 20. At that time, they will stand before Christ, the Judge, for their final judgment.

11:19: When we see the church again, it will be in the New Jerusalem, and we are definitely told that there is no temple there; but here, there is a temple in heaven. The temple, which Moses made, was made after the pattern in heaven (Exodus 25:9, Hebrews 8:5). Therefore the phrase "God's temple in heaven was opened" means that God is here dealing with the nation of Israel. The vision of the Ark of the Covenant could be a reminder to Israel that they are dealing with a covenant-making and covenant-keeping God, and on the basis of His past faithfulness the redemption of the remnant of the nation of Israel is guaranteed. The writer of Hebrews tells us, "The time is coming, declares the Lord, when I will make a new covenant with the house of Israel and with the house of Judah …" (Hebrews 8:8 – 13). At that time the Law will be written on their hearts instead of hard cold tablets of stone.

The "lightning, rumbling and peals of thunder" speak of judgment yet to come.

This chapter is a reaffirmation of God sending His final witnesses and making one last attempt to say to the nation of Israel that there is one true God, Jehovah, and Jesus is His Christ (Messiah).

In view of the destruction and misery that awaits the earth during the Tribulation,
any intelligent being is left with only one decision:
Avoid this dreadful period in the world's future by repenting and receiving
Jesus Christ as your Lord and Savior by personal invitation.

Review Questions

1) The nation of Israel will finally rebuild their temple during the first half of the Tribulation Period most likely as a result of _____

_____.

2) In our discussion of the proposed site plan of the third temple, it locates the present day Dome of the Rock in the middle of _____.

3) The lampstand is symbolic of _____.

4) The olive oil provides the fuel for the lamp, which symbolizes _____

_____.

5) The two witnesses are endowed with supernatural power for the purposes of _____

_____.

6) The two witnesses will be killed by Antichrist and after three and a half days these men will be

_____.

7) The blowing of the seventh trumpet is much like the breaking of the seventh seal in that it

_____.

Up For Discussion

"And there was given me a reed like unto a rod: and the angel stood, saying,
Rise, and measure the temple of God, and the altar,
and them that worship therein."
(Revelation 11:1 KJV)

As stated in our explanation (v.1 – 2), it is possible that Israel's third temple could be located and constructed without any displacement of the Muslim Dome of the Rock. Of course it would take a miracle to make that happen, a miracle in the form of a peace treaty or covenant confirmed by the "ruler to come" (Daniel 9:27). The Apostle John calls him the Antichrist. We will study him further in chapter 13.

Using the illustration entitled, "Jerusalem's Four Temples," review on your own or as a class. Discuss each block, moving from left to right, and read the Scripture references associated with each. Review the illustration, "The Temple Mount" for further discussion.

Some scholars believe the identity of the two witnesses is irrelevant. What is more important is the message of grace through the gospel of Jesus Christ to an unrepentant world in tribulation. Do you agree, or do you find it interesting or challenging to speculate as to their identities based on Christian writings?

Jerusalem's Four Temples

First Temple	Second Temple		Dome of the Rock	Tribulation Temple	Millennial Temple
King Solomon's	Zerubbabel's and Herod's		Mosque dominates the Temple Mount, Jewish Dispersion	Antichrist Desecrates	Christ's Memorial Temple
Shekinah Present	Roman Insignia		Church Age Gentile Inclusion Romans 9-11	"Abomination that causes Desolation"	Glory Returns Ezekiel 43:1-5
(Glory of God) 1 Kings 5-8	Ezra 3:7-6:18			Daniel 9:27 2 Thessalonians 2:4 Revelation 13:14-15	Jesus Christ Reigns
					Ezekiel 40-43 Isaiah 56:7

70 Year Exile

374 Years	586 Years		"Age of Grace"	7 Years	1,000 Years
Israel's Monarchy	Gentile Domination		The Church	Tribulation Period	Millennium
1st Temple built by Solomon 960 B.C.	2nd Temple built by Zerubbabel 516 B.C.		Believer's body as the temple 1 Corinthians 3:16 and 6:19	3rd Temple	Messianic Age Isaiah 2:2-4 Jeremiah 23:5-6 Zechariah 14:9-21 Acts 3:16-24 Revelation 20
Temple destroyed by Babylon 586 B.C.	Temple enlarged by Herod 19 B.C.		Temple destroyed by the Romans 70 A.D.	Temple is desecrated by Antichrist. Matthew 24:15	4th Temple built by the Lord Jesus Christ

Midpoint

67

The Temple Mount and the Tribulation Temple Under the Covenant of Antichrist

Many things coincide with the mid-point of the Tribulation Period, one of which is Antichrist's persecution of the nation of Israel. It is at this time that Antichrist breaks his covenant of peace with Israel as his false prophet initiates idol worship in the newly rebuilt temple in Jerusalem. It may be that Israel, who does not accept Jesus Christ as the Messiah during the first half of the Tribulation Period, will embrace Him in the second half; thus rejecting the deceiving idolatrous religion of Antichrist.

The nation of Israel will become the dividing line for the entire world during the second half of the Tribulation Period. Those who receive the mark of the beast and worship Antichrist will assist him worldwide in his persecution of the Jews (and Christians). Those who have receive Jesus Christ as Lord and Savior [Tribulation Saints] will provide aid and protection to the Jewish remnant, while sharing with them the long anticipated message of mercy and grace from their true Messiah, Jesus Christ.

Below is an example of how the Temple Mount might appear under Antichrist's coexistent covenant.

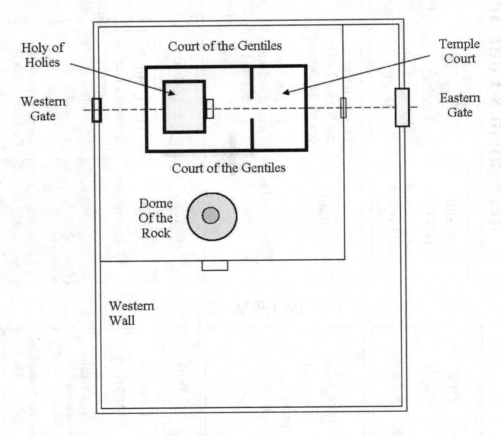

The Rebuilding of the Temple during the First Half of the Tribulation Period
*Sketch is for illustration proposes only and not to precise scale.

Chapter 12

This chapter introduces the second half of the Tribulation Period by giving a heavenly recap of the great conflict of the ages. It brings us up-to-date in our study. In chapters 12 and 13, we will take a close look at seven key figures or groups. The identification and clarification of these are essential for a proper understanding of the Book of Revelation. Please keep in mind that what John is seeing here is past, present, and future.

1) The Woman – Israel

12:1 – 2: The woman is referred to as a "great and wondrous sign" that appeared in heaven. The word "sign" indicates that the woman is not to be taken literally as a woman, but as a symbol of something else. At its most basic level, the Roman Catholic Church symbolically views the "woman" as the Blessed Mother – the Virgin Mary. The "pain" is viewed on a deeper level in her suffering, as that of the mother of our Lord as she stood beneath the cross upon which her Son died. However, literally speaking, it seems impossible to imagine Mary giving birth to her child "in heaven." Instead, I lean more toward the belief that the "woman" here represents the nation of Israel, which gave birth to the Messiah, Jesus Christ. From Abraham to the days of Mary, the nation of Israel was preparing to bring forth a man-child that would bless the entire world. The fact that this woman is seen "clothed with the sun, with the moon under her feet" illustrates illumination. The sun as a generator of light and the moon as a reflector are both symbolic of Israel being God's light-bearer to mankind. The sun, moon, and stars also belong to Israel as seen in Joseph's dream (Genesis 37:9). The "crown of twelve stars" is representative of the twelve tribes of Israel.

Remember in our previous chapter we learned that it was the responsibility of the nation of Israel to be "light" to the pagan Gentile world and to proclaim the one true God. However, when Israel rejected Jesus Christ as Messiah, God gave that responsibility over to the church.

2) The Red Dragon – Satan

12:3: Here we see "another sign"; meaning again, we are not to take it literally. Satan is identified by name in verse 9 and is here described as an "enormous red dragon." The King James Version uses the word "great" meaning he is very powerful. He is red because he is the motivating force behind all of the bloodshed throughout human history. He is called a dragon because of the viciousness of his character. Satan is the most dangerous being in all of God's creation. Although I cannot be certain here, many scholars suggest, and I agree, that the "seven-crowned heads" most likely represent governmental powers, or possibly the seven stages of the Roman Empire. These are the empires or kingdoms throughout history that Satan has used to enslave, persecute, and war against the nation of Israel and to blaspheme God. First was the kingdom of Egypt during the time of Moses. Second was the Assyrian Empire during the time of the divided kingdom. The Prophet Daniel identified the next four great empires as Babylonia, Media/Persia, Greece, and Rome. In fact, Roman government or Imperialism is still today in its sixth stage (or head symbolically) and governs a great deal of the earth's population. Any dictatorial government belongs to this category. The seventh head belongs to the future kingdom of the end-times Antichrist.

The "ten horns" refer to ten kings who will be dominant during the Tribulation Period, from whom Antichrist (the seventh head) will receive his power and authority. Antichrist is the human pawn of Satan himself, for throughout history Satan has stirred up and used governmental power to accomplish his purpose. Nothing has brought more havoc and evil to mankind than government. Political power in the hands of evil men has given license to torture, murder, war, famine, heartache, and suffering beyond human comprehension. Satan's intent has always been to keep nations fighting one another, and his energy has always been directed at the nation of Israel. This is why the Middle East will never be at peace – they will always be in conflict. During the last half of the Tribulation Period (forty-two months of Gentile rule), Satan will have the nations of the earth raging war against the nation of Israel. All of his efforts will be directed at Israel.

12:4: This verse tells us "his tail swept a third of the stars out of the sky and flung them to the earth." Because of Satan's pride, which encourages rebellion, we see the casting from heaven of one-third of the angels, those who chose to rebel against God and follow the dragon. Other references include Matthew 25:41 and Jude 6.

The original casting of Satan out of heaven was not his final overthrow, for although his forces have been limited to the atmospheric heaven around the earth; Satan himself still has access, even today, to the throne of God to accuse believers. In the first and second chapters of the Book of Job, we are told that Satan came with other angels to appear before God. This fact is further confirmed by the words of our Lord Jesus when He told Peter: "Simon, Simon, Satan has asked to sift you as wheat" (Luke 22:31).

The vision of Satan standing before the woman "who was about to give birth, so that he might devour her child the moment it was born" refers to Satan's hatred of the Male Child because it was predicted from the very beginning that this child would be his downfall (Genesis 3:15). Satan initiated what biblical scholars call the "conflict of the ages," attempting to stamp out the seed of the woman from the time of Adam and Eve to the end of the Tribulation Period; in other words, from the time of Genesis through the time of the Revelation.

3) The Male Child – Jesus Christ

12:5: Only the Lord Jesus Christ fits this description. The man-child "who will rule all the nations with an iron scepter" refers to Christ's rule during the Millennium, when He will be the absolute ruler of the world. In chapter 4 of Acts (v.25 – 26), the persecuted Christians quoted the second Psalm, identifying the Lord Jesus as the One to rule with a rod of iron. His identity is further clarified in our text here with the phrase, "her child was snatched up to God and to his throne." This is exactly what happened to Jesus forty days following His death and resurrection. In the Book of Acts, we read about Jesus' ascension: "He was taken up before their very eyes, and a cloud hid him from their sight" (Acts 1:9). Further in Acts, the Apostle Peter preached to the crowd at Pentecost proclaiming, "God has raised this Jesus to life and … Exalted to the right hand of God" (Acts 2:32 – 34). The Book of Revelation is the unveiling of the ascended Christ, the glorified Christ, and the Christ who is to return to earth one day in glory. The writer of Hebrews tells us: "Let us fix our eyes on Jesus, the author and perfecter of our faith, who for the joy set before him endured the cross, scorning its shame, and sat down at the right hand of the throne of God" (Hebrews 12:2). The King James Version uses the phrase "finisher of our faith."

12:6: This verse brings us up-to-date in our study and to the mid-point of the Tribulation Period with the phrase, "the woman fled into the desert to a place prepared for her by God." We are not told specifically where she (the nation of Israel) will flee to; the important thing to note is that God will protect and provide for her. Recall how God provided for the Israelites during the forty years in the desert after their exodus from Egypt. Remember also how God protected and provided for Joseph and Mary following the birth of Jesus when they fled into the desert to escape the murderous decree of Herod (the Great, 37 – 4 B.C.). During the last half of the Tribulation Period (1,260 days), God will protect and provide for the remnant of the nation of Israel. The Jewish remnant will flee from persecution during the greatest anti-Semitic crusade Satan has ever unleashed against them.

4) The Angel – Michael

12:7 – 9: The two angels whose names are given in Scripture are Gabriel and Michael. Gabriel is the "announcing angel," and Michael seems to be the "commanding general" of the heavenly host. We are told in the Book of Jude (v.9) that Michael is the "archangel." In the sixth century B.C., the Prophet Daniel had a vision and wrote the following: "At that time Michael, the great prince who protects your people, will arise. There will be a time of distress such as has not happened from the beginning of nations until then. But at that time your people – everyone whose name is found written in the book – will be delivered" (Daniel 12:1). We see from this that Michael is the angel specifically assigned by God to work for the protection of Israel as a nation. In the middle of the Tribulation Period, the conflict between Michael, with his army of heavenly host and Satan, with his demons will reach its climax. When God gives the order, Michael will cast the great dragon down to earth, "and his angels with him." Satan and his demonic host will now be banished and confined to earth. He will no longer have access to the throne of God. His fury will know no limitations, except the power of God. This passage details several things about Satan:

1) The ancient serpent: This refers to the first time he is seen in Scripture, in the Garden of Eden (Genesis 3:1).
2) The devil: This is the name used in the gospels for this enemy of God. It means "slanderer" or "accuser." In verse 10, he is called "the accuser of our brothers." This is why all believers need an Advocate and why the apostle wrote: "But if anyone does sin, we have one who speaks to the Father in our defense – Jesus Christ, the Righteous One" (1 John 2:1).

3) Satan: This name means *adversary*. Satan is the enemy of everything that is good and the adversary of all of God's children.

4) The one who "leads the whole world astray": He is the great deceiver. The Apostle Paul wrote on this very point: "The god of this age has blinded the minds of unbelievers, so that they cannot see the light of the gospel of the glory of Christ, who is the image of God" (2 Corinthians 4:4).

12:10: The fact that Satan is once and for all cast out of heaven along with his evil host and confined to earth will be cause for great rejoicing in heaven. This opens the way for the coming of four precious heavenly freedoms when Christ returns to earth:

1) Salvation: Salvation is consummated in the person of Christ. Our salvation (sanctification) is made complete when we finally come into the presence of Christ. For the surviving Tribulation Saints, this speaks of Christ's physical return to earth.

2) Power: Throughout history, the nations have corrupted and abused power. However, when Christ returns to earth, He will abolish all wickedness and assume all worldly power; and finally, true righteousness will reign over all the nations.

3) The kingdom of our God: Only when Christ returns to earth and establishes His Millennial Kingdom will there be true peace and harmony and freedom for all of God's creation.

4) Authority: This refers to the governmental authority that Christ will establish upon His return. His authority will be absolute and final.

12:11: The rejoicing in heaven continues in these verses that give us three sources of victory for the saints over Satan the accuser:

1) "They overcame him by the blood of the Lamb." The blood of the Lamb, which takes away the sins of the world, is the only true means of victory. The continued mention of the "blood of the Lamb" in the Book of Revelation is not to be taken as crude, but rather the crudity is in our sins which made it necessary for Jesus Christ to shed His blood. It is only through the blood of the Lamb that any of us overcome Satan.

2) "By the word of their testimony." Another way to overcome Satan is with a decisive testimony for Jesus Christ. The place to give your testimony is not in a well-fed church, but out in the world. Let the world around you know that you belong to Christ and that the love of Christ lives in you. Before sending out his disciples, the Lord told them, "Whoever acknowledges me before men, I will also acknowledge him before my Father in heaven" (Matthew 10:32).

3) "They did not love their lives so much as to shrink from death." Those who overcome are more concerned with obeying and glorifying God than they are with pleasing men or saving their own lives. When we put Jesus Christ first, others second, and ourselves last, we find that our love is the very basis of Christian service. Our Lord when speaking to Peter said, "Do you love me ... Feed my sheep" (John 21:15 – 17). Then the Lord used Peter, and in his first sermon to the church we read that, "about three thousand were added to their numbers" (Acts 2:41).

The Third Woe

12:12 – 13: Although heaven will rejoice because Satan is cast out, the earth will not share in this rejoicing. In fact, verse 12 warns us: "Woe to the earth and sea." This is the "third woe" of the Book of Revelation as Satan's confinement to earth extends through the final set of judgments and up to the final day of the Tribulation Period. Satan will now personally take command of the earth and step up his crusade against his greatest enemy, the nation of Israel. Let us keep in mind that it is through the nation of Israel that we have our blessed Savior Jesus Christ, our Holy Scriptures, the ministry of the apostles, and everything else associated with the faith we hold so dear. Satan and all his energy will be directed at Israel. Knowing he has but a short time, he will be filled with rage and hatred.

12:14: John's vision continues as he describes the "two wings of a great eagle." This has become a symbol to Israel representing that God will deliver them to safety, for this is the same symbolism used by God in His past deliverance of Israel from Egypt. God told Israel through His servant: "You yourself have seen what I did to Egypt, and how I carried you on eagles' wings and brought you to myself" (Exodus 19:4). The important thing is not the specific place they go or how they get there, but the fact that God will protect them by His mercy and grace. The phrase "time, times, and half a time," means three and a half years. The Prophet Daniel used the same phrase (Daniel 12:7) in describing his similar vision of this future time of distress for the people of Israel. During the second half of the seven-year Tribulation Period, God will care for, or "nourish" (KJV) the nation of Israel as He did in the days of Moses when He rained manna from the sky and streamed water from the rocks.

12:15 – 16: "Then from his mouth the serpent spewed water like a river, to overtake the woman and sweep her away with the torrent." Since this chapter has already used various symbols, such as that of the "woman" and the "enormous red dragon," the word "torrent" may be a symbol as well. This word might be likened to the word "flood" as used by the Prophet Isaiah (59:19) in his description of the enemies of God and their massive armies advancing from the west and the east. As in the days of the rebellion of Korah (Numbers 16:31 – 33), so also during the Tribulation Period, the earth will swallow up these anti-Semitic armies of Antichrist.

5) The Remnant of Israel

12:17: Who is the "rest of her (Israel's) offspring"? The King James Version uses the phrase "remnant of her seed." Throughout the Old Testament the prophets spoke of a remnant of the house of Israel that would survive. The Old Testament prophet wrote: "I myself will gather the remnant of my flock out of all the countries where I have driven them and will bring them back to their pasture, where they will be fruitful and increase in number" (Jeremiah 23:3). Centuries later, the Apostle Paul also wrote: "So too, at the present time there is a remnant chosen by grace" (Romans 11:5). Hence, in every age God has chosen to protect and save a remnant of Israel, His covenant people. We read earlier in this chapter that a remnant of the nation of Israel will flee into the wilderness to escape persecution by Antichrist. However, I believe the Jewish remnant referred to here by John might be the 144,000 witnesses of chapter 7 that are evangelizing throughout the world. This is evident by the words of our last verse here: "Those who obey God's commandments and hold to the testimony of Jesus." Even though Satan will "make war against" and eventually fail in his attempt to exterminate the Jewish race, he will never stop trying. We will see his final fate later in chapter 20.

Review Questions

1) The woman is symbolic of _____.

2) Her crown of twelve stars represents _____.

3) The enormous red dragon is identified as _____.

4) The man-child who will rule all the nations with an iron scepter refers to _____
_____.

5) Why does the woman flee into the desert in the middle of the Tribulation Period? _____
_____.

6) What is the third woe? _____
_____.

7) The two wings of a great eagle have become a symbol to Israel representing _____
_____.

Up For Discussion

"And there appeared another wonder in heaven; and behold a great red dragon …."
(Revelation 12:3 KJV)

Read on your own or as a class the following two lessons entitled "The Dragon" and "The Sovereignty of God." Consider how they reinforce or give added insight to the message of the Book of Revelation.

In "The Dragon," we look at the origins of Satan and how his fall from grace was the result of a prideful heart. As we move further into our study of the Book of Revelation, we will see Satan's rise to power during the second half of the Tribulation Period and his final doom when Christ returns to reclaim the earth from all unrighteousness.

In "The Sovereignty of God," we emphasize that God is in complete control, nothing happens outside of His will, and whatever He allows He will turn to our good. Indeed, we are to live our lives with that understanding.

The Dragon

The Dragon is introduced to us in chapter 12 of the Book of Revelation beginning in verse 3. In verse 9 he is identified by name – Satan, "that ancient serpent called the devil … who leads the whole world astray." John described the dragon first as "another sign … in heaven." This sign was symbolic of his character, not his physical appearance. Satan is a created being. He was created as an angel. In fact, the Lord called him "a guardian cherub" (Ezekiel 28:14). By nature, angels are spiritual beings (Hebrews 1:14) and exist in the spiritual realm where they remain unseen by mankind, unless God so wills otherwise.

The origin of Satan is found in the words of the Lord given to the Prophet Ezekiel (28:12 – 17). In these verses we find the judgment of the king of Tyre; but obviously, there was never a king of Tyre in the Garden of Eden. This prophecy looks beyond the local ruler to the one who is behind the kingdoms of the world – Satan. Recall that Satan offered the kingdoms of the world to our Lord Jesus during his temptation in the wilderness (Luke 4:5 – 7). The Lord rejected Satan's offer. Apparently, Satan had the authority to make the offer – at that point in time. Ultimately, as John the Revelator tells us, Christ will rule over the kingdoms of the world, but not as some prince of Satan. Unfortunately, Satan still functions today, in the words of our Lord, as the "prince of this world" (John 12:31, 14:30, and 16:11). Satan is the one behind all the kingdoms of the world. He has always used governmental power, that is, kings and kingdoms to accomplish his purpose. Let's take a closer look at the words of the Lord given to the prophet in Ezekiel 28:12 – 17:

28:12: Satan was created as "the model of perfection, full of wisdom." Satan is the wisest creature God ever created. He is smart, clever, and wise. You and I am no match for him. We will be overcome if we try to stand in our own strength against him. This is why the Apostle Paul counsels us to "be strong in the Lord and in his mighty power. Put on the full armor of God so that you can take your stand against the devil's schemes …" (Ephesians 6:10 – 18).

Satan was created "perfect in beauty." He is not some creature with horns, a forked tail, and webbed feet as might be found in Greek mythology. No, the word of God presents him as "perfect in beauty." And when God says perfect, that is exactly what He means. If you could see him, I believe you would find he is the most beautiful creature imaginable.

28:13: Satan was the ancient "serpent" who, so long ago, enticed Eve into disobeying God's command not to eat the fruit from the tree in the middle of the Garden of Eden (Genesis 3:1).

"Every precious stone adorned you. Your settings … made on gold." Imagine what a beautiful creature he must be.

The New International Version leaves out the following verse found in the King James Version: "The workmanship of your timbrels and pipes was prepared for you on the day you were created." You see, Satan was also created as the pinnacle of music itself.

28:14: Satan was "anointed as a guardian cherub," meaning he protected the throne of God. This is not Eden on earth. Apparently, "the holy mount of God" mentioned here is a picture of heaven itself. You might ask, "Why does the throne of God need a guardian, and protected from what?" Yes, God is all-powerful, all-knowing, and all-present. He simply has to speak, and His will is accomplished. Angels, like mankind, were created for God's pleasure and His good purpose. We were all created to praise, worship, and serve our Creator; and just as with mankind, angels too were evidently given free will. Consequently, we find in Revelation (12:4), that "a third" of the angels in heaven chose to rebel against God and follow Satan. As a result, the war between the forces of God and the forces of Satan, or in other words, the war between the forces of good and evil has continued down through the ages.

28:15: Satan protected God's throne. He had the highest position a created being could have. So what was it that brought him down? Ezekiel will tell us shortly in verse 17, but even before Ezekiel, the Prophet Isaiah has already told his story (Isaiah 14:12 – 15; read aloud for class discussion).

The thing that brought Satan down was pride. He wanted to lift up his throne "above the stars of God." He wanted to separate himself from God and become God. He was in rebellion against God. Now God cannot tolerate rebellion, so what is He going to do?

28:16: Satan will be judged for his sin. He is only a creature. This should be comforting to us all. Although we are no match for him, we can be thankful God is going to deal with him; and we will see the fate that is reserved for him later in chapter 20 of our study.

28:17: The prophet tells us here, "Your heart became proud on account of your beauty, and you corrupted your wisdom because of your splendor." Pride is number one on God's hate list (Proverbs 6:16 – 17). "To fear the Lord is to hate evil, I hate pride and arrogance" (Proverbs 8:13). King Solomon, who was considered the wisest man to have ever lived, became prideful. Although God had forbidden the Israelites to intermarry, he took on wives from all the surrounding nations. Subsequently, these wives caused him to sin against God by seducing him into worshipping their gods and idols. Now we have the greatest creature God ever created, perfect in wisdom and beauty, but prideful and in rebellion against his Creator. God says He is going to make "a spectacle" of Satan someday. At some time in the future God is going to rid Satan from His universe.

As we study the Book of Revelation, we find in chapter 12 that at the mid-point of the Tribulation Period the conflict between good and evil reaches its climax. At that time, when God gives the order, Michael, the archangel, and his forces will cast Satan and his demons down to earth. They will no longer have access to the heavenly realm but will be banished and confined to earth.

Chapter 13 then opens with Satan standing on the shore of the sea. Now you may ask yourself, if I was standing on that beach would I see him? The answer is no. Satan is still an angelic being, but of the fallen order. He still operates in the spirit realm, unless God allows otherwise. Satan will enter the body of Antichrist, who "had a fatal wound" (was slain) that had been healed (causing a resurrection). At the mid-point of the Tribulation Period, Antichrist will become the incarnation of Satan for in verse 2 we read that, "The dragon gave the beast his power and his throne [the kingdoms of the world] and great authority." The false prophet was also given power and authority by Satan (the dragon) to "perform great and miraculous signs" and to erect an image of the beast (Antichrist) and to "give breath to the image." This leads me to wonder if Satan will also possess the body of the false prophet in order to accomplish these wonders.

In his vision, the Apostle John says he saw "three evil spirits that looked like frogs; they came out of the mouth of the dragon, out of the mouth of the beast, and out of the mouth of the false prophet"

(Revelation 16:13). These evil spirits are deceiving spirits, and they again operate in the spiritual realm. Our Lord Jesus was referring to Satan when He proclaimed the following: "When he lies, he speaks his native language, for he is a liar and the father of lies" (John 8:44). All lies originate from Satan, and here Satan is the power and authority behind both Antichrist and the false prophet. They will use their power of speech, represented by these evil spirits, to deceive the armies from the East. They will con these kings into coming over to their side to assist them in their efforts to further persecute the nation of Israel and to oppose our Lord.

All of Satan's efforts will ultimately come to naught. His end has already been determined, revealed, and recorded by the Apostle John in chapter 20 of the Book of Revelation. Satan's fate, and the fate of all who choose to reject and rebel against God in favor of pride and self-reliance, will be an eternity spent in everlasting torment and separation from the God that created them, and gave His worldly life to demonstrate just how much He loved all of His creation.

> "Therefore rejoice, ye heavens, and ye that dwell in them.
> Woe to the inhabiters of the earth and of the sea!
> For the devil is come down unto you, having great wrath,
> because he knoweth that he hath but a short time."
> (Revelation 12:12 KJV)

The Sovereignty of God
Taken from a Sermon by Dr. Charles Stanley

The message of the Book of Revelation is God will be victorious. God has made promises to the nation of Israel throughout history and has kept every single one. There is not a single unconditional promise in the Old Testament God has not kept, unless it is something that has to do with future times such as those we are studying in the Book of Revelation. If God has been that faithful to the nation of Israel who has been corrupt, idolatrous, living in sin, disobeying God, and turning away from God; and if God remained faithful to them, no matter what, to keep His promise to a small remnant, then what does that say to you and me? God will also be faithful and keep His promises to you and me no matter what goes on around us.

The truth is – God is sovereign.

God is sovereign. He is in complete and absolute control of everything. If at any point in our lives we believe ourselves to be victims of circumstance, then God ceases to be sovereign. If God is sovereign, then we are not victims of anything. He may allow some tragedy to attack, afflict, or harm us – as it may appear – but if God is sovereign, then He will turn it to our good. Therefore, God is faithful and keeps His promises. God is sovereign and in complete control of our lives. The wisest thing we can do as children of God is to walk in His perfect will day by day, obeying His Word and giving thanks for His grace. If we do so, then we can take every single promise in His Word and claim it for ourselves.

He is the sovereign God of this universe. He is the ultimate and final authority, and nothing happens without His permissive will. Therefore, we can walk every single day with complete confidence and assurance that nothing is going to happen to us unless God allows it; and if He allows it, then He has a purpose that is higher and far wiser than ours. Whatever God allows, He will turn it to our good. That is how the children of God should live.

We must also realize God works His sovereign plan through our choices and decisions. This should motivate and encourage us. God uses our choices to direct us – our wise choices to bless us, our unwise choices to teach us. This is known as the doctrine of providence; and it teaches us (believers) that we are never in the grip of blind forces such as luck, chance, or fate. Everything that happens to us is divinely planned; and each event should come as a summons to trust, obey, and rejoice.

The Apostle Paul wrote these comforting words: "And we know that in all things God works for the good of those who love him, who have been called according to his purpose" (Romans 8:28).

It bears repeating – whatever is going to happen, God is going to turn it to our good, no matter what.

To live our lives any other way is to say that God is not sovereign. The essence of the Christian life can be summed up in these words: trust and obey. If you believe God is sovereign then you will trust God wholeheartedly – you are not going to worry about anything or let anything upset you. God will allow us to go through all kinds of trials in life, but He will turn it to our good.

Why, then, do Christians suffer in many of the same ways as the rest of the world? Christians die of cancer, and in automobile accidents, and at the hands of terrorists, and in some parts of the world, even suffer and die for their faith. Jesus made it very clear: "I have told you these things, so that in me you may have peace. In this world you will have trouble. But take heart! I have overcome the world" (John 16:33). The Apostle Peter likewise wrote: "Dear friends, do not be surprised at the painful trial you are suffering, as though something strange were happening to you" (1 Peter 4:12).

God allows us to go through suffering for a purpose. Sometimes He wants to teach us about ourselves. Sometimes He wants to build deeper character and faith in our lives so we may be of comfort to others in times of trial. Sometimes He wants to show us His goodness in the midst of the trial. Sometimes He just wants to move us to a new place. Regardless, God always has a specific purpose for hardships in our lives.

Knowing our troubles are part of God's plan for us, we can be grateful and thank Him for leading us through times of trial. Does this make the pain of hardship any less? Sadly, it does not. However, because God is at work, we can nonetheless rejoice that He is using the hard time to bring us to spiritual maturity.

The Book of Revelation tells us when Jesus Christ returns to earth, sin will be judged and brought to an end. Until that time, pain and death will be the experience of all who live in this fallen world, without exception. The Book of Revelation also reminds us that our Lord will wipe away every tear from the eyes of His children and death will be no more.

God is sovereign and if He has kept a remnant of the nation of Israel down through history, then He will keep you and me.

The Word of God that was given to Moses and spoken to Joshua just before he was to lead the nation of Israel across the Jordan to take possession of the Promised Land comforts us even today: "The Lord himself goes before you and will be with you; he will never leave you nor forsake you. Do not be afraid; do not be discouraged" (Deuteronomy 31:8).

Chapter 13

As we begin to study this chapter of God's Word, we see the dragon (Satan), having been cast out of heaven, angry and standing on the "shore of the sea." It is Satan who will bring the beast out of the sea and dominate him. We are now at the mid-point of the seven-year Tribulation Period, also referred to by our Lord as the Great Tribulation (Matthew 24:21 KJV).

6) The Beast Out of the Sea – Antichrist

13:1 – 2: Since chapter 13 is a continuation of chapter 12, whereas symbols are being used to describe personalities, and since there are no seven-headed beasts, we will conclude this composite picture of a leopard, bear, and lion must be a symbol as well. This is not the first time the Holy Spirit has used the symbol of these three beasts to describe either a king or a kingdom. In chapter 7 of the Book of Daniel, we find these same three beasts used to represent and describe the vicious character of three former world empires. Some details about this beast can apply only to an individual, whereas others apply to his kingdom. Here begins our description of the end-times king and his kingdom. This first beast (king) is Antichrist and his one-world government.

The beast rose "out of the sea." In Scripture the sea is symbolic of the nations of the world (Isaiah 17:12). The Prophet Daniel tells us: "After the sixty-two 'sevens,' the Anointed One will be cut off and will have nothing. The people of the ruler who will come will destroy the city and the sanctuary" (Daniel 9:26). The Anointed One is a reference to Jesus Christ, Israel's rejection of Him as their Messiah, and His subsequent crucifixion. Who destroyed the city and the temple? It was the Romans. Therefore, Antichrist (the ruler to come) will arise, as most scholars believe, out of the nations of Europe to establish a new one-world government – the revised Roman Empire.

The ten horns speak of the tenfold division of this new global government and represent the kings who give Antichrist their power during the Tribulation Period. The seven heads of this beast are mentioned later in chapter 17 (v.10) as kings of the Roman Empire. They represent five kings up to the time of the Apostle John; the sixth, Domitian, was the Roman emperor at the time of John; lastly, John skips forward to the end-times for the seventh king (head), Antichrist. All seven kings are guilty of blasphemy. Blasphemy manifests itself in two ways:

1) Making oneself equal to God.
2) Slandering and taking God's name in vain.

At the time of John and his writing of the Revelation, much of the prophecy of Daniel 7 had been fulfilled. The first three beasts (kingdoms) – Babylon, the lion; Media-Persia, the bear; and Greece, the leopard – had all come to pass. John focused next on the prophet's fourth beast and upon the "little horn" because the fourth beast, the Roman Empire, had appeared. The emphasis of the Book of Revelation is on the rule of the "little horn" of Daniel (7:8). The "little horn" of Daniel 7 and the "beast out of the sea" of this chapter are one and the same. We are looking at the man who becomes the final dictator of the world during the Tribulation Period. Read the prophet's description of Antichrist, "The king who exalts himself" (Daniel 11:36 – 39).

The Apostle John wrote extensively about Antichrist in his letters, and John is the only writer in Scripture to use that term or designation. John speaks of two characteristics of Antichrist:

1) Antichrist is one who is against Christ.
2) Antichrist is one who imitates Christ.

This beast (Antichrist) is both. The apostle writes: "Dear children, this is the last hour; and as you have heard that the Antichrist is coming, even now many antichrists have come. This is how we will know it is the last hour" (1 John 2:18 NKJV). Note that John not only says there is going to be an Antichrist, but there were many antichrists already present in his day. The apostle continues and states one key characteristic that identifies an antichrist: "Who is the liar? It is the man who denies that Jesus is the Christ. Such a man is the antichrist – he denies the Father and the Son" (1 John 2:22). The apostle gives us some additional facts concerning antichrist: "Dear friends, do not believe every spirit, but test the spirit to see whether they are from God, because many false prophets have gone out into the world. But every spirit that does not acknowledge Jesus is not from God. This is the spirit of antichrist, which you have heard is coming and even now is already in the world" (1 John 4:1, 3). In other words, any person, any group, or any publication that denies the deity of Jesus Christ is antichrist. Last of all, the apostle counsels us: "Many deceivers, who do not acknowledge Jesus Christ as coming in the flesh, have gone out into the world. Any such person is the deceiver and the antichrist" (2 John 7). Antichrist is a deceiver – he pretends to be Christ.

The Lord Jesus told His disciples: "For many will come in my name, claiming 'I am the Christ,' and will deceive many" (Matthew 24:5). We all need to be testing the little groups in which we are interested these days. Instead of being solid Christian believers, some may actually be following an antichrist. Can you identify any antichrist today?

13:3 – 4: These verses indicate that the beast, or Antichrist, will be given a deadly wound. Antichrist will apparently be killed. Revelation (17:8) indicates that his spirit will go down into the Abyss where it belongs, but that it will also return; in other words, it will be resurrected. We must keep in mind that this beast is the end-times Antichrist, and Satan will use this beast to duplicate things Jesus Christ has done. In the words of our Lord: "I tell you the truth, a time is coming and has now come when the dead will hear the voice of the Son of God and those who hear will live" (John 5:25). My friends, only He who created life can resurrect life – the Lord Jesus Christ. I believe this resurrection of Antichrist is a fake resurrection, a ruse. This is an embodiment of Antichrist by the dragon, Satan, in order to imitate the resurrection of Jesus Christ. Let me rephrase: In the middle of the Tribulation Period, when Antichrist is fatally wounded; Satan will evidently enter the body of Antichrist, in spirit, in order to resurrect him back to life. I do not know of any other way Satan can duplicate a resurrection, unless he is capable, in some way, of sharing a portion of his life spirit with Antichrist.

Now, there may very well be things that we are not meant to know. Just remember that Satan is the most dangerous and deceitful being in all of God's creation. Presumably after his resurrection, thousands of individuals around the world, previously undecided about Antichrist, will make him an object of worship and fall down before him. This is the very moment Satan has waited millenniums for, that is to be worshiped. Antichrist becomes the incarnation of Satan, for verse 2 tells us, "The dragon gave the beast his power and his throne and great authority," meaning all the kingdoms of the world that he once offered Christ (Matthew 4:8 – 9).

13:5 – 6: Satan has long been the source of blasphemy against God. He is against Christ and His church, which are in heaven. During the second half (forty-two months) of the Tribulation Period, Antichrist will seem to manifest even greater supernatural powers. People will worship the dragon, as the Apostle Paul predicted: "He will oppose and will exalt himself over everything that is called God or is worshiped, so that he sets himself up in God's temple, proclaiming himself to be God" (2 Thessalonians 2:4). This prophecy is also foretold by the Prophet Daniel (9:27) and by our Lord Jesus Christ in His Olivet Discourse (Matthew 24:15).

13:7: "He was given power to make war against the saints and to conquer them. And he was given authority over every tribe, people, language and nation." During this time many believers, whom we call Tribulation Saints, will suffer martyrdom at the hands of this brutal beast. This will be, without a doubt, the darkest hours in the history of the world. I call it a dictatorship on steroids!

13:8: Today the world is being prepared for a one-world government philosophy. That philosophy, inspired by Satan and promoted by the atheistic and secular leaders of world governments today, is rapidly spreading across the earth. During the Tribulation Period, Satan will provide a visible god with seemingly divine powers. On the basis of this verse alone it seems the majority of people on the earth will worship Antichrist rather than the Lord Jesus Christ.

The book of life is mentioned in several passages of Scripture, particularly in Revelation: "If anyone's name was not found written in the book of life, he was thrown into the lake of fire" (20:15). When a child is born, God records that infant's name in His book. If he or she matures and dies without receiving His Son Jesus Christ as their Savior, then that name is blotted out of the book (Revelation 3:5). The names remaining make up the "book of life belonging to the Lamb." There is no doubt as to the identity of the Lamb, for John the Baptist pointed to Jesus Christ as "the Lamb of God, who takes away the sin of the world" (John 1:29). The Lamb's book of life contains only the names of those who by faith have accepted the Lamb of God. Jesus Christ offers us eternal life if we simply receive Him into our hearts as Lord and Savior. Once He enters our lives, the recording angel writes our name into the Lamb's book of life, from which it can never be blotted out.

13:9 – 10: John is speaking here to God's saints who will be in the world at this time. He is telling them that they are going to have to bear, with patience and faith, the awful trials and sufferings that come even upon God's children.

7) **The Beast Out of the Earth – The False Prophet**

The first beast, Antichrist, is a political leader, and his power will become worldwide. Satan will provide another leader to promote his own form of worship. This second beast is a religious leader, and he is called the false prophet (Revelation 16:13; 19:20). During the second half of the Tribulation Period, the false prophet will command and facilitate global worship of the first beast – Antichrist.

13:11 – 12: These verses give us five characteristics of the false prophet:

1) "Coming out of the earth." Unlike the first beast, the "earth" from which the second beast arises is symbolic of Palestine and most scholars assume it to be from the nation of Israel. This beast, "out of the earth," is apparently prophet-like in some manner. You see, Israel would not trust him unless he had come from their land and was of Jewish descent. He will lead Israel into signing the covenant with Antichrist, (chapter 6) which triggers the seven-year Tribulation Period. This covenant of peace, we said earlier, is likely the instrument which permits the rebuilding of the temple. Will Israel see him as their long-awaited Messiah because of the peace he and Antichrist initially bring to the world? Consider personally or as a class.

2) "He had two horns like a lamb." Lambs do not have horns, which are symbolic of power or authority. As with the first beast, his power also comes from Satan. This demonstrates an imitation of the Lamb, Jesus Christ. You see, the first beast is opposed to Christ – he is antichrist. Now this second beast imitates Christ – he also is antichrist. Satan will likely cause the resurrection of the first beast, Antichrist (as we discussed earlier) to appear as though it was performed by this second beast, the false prophet. Speaking to His disciples, our Lord predicted: "Watch out for false prophets. They come to you in sheep's clothing, but inwardly they are ferocious wolves" (Matthew 7:15).

3) "He spoke like a dragon." This indicates that he will derive power of speech from Satan and deceive human beings by acting like a lamb; but really he speaks the word of the devil.

4) "He exercised all the authority of the first beast on his behalf." The false prophet will be given authority by Antichrist himself. During the second half of the Tribulation Period, his purpose will be to work toward the extermination of the apostate (false) church (the prostitute of chapter 17) left on earth after the rapture of the true church.

5) "Made the earth and its inhabitants worship the first beast." He will not exalt himself but will work solely for the purpose of facilitating global worship of the first beast, Antichrist. The phrase "whose fatal wound had been healed," indicates that both beasts will be capable of all kinds of counterfeit miracles, signs, and wonders. This is the big lie, the "powerful delusion," that the Apostle Paul spoke of in 2 Thessalonians (2:9 – 12).

13:13 – 15: The false prophet will be equipped by Satan and Antichrist with authority and power to do such supernatural and miraculous signs so as to "deceive the inhabitants of the earth." The fact that he will cause "fire to come down from heaven" should not surprise us, for Satan, the real force behind the false prophet, brought fire down from heaven and burned up Job's sheep and servants (Job 1:16). The Lord Jesus Christ warned us that in the last days "false Christs and false prophets will appear and perform great signs and miracles to deceive even the elect – if that were possible" (Matthew 24:24).

The false prophet will cause an *image* (the Greek word is *eikon* which means likeness) of Antichrist to be built and erected in the new temple in Jerusalem. This is "the abomination that causes desolation" as foretold by the Prophet Daniel (9:27) and by our Lord Jesus Christ (Matthew 24:15). He will even have power to "give breath" to this idol. An idol that speaks! How many times have the Old Testament prophets and even Paul in the New Testament told us that idols, made by men of gold, silver, and wood, cannot hear or speak? Evidently this one will, and it will issue an order that all who do not worship it will be killed. We are told later in chapter 20 (v.4) that many will be slain by the guillotine.

Many things coincide with the mid-point of the Tribulation Period, one of which is Satan's persecution of the nation of Israel. When the false prophet establishes and decrees his idol worship in the newly rebuilt temple in Jerusalem, it may well be that Israel, who does not seem to receive Jesus Christ as the Messiah in the first half of the Tribulation Period, will embrace Him in the second half, thus rejecting the deceiving idolatrous religion of Antichrist and his false prophet.

The Mark of the Beast

13:16 – 18: We know that six is the number of a human being. It is one short of the complete and perfect number seven; and mankind was created on the sixth day. Therefore in Bible numerology the number six is used to refer to mankind. We cannot be certain as to why three digits are used here, but it has without a doubt been puzzling to biblical scholars throughout history. The text also suggest that it will somehow mathematically represent the "name of the beast," Antichrist. What is more important than the meaning of 666, is that the false prophet will use this as a means of forcing people to worship Antichrist. Additionally, he will mandate that everyone have this mark on his or her forehead or right hand in order to buy or sell. One can hardly imagine the pressure of having to possess such a mark to secure the necessary food for his family.

Physically speaking, it will be necessary for every human being to have the mark of the beast. Spiritually speaking, it will be fatal. We have seen that those who are redeemed by the Lamb, those who have the seal of God, have made the choice to receive Jesus Christ as their Savior. However, those who receive Antichrist's mark will have made their final decision for eternity to reject Christ and worship his enemy (Satan); and thus share in his fate.

The nation of Israel now becomes the dividing line for the world during the second half of the Tribulation Period. Those who receive the mark of the beast and worship Antichrist will assist him worldwide in his persecution of the Jews (and Christians). Those who receive Jesus Christ as Lord and Savior (Tribulation Saints) will provide aid and protection for the Jewish remnant, while sharing with them the message of mercy and grace from their true Messiah, Jesus Christ.

Instead of wasting time trying to identify a person by this number 666, I'd rather spend my time getting to know Jesus Christ as my Savior. I join with the Apostle Paul as he writes: "I want to know Christ and the power of his resurrection and the fellowship of sharing in his sufferings, becoming like him in his death, and so, somehow, to attain to the resurrection from the dead" (Philippians 3:10).

Review Questions

1) The seven-headed ten-horned beast out of the sea symbolically represents _____
_____.

2) In Scripture, the sea is symbolic of _____.

3) Blasphemy manifests itself in what two ways? _____
_____.

4) What are the two characteristics of Antichrist described by the Apostle John? _____
_____.

5) How does Satan fake the resurrection of Antichrist? _____
_____.

6) The second beast, the false prophet, is a religious leader. He will promote a religion that solely
worships _____.

7) The mark of the beast will be used as a means of forcing people to _____
_____.

Up For Discussion

"And all the world wondered after the beast."
(Revelation 13:3 KJV)

How much do you follow the news and current world events? Discuss events that may appear as though the world, including the United States, is moving closer to a one-world order. One example might be our nation's massive debt resulting in the eventual devaluation of the US dollar and the call for a global currency. In 1999, the euro was introduced and is today the single currency shared by eighteen of the European Union's Member States, which together make up euro area.

Another example might be the continued growth in the size of government and the freedoms we compromise for the good of the greater population.

Keep in mind this is an area of great debate, so be sensitive and tolerant of the opinions of others in the class.

Do more: Read the following lesson entitled "Ezekiel's Latter Days Vision" on your own. Compare God's judgments upon the enemy that invades Israel with the six seal judgments of chapter 6 and the first four trumpet judgments of chapter 8.

Ezekiel's Latter Days Vision
(Ezekiel 37 – 39, amended from an earlier printing)

In chapter 37 of Ezekiel we have the vision of the valley of dry bones which concerns the future restoration of the nation of Israel. The Prophet Ezekiel was among the Jews exiled to Babylon by Nebuchadnezzar in 597 B.C. This vision was given to Ezekiel to reassure the exiles that God would be faithful to His promises; in other words, to give them hope. Israel's restoration not only had to do with them as a national entity, but also with their spiritual revival which the Lord had promised as well (Ezekiel 36: 24 – 27; Hebrews 8:8 – 10).

The "valley" represents the world where the Jewish people have been scattered. God told Ezekiel to "prophesy," which meant to speak or give out the Word of God. The Word of God is trustworthy; it is faithful and true, and His Word endures forever (Matthew 24:35). Ezekiel was faithful and obedient to God's call.

The restoration of the nation of Israel occurs in stages as represented by the coming together of these bones that were dead and dry and then coming to life. There are three distinct stages:

1) The scattered bones, as mentioned above, represent Israel's dispersion throughout the world and dead in their relationship to God because of their disobedience and rejection of God's Son, Jesus Christ, the Messiah.
2) The coming together of the bones with tendons, flesh, and skin represent Israel's re-gathering; beginning with their pre-1948 return and to their present state as a nation, and even further into the future including the Tribulation Period of the latter years.
3) Breath entered them represents their final conversion as a nation. They are made alive when they choose, at the mid-point of the Tribulation Period, to turn in faith to Jesus Christ as Messiah rather than worship Antichrist and take his mark. The breath could also be viewed symbolically as the Holy Spirit. The restoration of a person (or nation) into a right relationship with God, through His Son Jesus Christ, results in the Holy Spirit indwelling that once spiritually lifeless person (or nation).

God has made it very clear: "He who has the Son has life; he who does not have the Son of God does not have life" (1 John 5:12).

The kingdom of David split in two after the reign of Solomon and became the nations of Israel and Judah. The joining together of the two sticks marked "Judah" and "Ephraim" (Israel, the Northern Kingdom, was often called Ephraim after its largest tribe) is another assurance to the Jewish people that all twelve tribes will be represented when the nation of Israel is finally united and restored during the Millennium. The earthly reign of Jesus Christ, the Messiah, over the children of Israel begins with the resurrection of David as their prince (Ezekiel 37:24 – 25) along with the rest of the Old Testament Saints (Daniel 12:1).

Invasion of Israel During the Tribulation

We read above that God has a definite purpose for the nation of Israel in the future, and chapters 38 and 39 focuses on stage two of their restoration and specifically during the Tribulation Period. These chapters tell of an enemy that will come against Israel "in future years," or "the latter years" (KJV). The sleeping giant that will invade Israel, I believe, is Russia.

Gog is the leader of this coalition. Magog (land of) is the territory and is identified with the land north of Israel around and above the Black and Caspian Seas. Magog was one of the sons of Japheth (Genesis 10:2), and his descendants occupied lands from Spain to southern Russia and were later called Scythians. This is from whom the Slavic people were thought to have descended. The Hebrew word for chief is *Rosh*, and has been translated "chief of Rosh." This taken as a proper name again identifies Rosh with the inhabitants of Scythia. Meshech and Tubal were also sons of Japheth; thus making the coalition in Ezekiel's vision inclusive and led by people descended from Japheth. In addition, Russia was originally called Muscovy which was thought to be derived from Meshech. Other nations will ally with Gog. Persia is Iran, and Cush and Put are nations from North Africa. These are nations with radical Islamic factions and leadership, and are long-time enemies of Israel. Finally, Gomer and Togarmah, "from the far north," will also join the alliance and again represent descendants of Japheth (1 Chronicles 1:6).

God is in absolute control of this invasion. God says He "will put hooks in your jaws and bring you out with your whole army." I believe we are already seeing the beginning of this – the preparation. I do not want to suggest political intent as to why Russia is currently on the move. However, I believe it is obvious to most people who follow world events that Russia invaded and took possession of Crimea, in 2014, primarily because of their need for a warm-water port with access to the world's waterways. It appears as though God has started bringing them out!

The prophet says that these nations, led by Gog, will invade Israel "in future years," or "latter years" (KJV) during a time when the people (the Jews) are "gathered from many nations to the mountains of Israel" and living "in safety" (Ezekiel 38:8). Our first clue as to the timing of this assault is the phrase "latter years," which we have found from our study of Daniel to be a reference to Daniel's Seventieth Seven – the seven-year Tribulation Period of Revelation. Our second clue is the fact that the Jewish people will have gathered back to Jerusalem and will be living "in safety," that is, in peace. This could only be possible during the first half of the Tribulation Period when the people of Israel are living under the covenant of peace and dominion of Antichrist (Daniel 9:27). During this time the temple will be rebuilt and the Jewish people that have long been scattered throughout the globe will flock back to Israel en masse. The attack will likely come sometime in the first year of the Tribulation Period when the rebuilding of the temple is well underway and the "gathering" of the Jewish people is near complete. Russia and its Islamic allies will come against the nation of Israel "like a storm" (Ezekiel 38:9).

I would suggest the following four reasons why this confederation of nations would invade Israel:

1) The first reason is given to us by the prophet (v.12 – 13) and that is to "plunder and loot" Israel's wealth.
2) The second reason would be to gain territorial control of the Middle East.
3) The third would be "to wipe Israel off the face of the earth," which is the ultimate desire expressed time and again by the leaders of Iran and their Islamic brethren.
4) The last reason would be to challenge the authority of Antichrist (Daniel 11:40 – 44). Israel will be living under his covenant of peace; therefore, an attack against Israel will be viewed as a direct attack against Antichrist as well.

Antichrist will muster his armies against the invading threat from the North and the South; however, unbeknownst to him, God is orchestrating this entire ordeal. God will deal with Russia.

As war breaks out, God will deliver His covenant people by destroying the invading forces with the use of four judgments:

1) A great earthquake (Ezekiel 38:19 – 20).
2) The troops will turn against one another (Ezekiel 38:21), as did the armies that invaded Judah during the reign of Jehoshaphat (2 Chronicles 20:22 – 23).
3) A judgment of plague and pestilence (Ezekiel 38:22).
4) Torrents of rain, hailstones, and burning sulfur (Ezekiel 38:22). God will even "send fire" upon Magog, the homeland of the invaders as a final consequence (Ezekiel 39:6).

This is God's judgment. After the armies of the Russian and Islamic alliance are supernaturally destroyed, the birds and wild animals will feast on the dead, the weapons will be burned for fuel for seven years (inclusive), and the dead will be buried in the valley (Ezekiel 39:4 – 11). Israel will rejoice in the Lord's deliverance all the way up to the mid-point of the Tribulation Period.

The final three and a half years, referred to by our Lord Jesus Christ as the Great Tribulation (Matthew 24:21 KJV) begins. With the defeat of his enemies, Antichrist becomes the first global ruler of the united world. Empowered by Satan, Antichrist's tyrannical reign begins, and his first action will be to break his covenant of peace with Israel and invade her himself (Daniel 11:41 – 44). He will put an end to the daily sacrifice and erect his idol image in the temple. Antichrist will exalt himself as god and demand that everyone worldwide worship him and take his mark – 666. The whole world under the rule of Antichrist becomes a battleground of war, persecution, fear, and distress. It is no wonder our Lord said, "If those days had not been cut short, no one would survive, but for the sake of the elect those days will be shortened" (Matthew 24:22). The elect are believers, Gentile and Jew. As a result of Antichrist's deceit and persecution, the people of the nation of Israel will reject Antichrist and turn instead to Jesus Christ. Finally, as a united people and as a nation, they will accept the Lord Jesus Christ as their long-awaited Messiah.

You see, during the first half of the Tribulation Period, God will use the covenant of peace signed between Israel and Antichrist along with the reconstruction of the temple as an incentive to gather all the Jewish people from around the world back to Israel once more. Then, as a nation, they will stand and watch as the Almighty God, through a series of judgments, completely destroys the invading hoards descending from opposite directions, leaving them nothing more than smoldering ruins scattered throughout the valley. "I will display my glory among the nations, and all the nations will see the punishment I inflict and the hand I lay upon them" (Ezekiel 39:21). The nations will witness God's deliverance of His people, and Israel will acknowledge God's protective power and sovereign plan for them as a nation. Israel's rebellion against God is "finally broken" (Daniel 12:7) as she rejects the rule of Antichrist and turns wholly as a nation in faith to Jesus Christ – the one true Messiah.

God will fulfill all His promises to Israel, including her restoration: "Therefore, this is what the Sovereign Lord says: I will now bring Jacob back from captivity and will have compassion on all the people of Israel, and I will be zealous for my holy name ..." (Ezekiel 39:25 – 29). God's plan for His people will be accomplished with the return of His Son Jesus Christ to earth at the end of the Tribulation Period – Daniel's Seventieth Seven – to put an end to all wickedness and rebellion and establish His eternal kingdom of righteousness. "Then the sovereignty, power and greatness of the kingdoms under the whole heaven will be handed over to the saints, the people of the Most High. His kingdom will be an everlasting kingdom, and all rulers will worship and obey him" (Daniel 7:27).

Chapter 14

This chapter is yet another interlude in our chronology and contains several events. The contrast between chapters 13 and 14 is remarkable. From the wicked and rebellious scene of earth during the Great Tribulation, we fast forward in time to the end of the Tribulation Period, where Jesus Christ's name is honored rather than profaned, and all voices are raised in praise and adoration. It is apparent from chapter 13 that the Lamb of God will not be on earth in the midst of the Tribulation Period. The scene is on earth, and these first five verses offer us a rare glimpse into the days following the end of the Tribulation Period. John's vision begins with a scene in the Holy City that opens the Millennium upon the earth, when heaven and earth are finally brought into beautiful harmony.

The Lamb and the 144,000

14:1: The "Lamb" is the Lord Jesus Christ. "Mount Zion" is Jerusalem, and the Lord Jesus is going to reign from Jerusalem for the Psalms proclaim it (Psalm 2:6 – 9, 9:11 – 12, 48:1 – 3, 110:1 – 2, to name a few).

I believe the 144,000 standing with Jesus are the same as the ones who were sealed back in chapter 7. Though Jesus is called the Lamb here, we also know Him as the Good Shepherd. Our Lord started out with 144,000 witnesses, and He came through seven years of tribulation with 144,000. He didn't lose a single one! In the words of the late commentator J. Vernon McGee: "They came through the Great Tribulation like the three Hebrews came through the fiery furnace."

14:2 – 3: The 144,000 Tribulation witnesses join the heavenly chorus during the Millennium. They "had been redeemed from the earth" in the same way that all are redeemed – by faith in Jesus Christ. They too were purchased by His precious blood so they may enter the Millennial Kingdom on earth. "No one could learn the song" simply refers to the fact that no one can sing praises to God except those who love God – those who are redeemed. Songs of the heart are only learned through personal faith experience. The psalmist proclaims: "Give thanks to the Lord, for he is good; his love endures forever. Let the redeemed of the Lord say this – those he redeemed from the hand of the foe, those he gathered from the lands, from the east and west, from the north and south" (Psalm 107:1 – 3). The redeemed from all corners of the earth are the result of the seven-year evangelizing efforts of these 144,000 bold witnesses for Jesus Christ, the Lamb of God.

14:4 – 5: These verses give us additional characteristics of the 144,000 as they endured through the entire Tribulation Period:

1) They were morally pure because they did not "defile themselves with women." This may mean that they either kept their marriage vows; or more likely, I believe they viewed their obedience to God and their evangelical commission to take the gospel message to every nation, language, and tribe of world to be paramount above all else. During the Tribulation Period there will be an exaggerated emphasis upon sex and, as we mentioned in chapter 9, immorality will abound. The 144,000 will have kept themselves separated from these sins, and thus in the eyes of God, were considered "pure" or as the King James Version states "virgins." This probably refers to chastity in both the literal and spiritual sense.

2) "They follow the Lamb wherever he goes" means they were obedient to the Lord.

3) They were offered as "firstfruits to God and the Lamb." This phrase has definite reference to the nation of Israel. Israel (and especially the 144,000) is described as the firstfruits by the Apostle Paul: "For if their rejection is the reconciliation of the world, what will their acceptance be but life from the dead? If the part of the dough offered as firstfruits is holy, then the whole batch is holy; if the root is holy, so are the branches" (Romans 11:15 – 16). These 144,000 Tribulation witnesses will evidently hold some special or unique position alongside the Lamb when He establishes His Millennial Kingdom on earth.

4) "No lie was found in their mouths" means that they did not participate in the big lie of the beast and his false prophet. They just did not fall for it.

5) They lived "blameless" lives. This does not mean they were perfect, but in their desire to serve Jesus Christ and walk with Him, they leaned on His power to live holy, consecrated lives. They're considered "blameless" because they possessed the righteousness of Christ through faith.

This ends our brief fore-glimpse of the bright days beginning the Millennium as John's vision now returns in time to the mid-point of the dreadful Tribulation Period.

The Three Angels

14:6 – 7: One of God's faithful practices in all generations has been to send adequate warning prior to judgment. "Another angel" suggests a change in the matter in which God will communicate with those remaining on earth. This angel is the first of six we will find in this chapter. The "eternal gospel" is Jesus Christ's sacrificial death and resurrection. During our age the gospel has been committed to men – the church – as the messenger of it. In the Old Testament angels as well as men were messengers of God. The writer of Hebrews tells us: "The message spoken by angels was binding" (Hebrews 2:2).

We have already seen that God will use 144,000 sealed witnesses and two supernatural witnesses to evangelize the world during the Tribulation Period. However, the times are so intense that even an angel is needed to help spread God's message of salvation throughout the world. Why do you suppose? One suggestion might be that angels are spiritual creatures and cannot be harmed by men, unlike the two witnesses of chapter 11. This angel will warn the people to "Fear and give glory" to God instead of Antichrist, and to worship God instead of Antichrist, for He created all things. Proverbs reminds us: "The fear of the Lord is the beginning of knowledge" (1:7). This seems to be God's final call to mankind to flee the wrath to come before accepting Antichrist and his mark.

14:8: "Fallen! Fallen is Babylon the Great." Our second angel announces that which is yet to come. The Book of Revelation makes reference to two Babylons, both are termed "Babylon the Great." They are:

1) Religious Babylon: This is the apostate church, and it represents a false religion that promotes idolatry and sexual immorality.
2) Governmental and commercial Babylon: This is the literal ancient city of Babylon in present day Iraq that becomes the global headquarters of the end-times Antichrist.

As we briefly touched on in chapters 2 (v.13) and chapter 9 (v.14), Babylon has been Satan's headquarters from the very beginning. Babylon is the place where idolatry began. Semiramis was the wife (some scholars say the mother) of Nimrod. She was queen of Babel, which later became Babylon. She devised a story (a lie) in which she stepped fully grown out of an egg in the Euphrates River, thus beginning a whole system of idolatry. The worship of Semiramis introduced the female deity of false religion. This identifies Babylon as the birthplace of all false religions. In this verse, we see a fore-glimpse of the judgment of religious Babylon. It takes place in the middle of the Tribulation Period and is explained in greater detail in Chapter 17. The prediction of the destruction of the literal city of Babylon is found in chapter 16 (v.18 – 19), and the judgment upon governmental and commercial Babylon is vividly described in chapter 18.

14:9 – 11: In chapter 13 we saw the awful alternative for not having the mark of the beast was starvation. On the other hand, this third angel announces that anyone who does receive the mark will bring down upon his or her head the wrath of God in "full strength." The "wine of God's fury" is symbolism taken from the Old Testament. The psalmist wrote: "In the hand of the Lord is a cup full of foaming wine mixed with spices; he pours it out and all the wicked of the earth drink it down to its very dregs" (Psalm 75:8). This angel issues a warning of the awful consequences to those who "worships the beast" and "receives his mark." During the second half of the Tribulation Period, not only will they experience the cataclysmic judgments sent by God upon the earth as outlined in the bowl judgments of chapter 16; but even worse, they will be "tormented with burning sulfur" for eternity. I do not know anyone who enjoys teaching eternal damnation for lost souls, but Scriptures present no explanation other than the "lake of burning sulfur" as being literal and eternal, and those who are condemned there will be tormented day and night forever and ever. John even says this torment will be in the "presence of," meaning visible to the holy angels and Christ. This is not something I care to witness.

14:12 – 13: One of the consistent chords of Scripture is the concept that present-day sufferings are inconsequential in view of the eternal blessings prepared for those who love the Lord. "For their deeds will follow them," reveals that the "saints" will be rewarded for their faithfulness, patience, and deeds during the Tribulation Period. God does not save anyone by his or her deeds (good works) but only through faith in His Son Jesus Christ. Just as crowns are heavenly rewards for good works done while on earth for those who make up the church, so too will God reward these Tribulation Saints for their good works. The greatest reward of all will be entry into the earthly kingdom Christ will establish and reign from at the end of the Tribulation Period.

The Harvest of the Elect

14:14: The next few passages, like the ones earlier, are also prophetic fore-glimpses of events to come. The phrase, "a white cloud, and seated on the cloud was one like the son of man" is a vision of the Lord Jesus Christ as He returns to earth at the end of the Tribulation Period. The cloud aids us in our identification for our Lord told His disciples: "At that time the sign of the Son of Man will appear in the sky, and all the nations of the earth will mourn. They will see the Son of Man coming on the clouds of the sky, with power and great glory" (Matthew 24:30). The "crown of gold" refers to the fact that when Jesus returns He will be King, the King of Kings – not as prophet or priest. The "sharp sickle" speaks of the judgment that is to come upon the wicked.

14:15 – 16: This fourth angel announces the first harvest – the harvest of the elect. These are believers, Tribulation Saints who have survived all the way to the end of the Tribulation Period when Christ returns to earth. Our Lord foretold this event: "And he will send his angels with a loud trumpet call, and they will gather his elect from the four winds, from one end of the heavens to the other" (Matthew 24:31). The "harvest" has long been identified with Christian witnessing. After Jesus had completed His first journey through the region teaching the good news of the kingdom, and just before sending His disciples out to preach to the lost sheep of Israel, He encouraged them with these words: "The harvest is plentiful but the workers are few. Ask the Lord of the harvest, therefore, to send out workers into the harvest field" (Matthew 9:37 – 38; Luke 10:2). Today however, believers are not urged to harvest, but to sow – sow the message of the gospel of Christ and the Word of God.

The Harvest of the Wicked

14:17 – 19: The fifth and sixth angels announce the second harvest – the harvest of the wicked. These are all who have rejected Christ and followed Antichrist. The fifth angel also has a "sharp sickle," and the sixth angel, likely the same angel we saw in chapter 8 (v.3), has "charge of the fire … from the altar." Both are symbolic references to the judgment of the wicked. Here we continue in our fore-glimpse with a preview of Armageddon. The "great winepress of God's wrath" is a picture of the fullness of the cup of God's wrath against the wicked left on earth. The prophet Joel set the time of the harvest with these words: "Swing the sickle, for the harvest is ripe. Come, trample the grapes, for the winepress is full and the vats overflow – so great is their wickedness! Multitudes, multitudes in the valley of decision! For the day of the Lord is near in the valley of decision" (Joel 3:13 – 14). What makes it possible that "the time to reap has come"? Our Lord Jesus Christ answered that question with the following words: "The harvest is the end of the age, and the harvesters are angels. As the weeds are pulled up and burned in the fire, so it will be at the end of the age. The Son of Man will send out his angels, and they will weed out of his kingdom everything that causes sin and all who do evil. They will throw them into the fiery furnace, where there will be weeping and gnashing of teeth" (Matthew 13:39 – 42).

14:20: "Outside the city" means outside Jerusalem. "As high as the horses' bridles" means about four feet deep. "1,600 stadia" is equal to about 184 miles. It is interesting to note when using the mileage scale on a map of modern day Israel, the distance from the northern point of the Golan Heights to the southern point of the Gaza Strip, north to south, is right around 180 plus miles. This is the scene of the final war referred to as Armageddon.

Ronald A. Clower

There is some debate among biblical scholars regarding verses 14 through 20. Many, including myself, see two harvests – that of the righteous and that of the wicked. This harvesting of the earth is also explained by our Lord in His parable of the "sheep and the goats" found in Matthew 25:31 – 46. However, there are others that see only the harvest of the wicked. Whichever way you choose to believe, just know that you are in exceedingly good company. When Christ returns to earth at the end of the Tribulation Period, He will judge all those remaining; and He will separate those who will enter into His Millennial Kingdom from those who will not. We will look at this closer later.

Review Questions

1) All 144,000 witnesses survived through the Tribulation Period because they had _____ _____ .

2) The first angel's proclamation was _____ _____ .

3) The second angel proclaims the judgment and fall of _____ .

4) The third angel issues a warning of the dire and eternal consequences to those who _____ _____ .

5) The one sitting on the white cloud and referred to as "like a son of man" is _____ _____ .

6) The fourth angel announces the harvest of the _____ .

7) The fifth and sixth angels announce the harvest of the _____ _____ .

Up For Discussion

"And I saw another angel fly in the midst of heaven ...."
(Revelation 14:6 KJV)

The events of the Book of Revelation are directed by our Lord Jesus Christ from heaven and are executed on earth, for the most part, through the ministry of His angels. We have seen the four angels that control the winds of wrath. We have witnessed the angel seal the 144,000 Tribulation witnesses. In chapters 8 and 9 we saw seven angels with seven trumpets execute their judgment on mankind. Further in chapter 8 we saw the angel who had the golden censer that ministers before the altar in heaven. Now in this chapter, we witnessed a parade of six more angels, each with a specific duty. Just as Gabriel is known as the announcing angel, the first three angels of this chapter are also sent, each to make a dreadful announcement to an unrepentant world in turmoil. The remaining three angels represent a fore-glimpse of the angels who will accompany and assist Christ when He returns to earth at the end of the Tribulation, to judge the earth and those surviving to the end.

Obviously, angels play a key role throughout the Book of Revelation; but, how about in our lives? While teaching in the temple, our Lord Jesus told His disciples: "See that you do not look down on one of these little ones. For I tell you that their angels in heaven always sees the face of my Father in heaven" (Matthew 18:10). Have you ever sensed the supernatural presence and/or assistance of an unseen force – a guardian angel? Does it give you a sense of comfort, hope, and/or security? Share with the class any experience that you have had that you feel may have involved a supernatural presence or intervention.

Chapter 15

In this chapter we will see the preparation for the final series of judgment of the Great Tribulation. Chapters 15 and 16 belong together, for in them we have the pouring out of the seven bowls of God's wrath. We have already seen the seven seal judgments, the seven trumpet judgments, and the seven figures/groups (ch.12 and 13). The coming seven bowls of wrath are the most intense and devastating of them all.

Seven Angels with Seven Plagues

15:1: The phrase "great and marvelous sign" indicates that this may be the most significant of all signs revealed to this point. The word *sign* means a symbol of revelation; in other words, it represents something that will be revealed in greater detail later, just as we saw in chapters 12 and 13 with the seven figures/groups. From chapter 12 to the return of Christ, there are a series of events or elements that are mutually related. This does not mean they are all in a precise chronological order, but rather a logical order used to retrace them with added detail. We mentioned this earlier in the introduction to our study and said it was a method used often by the Holy Spirit throughout Scripture. John, however, immediately identifies the sign as the "seven angels with the seven last plagues." The apostle makes it clear that this will be the "last" or final set of judgments of the Great Tribulation before the return of Christ. The psalmist wrote: "The Lord says to my Lord: Sit at my right hand until I make your enemies a footstool for your feet" (Psalm 110:1). Remember these judgments are the wrath of God upon the earth; they proceed from heaven and are directed by our Lord Jesus Christ as Judge of the earth, and not from Satan or the beast.

15:2: This "sea of glass" is most likely the same sea observed before the throne of God in chapter 4 (v.6). We said it represented the Word of God, and here includes the Tribulation Saints who held firm to God's Word. The "fire" refers to the trial of fire (persecution) endured by these slain saints of the Great Tribulation "who had been victorious over the beast and his image." This is why our Lord Jesus responded to John, a disciple at the time, with the following words: "I tell you the truth, anyone who gives you a cup of water in my name because you belong to Christ will certainly not lose his reward" (Mark 9:41). During the second half of the Tribulation Period, Antichrist and the false prophet will persecute those who refuse to worship his image and receive his mark. These saints suffered through the fires of persecution on the earth and never lost their song. The "harps given them by God" show us they are playing the heavenly instrument in a beautiful symphony of praise and worship.

15:3 – 4: These Tribulation Saints are singing the song of victory over their enemy. The "song of Moses," found in Exodus (15:1 – 21), speaks of God's deliverance, salvation, and faithfulness. They couple this with the "song of the Lamb" we saw in chapter 5 (v.9 – 12) which praises our Lord Jesus Christ as the Redeemer. Let me remind you that the Book of Revelation is Christ-centered. Do not let anything else we study distract your focus from Christ. In this book we have the unveiling of Jesus Christ in His holiness, His power, and His glory. The song of Moses and the Lamb here clearly identifies the Lord Jesus Christ with the attributes of God the Father. While teaching in the temple, our Lord told those standing around Him, including the Jews: "I and the Father are one" (John 10:30). Let's take a look at the characteristics attributed to our Lord and Savior Jesus Christ:

1) "Great and marvelous are your deeds, Lord Almighty" refers to His creation.
2) "Just and true are your ways" refers to His justice and His righteousness.
3) "King of the ages. Who will not fear you, O Lord, and bring glory to your name?" This refers to our Lord as omnipotent, meaning all-powerful and the object of universal worship. This is the primary purpose of God the Father – to glorify His Son, Jesus Christ, in His created universe!
4) "For you alone are holy." This is a reference to His purity and His holiness. Only Jesus lived a sinless life; and it is only through faith in His death, as the perfect blameless sacrifice and subsequent resurrection, that we too are made holy.
5) "All nations will come and worship before you, for your righteous acts have been revealed." This refers to His absolute rule during the Millennium. As their righteous king, all the nations on earth will eagerly journey to worship Him.

The Book of Revelation clarifies who Jesus Christ truly is. This book is worthy of our study because it does what its introduction says. Chapter 1 (v.1) announces "the revelation of Jesus Christ." The late J. Vernon McGee once stated the following: "The Man Christ Jesus is wonderful! Only He can put one hand in the hand of God and the other in the hand of man and bring them together. He can do this because He is God." What awesome insight!

15:5 – 6: Beginning with chapter 4, the scene of the "throne" and/or "temple" in heaven is referred to many times. Its prominence cannot be ignored. There is no temple in the New Jerusalem (where the church is going) because the church is never identified with a temple. This fact makes itself abundantly clear that God is dealing with the nation of Israel, for only they had a temple. Both the temple and the Ark of the Covenant were patterned after the originals in heaven (Exodus 25:9, 40). Recall earlier in chapter 11 (v.19), "Then God's temple in heaven was opened, and within his temple was seen the Ark of his Covenant." The "tabernacle" of the temple of God is the Holy of Holies, the dwelling place of God during the desert wandering of the Israelites. Great significance should be given to this scene. The "testimony" that radiates from the tabernacle is seen in the Ark of the Covenant. The action of God here is based on Israel's violation of His covenant, or in other words, their disobedience resulting in the broken Law. God is righteous in what He is about to do. He will judge, and then He will fulfill His new covenant with the nation of Israel.

When you read the Old Testament prophets, you cannot miss the fact that God is going to return the children of Israel back to their land. The Prophet Jeremiah wrote extensively concerning the restoration of Israel in chapters 30 and 31. The writer of Hebrews (8:8 – 12) quotes Jeremiah's prophetic announcement and definition of the new covenant. The writer goes further to state that the new covenant is established upon better promises with "Christ as the Mediator" (Hebrews 9:15).

The temple of the tabernacle in heaven is opened so that the "seven angels with the seven last plagues" could go forth. Created as holy beings, angels are permitted entrance into the true tabernacle in heaven. These seven angels depart from the presence of God, who dwells upon the mercy seat. But now, God acts in justice instead of mercy. These angels "dressed in clean, shining linen" and with "golden sashes around their chest" are described in a priest-like adornment (Exodus 28); however, as servants of the Lord Jesus Christ, they are used to bring judgment upon the earth.

15:7 – 8: Seven is God's number for completeness, and in the Revelation we see a series of sevens that I believe all represent completeness. We have seen that the seven churches represent Christ's complete message to the church of all ages. After the church is removed from the earth, we have a complete seven-year Tribulation Period. With these "seven angels" and "seven golden bowls filled with the wrath of God," God's judgment upon the earth will be complete.

The "bowl" reminds us again of the temple because it was used in the service of the temple. Once a year, a bowl of blood was taken by the high priest into the Holy of Holies on the Day of Atonement. That bowl of blood represented redemption for sins. A world that has rejected the blood of Jesus Christ must now bear the judgment of its sin. The Apostle Paul warned the Jews with these words: "But because of your stubbornness and your unrepentant heart, you are storing up wrath against yourself for the day of God's wrath, when his righteous judgment will be revealed" (Romans 2:5).

As soon as the angels come out of the temple, great smoke from the "glory of God" and "his power" fills the temple so "no one could enter the temple until the seven plagues of the seven angels were completed." From this time forward, no created being will have access to the presence of God on His throne until the end of the Tribulation Period. God will not be dealing with humanity in mercy, as is His usual custom. During the second half of the Tribulation Period, referred to by our Lord as the "Great Tribulation" (Matthew 24:21 KJV), God will deal with mankind in judgment.

Even though our evangelical responsibility may include warning the world of the coming judgment of God, it is of greater importance we offer them the gospel of grace – that is, the message that God loves them and is willing to save them through His Son Jesus Christ. I truly believe more people are brought to salvation by the love of God than by the judgment of God. God has shown His love for the world for almost two thousand years of the church age (the age of grace). These last three and a half years of the Tribulation Period are God's final attempt, through judgment, to save a rebellious people.

The truth is, when a person hears or reads the Word of God,
that person is simply foolish not to accept Jesus Christ as their Lord and Savior.

Review Questions

1) In Scripture, the word sign means _____.

2) The sea of glass in heaven represents _____.

3) The fire refers to _____.

4) The song of Moses speaks of _____.

5) The song of the Lamb speaks of _____.

6) The visions of the temple in heaven indicate that _____.

7) With the seven angels and the seven bowls of God's wrath, God's judgment upon the earth will be _____.

Up For Discussion

"And after that I looked, and, behold, the temple of the tabernacle
of the testimony in heaven was opened."
(Revelation 15:5 KJV)

Up to this point in our study we have witnessed the scene of God's temple in heaven several times. John has given us his vision of the glory (Shekinah) of God on His throne. He has described for us the rainbow like crystal sea and the four seraphim that surround the throne. We have seen the twenty-four elders, a multitude of angels, and the souls of Tribulation Saints before the throne singing praises to God and to the Lamb. In addition, John shares his vision of the temple opened in heaven and of the Ark of the Covenant. Now, at the conclusion of this chapter, the temple is emptied (except for the glory of God) until the last seven plagues are completed. God is using these visions of the temple in heaven to emphasize a point to the nation of Israel: During this time of tribulation and judgment on earth, He is still working out His plan for the Jewish remnant – His chosen people.

In speaking of the future nation of Israel, God told Abram: "I will bless those who bless you and whoever curses you I will curse" (Genesis 12:3). Israel remains one of America's closest allies in the world. Do you believe we have been blessed as a nation because of our past alliance with Israel? Do you think recent events have damaged our relationship with Israel? Cite some examples where we, as a nation, have disregarded Israel in favor of others in the region. One example might be the 2015 Iran Nuclear Deal.

Chapter 16

16:1: The seven angels, each holding a bowl containing the wrath of God, are obedient to the "loud voice" of our Lord Jesus when He speaks: "Go, pour out the seven bowls of God's wrath on the earth." The Father has committed all judgment to the Son, as we have already read (John 5:22). The power, the glory, and the majesty belong to Him. The Lord Jesus Christ is in complete control. He is the One who gives the command from heaven, and the seven angels execute His command on earth.

The Bowl Judgments

Should we take these judgments as literal? It is worth noting that four of these seven judgments occurred among the ten plagues in Egypt; and as such, the plagues of Egypt have never been viewed by credible scholars of God's Word as anything but literal. In addition, part of the sixth judgment, the drying up of the Euphrates River and the menacing frogs, was literally fulfilled as well during the time of Israel's exodus from Egypt. Hordes of frogs were generated in the second plague of Egypt, and both the Red Sea and Jordan River were rolled back so God's people could walk forth on dry ground. If the plagues of Egypt were literal (and we certainly believe they were), then we should also expect these awful judgments to be literal as well.

16:2: The first bowl:

This judgment causes grievous and painful sores to come upon human beings. This parallels the sixth plague of Egypt as found in Exodus (9:8 – 12). It is interesting to note that Moses predicted coming judgment upon Israel similar to this, and it has yet to be fulfilled (Deuteronomy 28:27 and 35). This judgment identifies two important points:

1) The time: This judgment occurs at the time when the "beast" (Antichrist) is "worshiped." This is further confirmation that the three judgments (seals, trumpets, and bowls) are sequential, not concurrent as some biblical scholars suggest. This judgment will fall on mankind because of their worship of Antichrist, which only occurs after the mid-point of the Tribulation Period as we learned in chapter 13.
2) The recipients of the judgment – the "people who had the mark of the beast." This indicates that God in His amazing grace will not bring judgment on believers during the second half of the Tribulation Period but will protect them as He did the Israelites during the plagues of Egypt.

16:3: The second bowl:

We have already seen that God will cause one third of the sea to turn to blood as a result of the second trumpet judgment; however, this second bowl judgment afflicts the remaining oceans. It does not take much imagination to see that when all living creatures in the sea die, they will likely start floating to the top. Their decaying bodies, discharging an unbearable stench and lining the shores, will produce widespread disease. People worldwide will die en masse. This judgment will obviously put an end to commercial shipping, not to mention destroy what is left of the fishing industry. This is very similar to the first plague of Egypt, which was the turning of the waters of the Nile River to blood (Exodus 7:20 – 25).

16:4 – 7: The third bowl:

With this third bowl judgment, God will destroy the only remaining sources of water, "the rivers and springs," by turning them to "blood." This will breed disease and pestilence and result in more human death on an even greater scale. People simply cannot live without water. This may also, in a symbolic way, represent "corrupt blood." Antichrist will have "shed the blood" of so many Christian martyrs, he will "deserve" exactly what he gets. His quest for the blood of God's saints will result in his water supply turning to blood in the second half of the Tribulation Period. The altar response is from the "souls under the altar" we saw back in chapter 6; here their prayers are answered. Their response is the result of God's earthly vindication of suffering martyrs from earliest times to the present. "The angel in charge of water" reveals another ministry of angels in charge of the physical elements of the universe. We have already seen four angels that control the winds. This angel declares that God is "Holy" and "just in these judgments." Whatever God does is righteous and just. If you do not agree with Him, then you are simply wrong.

16:8 – 9: The fourth bowl:

When the fourth bowl is poured out on the earth, mankind will suffer from a sun-induced heat wave, the likes of which has never been experienced. Even though one third of the sun will have been darkened as the result of the fourth trumpet judgment, the remaining sun light will be so powerful it will "scorch people with fire." Even worse, without water to quench their thirst, we find people literally tasting the torments of hell as described by our Lord (Luke 16:23 – 24). Jesus also predicted: "There will be signs in the sun, moon, and stars. On the earth, nations will be in anguish and perplexity at the roaring and tossing of the sea" (Luke 21:25). The Old Testament prophets had a great deal to say regarding this specific judgment of the Great Tribulation (Deuteronomy 32:24 (KJV); Isaiah 24:6; Malachi 4:1). Instead of driving people to their knees in repentance to God, we see the first of three occasions when people "cursed the name of God … but they refused to repent and glorify him." This proves that the human heart is incurably wicked and by this time no amount of punishment will change it. This is judgment upon an unrepentant world.

However, believers during the Great Tribulation will find comfort in God's words as recorded by the psalmist: "The Lord watches over you – the Lord is your shade at your right hand: the sun will not harm you by day, nor the moon by night" (Psalm 121:5 – 6).

16:10 – 11: The fifth bowl:

The fifth bowl is a special judgment that seems to center on the headquarters of Antichrist, for it is poured out on "the throne of the beast, and his kingdom was plunged into darkness." This is very similar to the darkness that covered all of Egypt (Pharaoh's dominion) for three days during the ninth plague (Exodus 10:21 – 23). The Old Testament prophets foretold this same judgment (Joel 2:1 – 2, 31; Amos 5:18; Zephaniah 1:15). Jesus, as well, warned His disciples concerning the distress of those days: "The sun will be darkened, and the moon will not give its light" (Matthew 24:29; Mark 13:24). Remember since the water supply has been turned to blood, mankind may well be incapable of producing electrical power and illumination from the rivers and bodies of water. Subsequently, battery operated, fuel generated, or other types of light generation will be supernaturally rendered useless as well. When God says darkness, He means darkness!

"Men gnawed their tongues in agony." Can you imagine the intensity of the suffering? Yet, for the second time, instead of falling down before Him in repentance, people only "cursed the God of heaven because of their pains and their sores." We must understand that those who reject the Lord do so not because of philosophical doubts, but as a result of hardness of their hearts. We read earlier the Apostle Paul's warning in his letter to the Romans: "But because of your stubbornness and your unrepentant heart, you are storing up wrath against yourself for the day of God's wrath, when his righteous judgment will be revealed" (Romans 2:5). This is God's righteous judgment.

16:12: The sixth bowl:

The sixth bowl judgment comes in two parts:

1) The drying up of the Euphrates River, which will be in preparation for the "battle on the great day of God Almighty."
2) The three frog-like demon spirits that will bring the rebellious armies of the world to the Valley of Megiddo for the purpose of opposing the Lord.

As mentioned earlier in chapter 9 (v.14), the Euphrates River is one of the most prominent rivers in Scripture. It has always stood as a natural barrier between east and west. The sixth bowl judgment will dry up that river to make way for the "kings from the East." The literal meaning is "the kings from the sunrising," a reference to the kings of the oriental nations of the world. This oriental alliance may be preparing to oppose Antichrist, whose capital lies in Babylon. However, because of the lying tongues of the three demonic spirits described in the next two verses, the armies instead will be deceived into coming across onto the side of Antichrist in opposition to our Lord. The bulk of the world's population is in the east, and there is very little gospel there. They will choose Antichrist. No wonder, as we read at the end of chapter 14, the blood will "rise as high as the horses' bridles."

16:13 – 14: These "three evil spirits" that will come from the mouths of "the dragon," "the beast," and "the false prophet" are deceiving spirits. They should not be taken literally as frogs because John only says they "looked like frogs." They are to be interpreted spiritually as demonic creatures (visible or invisible – I am not certain) that will work miracles before the "kings of the whole world." In some deceitful manner, they will con these kings into coming together for the "battle on the great day of God Almighty." The timing of this event must be the very last days of the Great Tribulation, since the next bowl concludes the Tribulation Period with, what I believe to be, the literal destruction of governmental and commercial Babylon.

16:15: This verse begins another interlude; and, as we have seen before with the seal and trumpet judgments, occurs between the sixth and seventh bowl judgments. This is our Lord's challenge to all the saints still living during the closing days of the Great Tribulation to continue faithfully to the very end.

"Behold, I come like a thief!" Christ will never come as a thief to the church. The Apostle Paul wrote: "But you, brothers, are not in darkness so that this day should surprise you like a thief" (1 Thessalonians 5:4). A thief is someone you shut out; you don't welcome him. However, the Lord Jesus Christ does come like a thief to the world at the end of the Great Tribulation. As we read earlier in chapter 1 (v.7), "the earth will mourn because of him." They do not want the Lord to come. Christ further challenges these saints to "stay awake and keep his clothes with him." This is a command to continue faithfully, clothed with the righteousness of Christ through faith.

16:16: This is the only occurrence of the word *Armageddon* in Scripture. It means "Mount of Megiddo." It stands on the southwestern edge of the Esdraelon (Greek for Jezreel) Valley. The Valley of Jezreel is a major travel route through the rugged Palestinian hills. It also separates the province of Galilee from the district of Samaria. Armageddon is an expression often used to describe the decisive battle between the God-opposing forces of Antichrist and our Lord Jesus Christ upon His return to earth. The actual scriptural expression, found above (v.14), is "the battle on the great day of God Almighty." It takes place in the Valley of Megiddo. This valley is a place where many battles have been fought in the past, from the Old Testament account of the thirty-one kings conquered by Joshua (Joshua 12:21), to the devastating march of Napoleon Bonaparte from Egypt to Syria. It was Napoleon who was said to have stated with deep emotion after his first sight of this great valley: "This is the ideal battleground for all the armies of the world." The "they" mentioned in this verse refers to the dragon trinity with their deceptive tongues; nevertheless, they unknowingly fulfill the Word of God.

16:17 – 18: The seventh bowl:

The seventh angel pours out his bowl "into the air," which means into the atmosphere or heavens, and at no specific location or target. The Lord Jesus Christ controls the heavens, and He is getting ready to come through them. "Out of the temple came a loud voice from the throne," conveying a most welcome message: "It is done!" This is the voice of the Son of God, our Lord Jesus Christ. This is the second time we have heard Him say this. As He hung from the cross, He murmured these final words, "It is finished." The Greek word for *finished* is *teleo* which means "complete" or "discharge" (a debt). At that point in history redemption was made and salvation became available to all mankind. There is nothing more man can do to add to his salvation, but to simply receive it in faith as the miraculous gift from a loving God.

"It is done" is most welcome because it signifies the end of the Great Tribulation, the conclusion of the day of God's wrath on the ungodly, and the end of the time of Jacob's (the nation of Israel) trouble (Jeremiah 30:7).

Earlier in chapter 4 (v.5), we saw proceeding from the throne in heaven "flashes of lightning, rumblings, and peals of thunder" beginning the Tribulation Period and announcing the coming judgment. Here at the conclusion of the Great Tribulation this scene is repeated; however, this time with the addition of a "severe earthquake." Likewise, in chapter 6 (v.12), we saw that the opening of the sixth seal brought about a "great earthquake," and that men hid from the "Wrath of the Lamb." This final judgment of God will include an even greater earthquake which will apparently shake the entire world, for our passage reads: "No earthquake like it has ever occurred since man has been on earth, so tremendous was the quake."

16:19 – 20: This earthquake will destroy the "great city." There is much debate about the meaning of the "great city." Many scholars believe it to be Jerusalem. But why did John not say Jerusalem since he was well familiar with that city? Others identify it as governmental and commercial Babylon, the capital of the world at that time. I lean toward the latter, for two reasons:

1) Governmental Babylon is referred to as the "great city" several times in chapter 18.
2) In chapter 18, Governmental Babylon is destroyed by a cataclysmic judgment from God. In fact, the next two chapters will give us the details concerning both great Babylons and their destruction.

The phrase, "The cities of the nations collapsed," refers to all the cities of the world and their ultimate destruction. Combined with the phrase, "Every island fled away and the mountains could not be found," would lead us to conclude that what we see here is a complete renovation of the earth's surface. We will discuss this further in chapter 20.

16:21: If this were not enough catastrophes, "huge hailstones of about a hundred pounds each fell upon men." Let us remember what the Lord told his servant Job: "Have you entered the storehouses of the snow or seen the storehouses of the hail, which I reserve for the times of trouble, for the days of war and battle?" (Job 38:22 – 23)

"They cursed God on account of the plague of hail." It is hard to imagine human beings so rebellious that they lift their faces in final defiance to God even in the midst of such disaster. All hopes and dreams will be ended with this final judgment because people will have chosen to worship Antichrist.

The hailstorm ends the Great Tribulation Period.

Review Questions

1) The first bowl judgment produced ugly and painful sores upon all who _____

_____.

2) The second bowl judgment turned the remaining parts of the sea into blood resulting in

_____.

3) The third bowl judgment turned the remaining fresh water supplies to blood. The angel said Christ was justified because _____

_____.

4) The fourth bowl judgment was poured out on the sun and as a result _____

_____.

5) The fifth bowl judgment of darkness affected only _____.

6) The sixth bowl judgment dried up the _____ so that the three demonic spirits could deceive the kings of the East into coming together to assist Antichrist in his opposition to _____.

7) The seventh bowl judgment was poured out into the air resulting in _____

_____

_____.

Up For Discussion

"And men blasphemed God because of the plague of hail ...."
(Revelation 16:21 KJV)

Imagine the magnitude of grief and suffering on human beings. The people on earth recognized that these judgments were from God, but they still refused to repent and turn to Him. When they rejected God and all the warnings He sent, and accepted the mark of the beast, their decision was cemented for eternity. God hardened their hearts just as He did Pharaoh's at the time of Israel's exodus from Egypt. Is this fair? Can you reconcile their decision with their fate and agree that God is just and righteous?

Read on your own or review as class time permits the FAQ: Tribulation Saints.

Read on your own or review as class time permits the FAQ: God Hardens the Heart.

Take a few minutes and look over the map of Ancient Israel and Judah. Locate and discuss:

1) Jerusalem: The capital city and worship center of the southern kingdom of Judah.
2) Samaria: The capital city of the northern kingdom of Israel.
3) Bethel: The location where Abraham first "pitched his tents" and "built an altar to the Lord." This is also where Jacob dreamed of the ladder reaching to heaven and referred to it as the "house of God" and the "gate of heaven." This city was early recognized as the worship center of Israel because the Ark of the Covenant was located there; but later, after the death of Solomon and the division of his kingdom, it became a great center of idolatry in the northern kingdom.
4) Megiddo: The site of battle between the nations of the world lead by Antichrist and our Lord Jesus Christ upon His return to earth.

If you have traveled to the Holy Land, share with the class some of your experiences and sites you enjoyed seeing the most. If time allows, bring some photos to share with the class as well.

ANCIENT ISRAEL
& JUDAH

Damascus

Zarephath

Tyre

Dan

TYRE

Hazor

SYRIA

Sea of Galilee

Aphek

Megiddo

Ramoth-gilead

Beth-shean

ISRAEL

Samaria ✪ • Tirzah

Penuel

Shechem

Jordan River

Joppa

AMMON

Beth-horon • Bethel

Rabbah

Gezer

Jerico

Ashdod

Jerusalem ✪

Heshbon

Shaphir • Gath • Bethlehem

• Adullam

Ashkelon   Moresheth-gath • • Achzib

• Mareshah

Dead Sea

Dibon

Gaza

PHILISTIA   Lachish   Hebron

Engedi

JUDAH

MOAB

• Beersheba

Kir-hareseth

EDOM

Kadesh-barnea

Bozrah

N
↑

FAQ: Tribulation Saints

Question: We learned in chapter 7 that 144,000 Jewish witnesses received the seal of the living God from an angel so as to protect them from the judgments of the Tribulation Period as they evangelize the world. Are the Tribulation Saints protected from God's judgments as well?

We defined Tribulation Saints as those who had not accepted the Lord Jesus Christ during the church age and were thus left behind on earth after the rapture. They, in turn, accept Jesus Christ as their Lord and Savior during the dreadful times of the Tribulation Period as a result of the faithful witness of the 144,000. It is believed by many biblical scholars, including myself that the only way these Tribulation Saints will die is by martyrdom – persecuted and slain by the beast (Antichrist) and forces loyal to him. They will not die from the judgments that are coming upon the earth because their judgment has been paid in full as well by the blood of the Lamb – Jesus Christ.

Revelation 12:6: We see that the redeemed remnant of Israel will flee persecution by Antichrist to a place in the "desert where she might be taken care of" by God. This occurs at the mid-point of the Tribulation Period when the Jewish remnant rejects the idolatrous religion of Antichrist and turns as a nation to the one true Messiah, Jesus Christ. God will protect and provide for them just as He did during their exodus from Egypt.

Revelation 13:7: We are told that the beast (Antichrist) will be "given power to make war against the saints and to conquer them." This is a reference to the above mentioned persecution and murder of God's children by Antichrist.

Revelation 20:4b: Sadly we see that these Tribulation Saints are "beheaded because of their testimony for Jesus and because of the word of God. They had not worshiped the beast and his image." They held fast to their new-found faith in the Savior and became martyrs for Christ.

The unrighteous, on the other hand, suffer as a direct result of the judgments (wrath) from God coming upon the earth.

We learned that both the seal judgments (6:8 – Hades, referring to the abode of the unrighteous dead) and the trumpet judgments (9:20 – "the rest of mankind … still did not repent … they did not stop worshiping demons and idols") only affected the unrighteous – the unbelievers.

In our study of the bowl judgments here in chapter 16, we see that Scripture only speaks of the judgments and their punishment as "poured out" upon the unrighteous – those "who had the mark of the beast and worshiped his image" (16:2).

Revelation 16:9: We see that "they cursed the name of God." They, referred to here, can only be the unrighteous because a child of God would never curse God's name. Unrepentant mankind becomes progressively worse in their rebellion against God on account of the bowl judgments.

Revelation 16:10: "The fifth angel poured out his bowl on the throne of the beast and his kingdom was plunged into darkness." This judgment is directed specifically onto the wicked governmental and commercial headquarters of Antichrist.

Revelation 16:11: "Men ... cursed the God of heaven ... but they refused to repent of what they had done." Again, these are the unrighteous, the wicked and corrupt associates of Antichrist and his kingdom.

Revelation 16:21: Lastly, we see that "they cursed God on account of the plague...." Three times in this chapter alone, the unrighteous, that is, unrepentant mankind curses God. When you live your life in complete rebellion to God, apparently no amount of judgment will cause you to turn around and repent.

Please do not misunderstand me; the Tribulation Period will be a time of extreme suffering for everyone during those days, including Tribulation Saints. Sadly, those who do die, their death will be the result of some dreadful persecution by Antichrist and not from any judgment from God. What about natural causes or accidental death? I cannot determine that from our study; however, I believe God will use every resource – the 144,000 witnesses (ch.7), the two divine witnesses (ch.11), angels (ch.14), and every Tribulation Saint in order to reach and convert as many souls as possible for the sake of the gospel of His precious Son Jesus Christ and His kingdom. Amen.

FAQ: God Hardens the Heart

As we read through the last set of judgments – the bowl judgments – we discussed the fact that these judgments are "poured out on," or affect only unrepentant mankind. The righteous, those who have made the decision to accept Jesus Christ rather than Antichrist are protected from these judgments, despite the extreme conditions of the times. We highlighted the fact that three times "people cursed the name of God … but they refused to repent." Recall the words of the Apostle Paul as he warned us regarding the "man of lawlessness": "For this reason God sends them a powerful delusion so that they will believe the lie and so that all will be condemned who have not believed the truth but have delighted in wickedness" (2 Thessalonians 2:11 – 12). For the vast many that have lived their entire lives in rebellion to God and in favor of self-reliance, God will harden their hearts, just as He did Pharaoh's as described in the Book of Exodus.

Question: Why does a loving God harden the hearts of men against Him?

This is a great question and one probably debated by scholars down through the ages as much as the meaning of 666. We have discussed in past Revelation study classes how some people are indoctrinated from childhood into other religions or raised with non-religious beliefs; consequently as adults, they refuse to believe otherwise despite hearing and/or reading the truth from the Word of God. I believe that has a great deal to do with it. However, during the dreadful Tribulation Period, God will use 144,000 witnesses, two supernatural witnesses, and an angel to get the message of the gospel of Jesus Christ out to the entire world – "every nation, tribe, people, and language" (7:9). Every single person on earth will have heard the gospel and been given the opportunity to make a choice – Jesus Christ or Antichrist.

As I thought on this question, God kept bringing my attention back to the words of our Lord Jesus Christ: "He who is not with me is against me, and he who does not gather with me scatters. And so I tell you, every sin and blasphemy will be forgiven men, but the blasphemy against the Spirit will not be forgiven. Anyone who speaks a word against the Son of Man will be forgiven, but anyone who speaks against the Holy Spirit will not be forgiven, either in this age or in the age to come" (Matthew 12:30 – 32). This message is highly significant since it is repeated again in both the Gospels of Mark (3:28 – 29) and Luke (12:10). The phrase "this age" is a reference to the present day up through the return of Christ at the end of the Tribulation Period; wherein the phrase "the age to come," I believe refers to the Millennium (ch.20).

We learned back in chapter 13 that blasphemy manifests itself in two forms: First, making oneself equal to God; and secondly, slandering the name of God. The context of the above statement by Jesus was in response to the Pharisees attributing the miracles of Jesus to Satan's power and not that of the Holy Spirit – making oneself equal to God. However, the statement has greater scope for us all regarding slandering the name of God. Once someone hears the gospel of Jesus Christ, it is the Holy Spirit that woos and leads that person into a personal commitment and relationship with Christ. If that person denies or rejects, or even worse "curses God," then they have slandered or "blasphemed" the Holy Spirit. They have rejected God's grace; and that, my friends, is the unpardonable sin that our Lord forbids.

Our lesson makes it abundantly clear that all people remaining on earth after the rapture will hear the message of salvation through faith in the Lord Jesus Christ during the seven-year Tribulation Period. By the time we get to the second half of the Tribulation and into the bowl judgments, most will have made their decision. Unfortunately, those who choose Antichrist and take his mark will have made an irreversible decision; and thus, God will harden their hearts.

Chapter 17

Religious Babylon Destroyed
(The False Church)

Historians tell us that Babylon is the cradle of civilization. Located on the shores of the Euphrates River, the ruins of this city have uncovered some of the most ancient documents of past generations. This was the first city established after the flood by Nimrod, grandson of Ham, son of Noah, and who grew to be a mighty warrior (Genesis 10:8 – 10). However, Nimrod rebelled against God. He initiated some of the greatest evils ever to fall on mankind. In those days Babylon appeared to be the capital of Satan's evil operation. It became the birth place of all false religion. From here, a system of false religion originated which emphasized idolatry and sexual immorality. Babylon was also the beginning of mankind's attempt at self-governance in defiance of God's will, and structures were built for commercial and social purposes contrary to God's commands.

In chapter 14 (v.8) we read: "Fallen! Fallen is Babylon the Great, which made all the nations drink the maddening wine of her adulteries." This chapter describes in detail the coming judgment from God on this religious system also referred to by some scholars as the apostate or false church. It will acquire its members from all the great systems of the world, especially pagan religions, cults, and "isms." Even in our churches today there are those who are not true believers; and during the first half of the Tribulation Period, they will join this organization that may call itself a church, but is not. God calls it the "great prostitute."

These verses portray through symbols two great institutions: One religious (the prostitute, i.e. apostate or false church) and the other governmental (Antichrist and his revised Roman Empire). Together they describe a powerful global religious system which gains a controlling influence in Antichrist's government during the first half of the Tribulation Period. Leaders of false religions of the world have always competed with political leaders for dominance over their countries or empires. This is in contrast to the true Christian Church, as we know it, which has never sought political power; in fact, Jesus told the Roman Governor, Pontius Pilate: "My kingdom is not of this world" (John 18:36).

17:1 – 2: "The great prostitute" is that faction of the church which will be left on earth after the true church has been raptured. It will be made up of those who have never trusted Jesus Christ as Savior. This is the group that enters into the Tribulation Period. Just as the "bride" (19:7) represents Christ's raptured and resurrected church, the "prostitute" represents an evil religious system, one that emphasizes idolatry. Later in this chapter (v.15), the angel defines the meaning of the phrase "many waters" as the "peoples, multitudes, nations, and languages" of the world. This phrase is used here to designate all of humanity. This prostitute is a worldwide system that has control over all people; this is why she is portrayed as sitting on them. You see, when you reject the genuine, you are wide open to the counterfeit. We have read before, but let's read again what the Apostle Paul wrote: "For this reason God sends them a powerful delusion so that they will believe the lie and so that all will be condemned who have not believed the truth but have delighted in wickedness" (2 Thessalonians 2:11 – 12).

The "punishment of the great prostitute" indicates that God's judgment will come down upon her. How will God put an end to this false church? During the first half of the Tribulation Period the beast (Antichrist) tolerates it; and even though he hates it, he will use this apostate church to control the masses. However, during the second half of the Tribulation Period, God will use the beast and the false prophet to destroy the "great prostitute" so that they may set up a religion making Antichrist the sole object of worship as he proclaims himself to be god.

This religious system, called a prostitute, will have gained worldwide dominance during the first half of the Tribulation Period, causing the "kings of the earth to commit adultery" and making the "inhabitants of the earth intoxicated with the wine of her adulteries." This clearly demonstrates a corrupt union – an unholy alliance between church and state during the first half of the Tribulation Period.

17:3: Recall in chapter 4, John was carried in Spirit to heaven to prepare him for the vision of the glorified Christ. Now here, the phrase "the angel carried me away in the Spirit," may likely refer to John's need for a fresh anointing of the Holy Spirit to prepare him for the awesome visions still to come.

In his vision, John's focus is now on a "woman sitting on a scarlet beast." The beast was identified in chapter 13 as Antichrist and his revised Roman Empire. John identifies the woman in verse 18 as "the great city that rules over the kings of the earth." Hence, the woman is also a city, and the city is most likely present-day Rome (Vatican City contained therein), considered by some to be the religious capital of the world. She is religious Rome, who at that time will have incorporated all religions of the world. The city is further identified in verse 9 as follows: "This calls for a mind with wisdom. The seven heads are seven hills on which the woman sits." Any internet search today would identify Rome, Italy as the "city set on seven hills."

"Covered with blasphemous names" refers to the irreverent and profane nature that has been characteristic of all world governments that continue in opposition to God's will.

17:4: "Dressed in purple and scarlet." Purple is the color of royalty and the predominant color of Roman imperialism. It was worn by every senator and consul as recognition of their position. In the Roman Catholic Church, scarlet is the color worn by a cardinal and is associated with the blood of Christ and Christian martyrs. "Glittering with gold, precious stones and pearls" details a beautiful outward appearance reminiscent of the Pharisees. Recall our Lord's rebuke of the Pharisees: "Woe to you, teachers of the law and Pharisees, you hypocrites! You clean the outside of the cup and dish, but inside they are full of greed and self-indulgence" (Matthew 23:25).

"A golden cup filled with abominable things" represents the religious intoxication – the lure or enticement of the false church and religion that emphasizes idolatry and sexual immorality. This is the cup that intoxicated the earth (v.2). The prophet foretold this: "Babylon was a gold cup in the Lord's hand; she made the whole earth drunk. The nations drank her wine; therefore they have now gone mad" (Jeremiah 51:7).

17:5: "This title was written on her forehead" indicates she does not wear a crown but the mark of her profession: "MYSTERY BABYLON THE GREAT." This false church is a mystery because it was not revealed until John wrote about it here. The true church is a mystery because it was never revealed in the Old Testament. After the true church is removed from earth at the rapture, only false members are left. As mentioned earlier, they are but a part of many factions that will make up the false church remaining on earth during the first half of the Tribulation Period. However, God does not call Babylon a church, He calls it a prostitute. The Apostle Paul wrote about wickedness in the church: "For the secret power of lawlessness is already at work; but the one who now holds it back will continue to do so till he is taken out of the way" (2 Thessalonians 2:7). You see lawlessness is at work in the church today, just as it was back in Paul's day. Our Lord spoke of this in His parable of the "sower," (Matthew 13:3 – 23). Here Jesus compares the lawlessness as the "thorns," or weeds that come up among the wheat (believers). Who is "the one who now holds it back"? It is the Holy Spirit. When will "he be taken out of the way"? I believe at the rapture. Does that mean the Holy Spirit will not be present during the Tribulation Period? Sure He will. He will continue in His same mission, to woo people to Christ through the evangelizing efforts of the 144,000 witnesses and the two supernatural witnesses. However, He will not hinder evil. Satan will have his day for a while.

"THE MOTHER OF PROSTITUTES AND OF THE ABOMINATIONS OF THE EARTH": This is one of Scripture's most expressive and vivid descriptions of abominable sin. Sex, idolatry, and false religions go hand-in-hand. Abomination in the Old Testament refers to the worship of idols and is exactly the form of religion Satan has used throughout the ages to deceive men and women and lead them away from a relationship with God.

17:6 – 7: "Drunk with the blood of the saints." The prostitute not only makes others drunk, as we saw above, with her emphasis on idolatry and sexual immorality, but she is also intoxicated by her own acts of persecution. "The saints," mentioned here, may refer to Old Testament Saints where the phrase, "those who bore testimony to Jesus" is a reference to New Testament Saints. Religious Babylon is a composite system made up of all religions, groups, and cults that remain on earth after the rapture of the true church. It was in Babylon where three Hebrew exiles were thrown into a fiery furnace because they would not worship the king's golden statue. Even today our greatest fears come from unpredictable acts of terrorism throughout the world perpetrated by extreme religious radicals.

When John saw the vision of the woman, he was "greatly astonished." John is in great wonder, or maybe even confused. Is the emphasis here on the revised Roman Empire aspect of the beast or on the Antichrist aspect of the beast – the kingdom or the man? As we look at the next few verses we will see that this is an area of debate among scholars.

17:8 – 10: We have already seen in chapter 13 (v.3 – 6) a description of the death of the beast (Antichrist) and his apparent resurrection by the dragon (Satan) at the mid-point of the Tribulation Period. Many scholars feel these verses reinforce that explanation, and that may well be correct.

However, let me explain another view that suggests the emphasis here is on the kingdom, the revised Roman Empire aspect of the beast rather than Antichrist himself.

The beast "once was" speaks of the past history of the Roman Empire. "Is not" refers to the present condition of the fragmented Empire. The Roman Empire did not die; it just fell apart becoming the nations of Europe as seen today. "Will come out of the Abyss" speaks of the restoration of the Roman Empire by Antichrist during the Tribulation Period. "Go to his destruction" refers to the destruction of the Roman Empire by the coming of Christ at the end of the Great Tribulation. The "inhabitants of the earth ... will be astonished." The re-establishment of the Roman Empire in its great power and glory will win the admiration of all the unredeemed remaining on earth. They will respect and worship Antichrist for his brilliant accomplishment.

The seven heads are "also seven kings" and probably represent kings of the Roman Empire throughout John's lifetime and would reinforce the above-mentioned explanation. They are:

1) Augustus
2) Tiberius
3) Caligula
4) Claudius
5) Nero

The "one is" would refer to the ruling king at the time of the writing of John's Revelation – Domitian. The "other has not yet come" refers to the future ruler of the revised Roman Empire – Antichrist. Other scholars, however, view these kings as representative forms of government as we discussed in our study of the dragon back in chapter 12 (v.3). Regardless, the end in view is the same – Antichrist rules over the revised Roman Empire until it is destroyed by the coming of our Lord Jesus Christ.

17:11: "An eighth king ... belongs to the seven," would suggest that king number eight is the same as king number seven. Here it signifies the last head (king), the final emperor – Antichrist – the incarnation of Satan himself, with his dictatorial form of the restored Roman Empire.

17:12 – 14: The "ten horns" are ten kings we saw in chapter 13 (v.1) who give their "power and authority" to Antichrist during the Tribulation Period. These are the same as the ten horns of Daniel 7:7. "One hour will receive authority as kings" probably refers to the fact they will reign with Antichrist but will be subservient to him.

The end is already recorded. Though they will "make war against the Lamb," Christ will "overcome them" because He is "Lord of Lords and King of Kings" (19:15 – 16). Christ will be accompanied by "His called, chosen, and faithful followers." I believe this phrase represents the entire host of heaven, including the redeemed and glorified church making up the bride of Christ. We will discuss this in greater detail later in chapter 19 (v.14).

17:15: As mentioned earlier, this verse defines for us the phrase "many waters" (v.1).

17:16 – 17: Antichrist will allow the prostitute (apostate church) to govern his actions during the first half of the Tribulation Period while he is gathering more and more power. However, in the middle of the Tribulation Period, when he firmly establishes his revised Roman Empire and lifts himself up as world dictator, he and the ten kings will eliminate the prostitute. Antichrist not only breaks his treaty with the nation of Israel, but he also terminates his relationship with the false church.

In reality, while sharing in their exalted position, the "beast and the ten horns … will hate the prostitute." Why? Because the glory is divided. When it is no longer necessary, Antichrist and the ten kings will "bring her to ruin and leave her naked," meaning they will destroy her temples and confiscate her many riches. This hatred is so violent that the passage further states: "They will eat her flesh and burn her with fire." This great hatred destroys the false church. In contrast to the true church in heaven, the false church on earth has no victory.

In doing so, Antichrist and his ten allies will unknowingly be instruments of God in destroying this dreadful Babylonian system of false religion once and for all: "For God has put it into their hearts to accomplish his purpose."

From then on the world does not worship Mystery Babylon but the image of the beast. As mentioned earlier, Mystery Babylon is likely Rome, and when it is destroyed in the middle of the Tribulation Period, the religious center shifts to Jerusalem. It is in the temple in Jerusalem that the false prophet will erect an image of Antichrist to be worshiped (Daniel 9:27; Matthew 24:15). The false prophet will do away with all religion except the worship of Antichrist (Satan), which he will mandate and enforce. The reign and worship of Antichrist will be the darkest hours earth will ever know. Having rejected the truth, the only alternative left for mankind is to believe the big lie.

17:18: The woman who rides the beast and gets her power from the beast is mentioned here by the Holy Spirit to illustrate how intertwined religious and governmental Babylon are during the first half of the Tribulation Period. However, they are destroyed at different times. Religious Babylon is destroyed in the middle of the Tribulation Period. Governmental Babylon, as we will see in the next chapter, will be destroyed at the end.

Even in the horrific second half of the Tribulation Period, the worship of Antichrist will not be universal. Those who have received the Lamb of God will resist him, even at the cost of martyrdom.

Review Questions

1) What are the two basic tenets associated with false religions? _____.

2) The great prostitute, or false church, is that part of the church that is left on earth after _____

    _____.

3) This false church is made up of those who _____.

4) During the first half of the Tribulation Period, Antichrist will tolerate this false church because
   he will use it to _____.

5) Religious Babylon is destroyed when? _____.

6) Who destroys religious Babylon? _____.

7) Why was religious Babylon destroyed? _____

    _____.

Up For Discussion

"And the habitants of the earth have been made drunk with the wine of her fornication."
(Revelation 17:2 KJV)

Religious Babylon, the false church, is that part of the church left on earth after the rapture of the true church. It consists of those who have never put their faith and trust in Jesus Christ as their Lord and Savior. I once read the following: "Take the simple gospel of Jesus Christ, which is God made flesh in the virgin birth, lived a sinless life, died on the cross for the sins of all mankind, on the third day He rose from the dead and now sits at the right hand of God, the Father in heaven, and will return again to earth one day. Now if you add to or take away anything from that simple gospel, then what you would have is religion," (author unknown). There are many books available today written on the subjects of other (false) religions. You might have read some; and if so, you may have even been surprised at some of the organizations listed in them. Is it important to our Christian faith to study and have some knowledge of the tenets of other religions?

Or is it of greater importance to prayerfully read and study our Bibles daily so we are better prepared, at a moment's notice, to defend the faith we hold so dear?

Share with the class any experiences you have had in another church and/or civil organization that conflicted with your faith in the gospel of Jesus Christ. How did you response?

Chapter 18

Governmental and Commercial Babylon Destroyed

In chapter 16 (v.19), we read: "God remembered Babylon the Great and gave her the cup filled with the wine of the fury of his wrath." Now in this chapter, we will discuss in greater detail the judgment of governmental and commercial Babylon, and the reaction of both earth and heaven to it. "Babylon the Great" is ancient Babylon (there or about) rebuilt as the governmental and commercial capital of the world. This city is the final capital of the political power of Antichrist. This judgment will not take place until the end of the Tribulation Period. The following four reasons establish the distinction between the destruction of Babylon in chapter 17 and that of chapter 18:

1) "After this …." In verse 1 this expression indicates that the events described in chapter 18 will not take place until sometime after the events of chapter 17 have been fulfilled.
2) Religious Babylon, the prostitute of chapter 17, will be destroyed by Antichrist and the kings of the earth. Governmental Babylon will be destroyed by a cataclysmic judgment from God.
3) The kings who destroyed religious Babylon rejoice because they hated the prostitute. In this chapter concerning governmental and commercial Babylon, we will see the kings and merchants lament and weep over her destruction.
4) If the events of chapters 17 and 18 both took place during the last days of the Tribulation, then there would be no time remaining for Antichrist and the false prophet to do away with the false church in order to decree and enforce universal worship of Antichrist and his image as described in chapter 13.

18:1: We begin our chapter with yet another awesome angel. Thus far, we have seen the phrase "mighty angel" described and used twice by John (5:2 and 10:1). Since this angel has such "great authority," he may likely be of a higher order than other angels we have previously seen, including the seven angels who had the seven bowls of God's wrath. These "great" or "mighty" angels may well be of the order of archangel, since they allegedly number seven in all. Michael and Gabriel are two who are mentioned by name in our Scriptures. If it is true that the archangels total seven, then should we not expect each to play a prominent role in these final chapters of earth's history leading up to the return of Christ? The fact that the "earth was illuminated by his splendor" seems to further illustrate the prestige of this angel.

18:2: The message of this angel who cries with a "mighty voice" is: "Fallen! Fallen is Babylon the Great!" Babylon, the great commercial center of the world, will be destroyed because it is in God's plan to do so. "She has become a home for demons and a haunt for every evil spirit, a haunt for every unclean and detestable bird." The Prophets Isaiah (13:19 – 22 KJV) and Jeremiah (50:39) both predicted that Babylon will be the place where wild beast and dragons, and unclean birds will dwell following its destruction – during the Millennium. These prophecies find their final fulfillment in this chapter with the destruction of the literal city of Babylon.

Since this chapter describes the destruction of a literal commercial city, the governmental capital of the world during the Tribulation Period, we naturally ask ourselves the question, "Where is this city?" Biblical scholars are not in agreement on this question. I agree with those who follow the Old Testament prophecies that point to the literal rebuilding of Babylon. God woos us through His Word and His Spirit to walk by faith; Satan woos us through government, commerce, and religious idolatry to walk by sight.

Several reasons for believing Babylon must be rebuilt relates to prophecies concerning her destruction that are yet unfulfilled:

1) Isaiah 13 – 14 and Jeremiah 50 – 51 describe the destruction of Babylon as being at the time of the "Day of the Lord." These verses refer to the overthrow of Babylon (the enemy of Israel) on the final day of their atonement and referred to as the Day of the Lord, marking the end of the Tribulation Period.
2) Contrary to the Prophet Jeremiah (51:26), the ruins of Babylon have been used to build other cities. It is reported that at least six cities bear the marks of having used stones from ancient Babylon in their building, including Baghdad, fifty miles north of the site of ancient Babylon. This fact alone demands the rebuilding of Babylon because, when God destroys it, the prophet tells us: "No rock will be taken from you for a cornerstone, or any stone for a foundation."
3) Jeremiah also foretold that, "Babylon will suddenly fall and be broken" (51:8). Likewise, the Prophet Isaiah wrote: "Babylon, the jewel of kingdoms, the glory of the Babylonians' pride, will be overthrown by God like Sodom and Gomorrah" (Isaiah 13:19). History reveals that ancient Babylon was never destroyed like that.
4) Furthermore, Isaiah foretold that the ruins of Babylon were never to be inhabited: "She will never be inhabited or lived in through all generations; no Arab will pitch his tent there, no shepherd will rest his flocks there" (Isaiah 13:20). Again, a look at history reveals that this prophecy regarding Babylon has never been fulfilled.

Much has happened in recent years in both Iraq and Babylon. Saddam Hussein, the former dictator of the country, spent over $800 million on reconstruction and re-establishment of ancient Babylon, which may well be taken over some day by Antichrist, renamed New Babylon, and made the political and commercial center of the world. Saddam was trying to restore ancient majesty to the city and his rebuilding program was progressing. It is interesting to note that among his first projects was rebuilding of the monumental staircase in the temple of Marduk, also called the Ziggurat. This should not be difficult to understand, as Saddam Hussein was a committed Satanist. He was a Muslim for political reasons, but at heart he worshiped the supreme god of the Babylonians. He also built a lavish palace for himself, which was featured in many televised news reports following his downfall and capture. In addition, he commissioned over 60 million bricks to be placed in the walls of Babylon, each engraved with the inscription: "To King Nebuchadnezzar in the Reign of Saddam Hussein."

18:3: As similarly mentioned in chapter 17 (v.2), this case illustrates an unholy alliance between government and business. The word merchants here mean "those who travel." It is not those who produce or manufacture goods; but those who are brokers, engaging in business for a big profit. God will judge godless commercialism. Man has always used business as the biggest excuse for not having any time for God. This is God's judgment on big business, which denies God's authority and promotes corruption.

18:4: Now we hear the "voice from heaven," our Lord Jesus Christ, calling God's people out of the city of Babylon before her destruction. This verse makes it clear that God's people are going to be in the world to the very end. Just as Lot was warned to get out of Sodom to escape the judgment of fire (Genesis 19), so too are these people of God warned. Such was also God's warning to Israel (Isaiah 48:20 and Jeremiah 51:5 – 6, 45). In these prophetic verses, the Lord warns Israel to have no fellowship with the sins of Babylon and to flee before judgment falls. Who are these people referred to as "my people," and what are they doing in the capital city without the mark of the beast? They may be Gentile Tribulation Saints, or they could be Jews who have not yet received Christ as their Savior. Christ's invitation to "come out of her" is typical of God in His call to sinners of all ages to repent and turn to Him for salvation. The mercy and grace of God is forever available. In every age, God receives those who, through faith in His Son Jesus Christ, are willing to repent of their sin and look to Him for mercy. I believe this may also be a warning to us today to separate ourselves from the world and our old sinful nature, and walk by the Spirit.

18:5: Babylon is the oldest city in the history of mankind. With the exception of Jerusalem, Babylon is mentioned more than any other city in the Bible, roughly 260 times (depending on your version). Babylon has a long history of accumulating sins, and God has kept a record. Finally God's judgment will come upon this city.

18:6: God is right and just in what He does. Listen to the words of the Prophet Obadiah: "The Day of the Lord is near for all nations. As you have done, it will be done to you; your deeds will return upon your own head" (v.15). Consequently, Babylon's own cup of iniquity will be pressed in "double portion" back onto her and all who have joined with her in sin and wickedness.

18:7: The riches and fame of Babylon blinded her to the judgment of God. "She boasts" is a reference to her arrogance – her prideful "glory and luxury" that are so often short-lived in life. Sin and self-deception characterized the spirit of this godless city. Recall the prophets from chapter 11, the two witnesses back in Jerusalem, who preached a warning to a world in rebellion to repent and turn to God; however, they were hated and eventually killed.

18:8: "In one day" illustrates the suddenness of her destruction and that it will be by "fire." So great is her grief that "mourning" is counted a plague along with "death" and "famine." Her destruction is total and final. The long history of this sinful city ends with the judgment of God upon her.

"For mighty is the Lord God who judges her." It is God who destroys this city because He alone is able to do so. I believe He does this as part of the seventh bowl judgment and just prior to the return of Christ to earth, as we read in chapter 16 (v.19 – 21). This occurs in the final days of the Tribulation

Period. In His return to earth, Christ is seen coming from Edom (Isaiah 63:1 – 4). It is my opinion He returns via Babylon, after executing judgment upon that wicked city. Christ is coming to rescue the remnant of Israel that has fled Jerusalem and the persecution of Antichrist as we read in chapter 12 (v.6). We will discuss Christ's second coming in the next chapter.

Next we will see the reaction to the destruction of this great city. There are two distinctly opposite views to her destruction. There will be anguish in the world and rejoicing in heaven because of the judgment upon Babylon.

18:9 – 10: In that day, Antichrist will have the first global dictatorship, and his capital will be Babylon. Babylon will dominate and rule the world. Everything will center in Babylon. Everything in that city will be in rebellion against Almighty God, and it centers in Antichrist. The kings of the earth love commercial Babylon. The "adultery" committed is a reference to the revenue she brought to these kings, in other words, corrupt profits. No one ever expected this great city to be judged. In spite of her splendor, this will be the most short-lived capital of the world, for by the end of the day, Babylon is nothing but smoldering ruins. When the word goes out, the world will "weep and mourn over her" and will be "terrified at her torment." As stated earlier in our introduction to this chapter, one of the contrasts between the destruction of religious and commercial Babylon is that the kings who destroyed religious Babylon rejoiced, where here they will "stand far off and cry."

18:11 – 17a: These verses illustrate the products of an affluent society. All are articles of a society accustomed to the better things of the material world. Now, with the destruction of the great city, the merchants are left without a buyer for their "cargoes anymore." Let's take a look at the costly products mentioned in these verses and try to categorize them:

1) "Gold, silver, precious stones and pearls" are monetary currencies and fine jewelry.
2) "Fine linen, purple, silk, and scarlet cloth" refers to luxurious articles of clothing.
3) "Every sort of citron wood, and articles of every kind made of ivory, costly wood, bronze, iron and marble" would refer to gift items and costly building materials.
4) "Cinnamon and spice, of incense, myrrh, and frankincense" are spices and cosmetics.
5) "Wine and olive oil, of fine flour and wheat" refer to expensive liquors and pastries.
6) "Cattle and sheep" not only refer to meat for the wealthy, but also leather and wool.
7) "Horses and carriages" refer to certain types of ground transportation.

This merchandise covers every phase of business. Even "men" were bought and sold, including their "souls." Slavery becomes acceptable everywhere and is big business. "The merchants who sold these things and gained their wealth from her will stand far off, terrified at her torment. They will weep and mourn and cry out: Woe! Woe." The merchants sit in front of their television screens and cry, for in "one hour" wealth so great lay desolate.

18:17b – 19: The last group of mourners are those who are engaged in transportation. Our text reads "all who travel by ship," and "earn their living from the sea." Though we concluded earlier (chapter 16) that oceanic shipping would be shut down due to the second bowl judgment turning the remainder of the sea to blood, I believe this may refer to other modes within the transportation industry in operation at the time, such as airline carriers, railroad, and trucking. In present-day language, these are all considered "ships." The "sea," as we stated back in chapter 13 (v.1), is symbolic of the nations of the world. They all became rich by transporting the merchandise of Babylon. Like the others, they weep and mourn, and they too marvel at the sudden destruction of the "great city."

The truth is: The things of this earth are passing away. Would it break your heart if you saw the things of this earth go up in smoke? Is your heart fixed on Christ and things in heaven? Dr. Charles Stanley stated the following in one of his sermons: "If you cannot part with a penny out of every dime, then you are materialistic, and to be materialistic is to be sinful." We are living in a Babylonian society today. Take a moment and read what our Lord Jesus Christ said regarding materialism and storing up treasures (Matthew 6:19 – 21), and on the subject of handling worldly wealth (Luke 16:10 – 12).

18:20: The scene is entirely different in heaven – there is rejoicing. It is the celebration of a long awaited event. The "saints" prayed for it; the "prophets" of the Old Testament and the "apostles" of the New Testament predicted it. Now it is fulfilled, and there is joy in heaven because God has vindicated His name. Judgment has come upon Babylon.

18:21: The phrase, "a large millstone and threw it into the sea," symbolizes the suddenness and permanence of the destruction of Babylon. Just as a huge boulder makes a big splash and then disappears beneath the water, so too will Babylon come to an end. "Never to be found again" coincides with the prophecies of Isaiah 13 as mentioned earlier, and is yet another illustration of the permanence of her destruction.

18:22 – 23: The music will be silenced, the storerooms and warehouses will be destroyed, and the bright lights will go out. It is all over. No more marrying or being given in marriage here. This city "led astray," meaning that it deceived the world with the worship of Antichrist. This is the strong delusion – the big lie. The tragedy of the ages is the millions of souls Satan has deceived about God and His grace. There is nothing in Scripture to even suggest they will not suffer forever for allowing themselves to be deceived.

18:24: She will be solemnly and finally judged because of her slaughter of the "prophets and of the saints" and those who would communicate God's truth to the world. Just as God chose Jerusalem as His city to win the souls of people, Satan chose Babylon as his capital to destroy them. This was Satan's city, and he was a murderer from the beginning.

This marks the final ruin of the most destructive religious and governmental system in the history of mankind, and the demise of the most godless and influential city ever built. With her destruction and the darkness in which Babylon will be permanently entombed, she will bear testimony to her lifelessness for eternity as we will see in chapter 19 (v.3).

This chapter brings to a conclusion the frightful period referred to by our Lord Jesus Christ as the Great Tribulation. In the next chapter we will see our Lord coming to earth to bring to an end this dark period of unrighteousness and to establish His Millennial Kingdom.

Review Questions

1) Commercial Babylon, also considered the political capital of Antichrist, is believed by most scholars to be located _____.

2) The Lord Jesus calling His people out from Babylon before her destruction is consistent with God's warning to Israel _____.

3) The fact that Babylon boasts of her glory and luxury refers to _____.

4) The adulteries committed with the kings of the earth refer to _____

_____.

5) Her destruction is sudden and is accomplished in only _____.

6) Commercial Babylon is destroyed by a cataclysmic judgment of God, most likely as a result of

_____.

7) Her destruction concludes the frightful period referred to by our Lord as _____

_____.

Up For Discussion

"The kings of the earth have committed fornication with her, and the merchants
of the earth are waxed rich through the abundance of her delicacies."
(Revelation 18:3 KJV)

Throughout history Satan has stirred up and used governmental power to accomplish his purpose. We mentioned earlier in chapter 12 that nothing has caused more grief to humanity than government. Power in the hands of evil men, in the form of government, has literally given license to genocide, war, famine, torture, and human suffering beyond comprehension. The history books testify to it. However, let us take a look closer to home and to our state and local governments. Satan has used them to inflict pain and suffering on people in both an economic and emotional sense. Corruption in government abounds; you need only watch the nightly newscast on television. Special interest groups take priority over real needs and desires of constituents. Taxpayers' money is oftentimes mismanaged and wasted on enormous salaries, perks, and pet projects. As a result, good hard-working people are laid off or furloughed, and legitimate needs and programs are cut out of budgets everywhere.

As we continue to endure through recession after recession, has your family been impacted in any way by the irresponsible or corrupt actions of your local government? One example may be new or increased taxes levied to compensate for mismanagement, such as a tax on rain and termed "watershed tax." This may seem a little personal; but if you are willing, please share your thoughts or experiences with the class.

Chapter 19

The destruction of Babylon, the capital of Antichrist's kingdom, marked the end of the seven-year Tribulation Period and the Great Tribulation of the latter days. This chapter begins a remarkable transition in our study. The shift is from darkness to light and from dreary days of judgment to bright days of blessing. This chapter is the link between the Great Tribulation and the Millennium. Here we will see two great and significant events. The first is the wedding of the Lamb. The second is the return of Christ to earth to abolish all wickedness and rebellion, and to execute judgment upon the beast and his false prophet. The hallelujahs open this chapter and the opening of hell concludes it. There are also two great suppers recorded in this chapter. The first is the wedding supper of the Lamb, and the second is the cannibalistic feast of the birds called the "great supper of God" following the conclusion of the Battle of Armageddon.

The Heavenly Hallelujahs

19:1: The "Hallelujah Chorus" from Handel's *Messiah* is usually considered the grandest and most majestic expression of praise and worship in the field of music. However this praise will be totally eclipsed by the magnificent heavenly "Hallelujah Chorus" of the future, described in these opening verses, which was the source of Handel's inspiration.

This chapter gives us a spectacular view of the rejoicing in heaven now that God's judgment has finally settled upon the earth; no longer will anyone be permitted to rebel against Him. This heavenly chorus results from the final triumph of good over evil, Christ over Antichrist, God over Satan, and the Holy Spirit over the spirit of evil. The "great multitude" here is distinct from the other beings in heaven for they are singing a song that includes salvation. This incorporates all believers – Old Testament Saints, Church Age Saints, and the Tribulation Saints. This is the first time that together, they can all join in this great chorus, proclaiming "Hallelujah!"

This is the only chapter in the New Testament where the word *Hallelujah* is found. It occurs four times in the next six verses. It is an Old Testament word taken from the Psalms and means "praise the Lord." Hallelujah is an exclamation of praise as the final phase of "salvation" is coming to pass. The Apostle Paul wrote explicitly about this in his letter to the Romans (8:18 – 23). This is that great day which is coming when the earth will be released from the bondage of sin.

Two additional words are used to express this praise to the Lord our God. The first is *glory*, which refers to God's moral glory in judgment; and the second is *power*, which speaks of His might displayed in the execution of His judgment upon the earth and its rulers.

19:2 – 3: These verses establish the cause for the judgment brought upon "the great prostitute," thus referring primarily to religious Babylon of chapter 17. However, the term prostitute here may refer to all three forces, or "adulteries" that corrupt and lead a person away from a basic quest for God; they are:

1) False religion.
2) A lust for money and material possessions.
3) A lust for power through government.

Recall from our study of chapter 17 that the kings of the earth and Antichrist destroyed religious Babylon, the prostitute; yet here we are told it was God who judged it. God uses different instruments, and He will even use Satan to accomplish His purpose. Those in heaven who have more perfect knowledge than you and I are able to say that God's judgments are "true and just." My friends, whatever God does is true and just!

All the iniquities of past ages will be justified in this ultimate destruction when God, in righteous judgment, "has avenged on her the blood of his servants."

As believers, we are not to seek revenge on those who do harm to us for the Apostle Paul wrote: "Do not take revenge, my friends, but leave room for God's wrath, for it is written: It is mine to avenge; I will repay, says the Lord" (Romans 12:19). God will take care of vengeance for you and me. The extent of God's judgment on the prostitute is seen in verse 3 as "the smoke from her goes up for ever and ever," indicating this judgment on Babylonian religion, politics, and commerce will be eternal.

19:4: Five times in the Book of Revelation the "twenty-four elders" express themselves, each time in praise and rejoicing, and this time along with the "four living creatures" of chapter 4. Recall from our study of chapter 4 that the twenty-four elders are representative of the church in heaven. This is the last time the elders appear as such, for the church is to become the bride of Christ. The word *church* is translated from the Greek word *ekklesia* which means "called out." While on earth, we who make up the church are the "called out" ones – called out or separated from the darkness of the world to be light and Christ's ambassadors (2 Corinthians 5:20); but when we leave the earth we become Christ's bride.

19:5: The "voice came from the throne." Notice the call to "praise" and worship comes directly from the throne of God, because the Lord Jesus Christ is preparing to take control of His world. This great heavenly chorus will be a mixture of human and angelic voices as they sing, "Hallelujah!" They all share one thing in common; through faith, they have all voluntarily become "his servants."

"Hallelujah! For Our Lord God Almighty Reigns"

19:6: This takes us all the way back to the Old Testament covenant that God made with David when the Lord declared: "Your house and your kingdom will endure forever before me; your throne will be established forever" (2 Samuel 7:16). The united song of all those in heaven anticipate the reign of the "Lord God Almighty," Jesus Christ. For almost two thousand years Christians have prayed in obedience to our Lord, "Your kingdom come, your will be done on earth as it is in heaven" (Matthew 6:10). That prayer will finally be answered when Christ returns physically to earth to rule forever.

The Wedding of the Lamb

19:7 – 8: The "wedding of the Lamb" is a phrase that beautifully describes the final and complete union of Jesus Christ and the church. It conveys an intimacy of relationship between Christ and believers that in this life has never been experienced, and one that will never be compromised or broken. Jesus spoke often in His stories and parables about weddings and wedding suppers. The wedding takes place in heaven after our Lord raptures His church from the earth.

In the parable of the "wedding banquet," our Lord Jesus tells us: "The kingdom of heaven is like a king who prepared a wedding banquet for his son. He sent his servants to those who had been invited to the banquet to tell them to come, but they refused to come" (Matthew 22:2 – 3). The bridegroom can only be "the king's son," the Lord Jesus Christ. John the Baptist made it clear he was not the Christ. He referred to Jesus as "the bridegroom," and to himself as "the friend who attends the bridegroom [and who] waits and listens for him, and is full of joy when he hears the bridegroom's voice" (John 3:29). Hence, our Lord Jesus Christ is here referred to as the Bridegroom as well as the Lamb.

The verses of importance regarding the identity of the bride are found in Ephesians (5:31 – 32). The Apostle Paul, speaking to husbands and wives of their relationship together, likens the husband to Christ and the wife to the church; here he writes: "For this reason a man will leave his father and mother and be united to his wife, and the two will become one flesh. This is a profound mystery – but I am talking about Christ and the church." This clearly illustrates that the perfect picture of the relationship between our Lord Jesus Christ and His church is that of a bridegroom and bride.

The apostle also indicates the manner in which the bride will be presented to Christ: "A radiant church, without stain or wrinkle or any other blemish, but only holy and blameless" (Ephesians 5:27). This condition will only exist after the judgment seat of Christ when all believers have been completely cleansed and the church is made whole. All Christians who have trusted in Jesus Christ during the age of grace, from the day of Pentecost to the rapture of the church, will make up His bride. In verse 8 we see that the "bride" makes herself ready with a wedding dress of "fine linen, bright and clean" that portrays "the righteous acts of the saints." The relationship of Christ and the church is intimate, delightful, and unique. No other creature will enjoy such sweetness. You see, Christ loved the church and gave Himself for it. Take a moment and read Christ's prayer for all believers found in John 17:20 – 26.

The Wedding Supper of the Lamb

19:9: The "wedding of the Lamb" will take place in heaven, but the "wedding supper of the Lamb" will take place on earth. This is illustrated in the parable of the "ten virgins" found in Matthew (25:1 – 13). The virgins are not the bride because Christ has only one bride, and that is the church.

The virgins are guests who await the return of the bridegroom. Christ will return not only to judge the earth, but also to have the wedding supper, which the ten virgins are hoping to attend. Sadly, as the story goes, five of the virgins were foolish and not prepared when the bridegroom arrived and were thus shut out.

"Blessed are those who are invited to the wedding supper of the lamb!" Those who are invited are friends or guests; they are "blessed" because of their personal relationship with Christ. As mentioned earlier, John the Baptist, one of the last Old Testament Saints, indicated he was a friend of the bridegroom (John 3:29). Therefore, all the Old Testament Saints who have the righteousness of God through faith will be guests at this feast. In addition, there will be those who have received our Lord and Savior during the Tribulation Period. They are the remnant of the nation of Israel and the Gentile nations; both groups enter into the Millennium as invited guests. Our Lord described this scene in His parable of the "sheep and the goats" found in Matthew (25:31 – 46). The wedding supper is apparently the Millennium. This thousand-year period is a long supper!

The supper is distinguished by the use of the sacrificial name of the Lord – "Lamb." Angels have never been the recipients of the blessings of the redeemed. This would lead me to suspect that only those who have lived a human existence, have sinned, and have been redeemed by the blood of the "Lamb" will be in attendance.

19:10: Here is another transition verse, this time between the wedding supper of the Lamb and the Revelation of Jesus Christ – the return of our Lord to earth.

At this point, John appears completely overwhelmed by the angel and the visions shown him. This angel is probably the same mighty angel we saw in chapter 18; and in his weakened state, John is compelled to worship him, but is restrained from doing so. John is an apostle of Jesus Christ – he knows better. He is commanded by the angel: "Do not do it!" Only God is to be worshiped.

In the Book of Revelation, we are considered fellow servants with the angels, because of our "testimony of Jesus." However, Dr. Charles Stanley once made this interesting statement in one of his sermons: "Through redemption we are lifted higher than the angels." The writer of Hebrews likewise wrote: "Are not all angels ministering spirits sent to serve those who will inherit salvation?" (Hebrews 1:14). The writer continued with these words: "Both the one who makes men holy and those who are made holy are of the same family. So, Jesus is not ashamed to call them brothers" (Hebrews 2:11). In his letter to the church in Corinth, the Apostle Paul wrote: "Do you not know that we will judge angels?" (1 Corinthians 6:3). The role of angels in God's plan for eternity is uncertain and for God to direct as He determines; our focus must remain on Jesus.

"The testimony of Jesus" represents the best description of the spirit of prophecy to be found in Scripture. Prophecy receives its value and meaning from its relation to Christ. From the first prophetic utterance of God (Genesis 3:15) to the last prediction of the Revelation, the heart of prophecy has been directed at the person of Jesus Christ. The study of the Book of Revelation should cause our hearts to "burn within us" (Luke 24:32) because it is the Revelation of Jesus Christ, who forms the heart of all prophecy.

The Revelation of Jesus Christ

The "blessed hope – the glorious appearing of our great God and our Saviour, Jesus Christ" (Titus 2:13) is the most exciting event that every Christian who knows anything about God's Word anticipates. That blessed day when our Lord will truly be glorified. In His first coming, He suffered Himself to be abused and beaten by His enemies, even to the point of allowing men to spit on Him and crucify Him. The next time our Lord will not come in humility, but in His own words, "They will see the Son of Man coming on the clouds of the sky, with power and great glory" (Matthew 24:30). His coming will be the final display of the wrath of God upon a sinful world. All rebellion and wickedness of mankind is finally crushed and judged at Christ's return so that He may establish His righteous kingdom on earth. Since the revelation of Christ is such a climactic event in the Bible, we can expect to find many references to it. They include, Isaiah 63:1 – 6, Zechariah 14:3 – 5, Matthew 24:27 – 31, and Jude 14 – 15 to name a few.

19:11: What an awesome scene! John's vision begins with "heaven standing open" to let the rider on the white horse out. Recall in chapter 4 (v.4), heaven was opened to allow John in where he saw the twenty-four elders surrounding the throne. Here heaven opens again, this time to let Christ exit. The Lord Jesus Christ is the rider of this white horse, which stands in stark contrast to the rider in chapter 6 (v.2), who was Antichrist. The significance of the white horse is typical of the difference between Christ's second coming and His first coming. While in His first coming, our Lord fulfilled the words of the Prophet Zechariah (9:9) by entering Jerusalem on a lowly donkey, which denotes peace. Our Lord's humiliation is long-past. Now, He will come in all His majesty riding a white horse, an animal of warfare, which emphasizes His awesome power and glory. In addition, Christ's eternal nature is revealed for He is called "Faithful and True." Christ is "Faithful" because He has come to execute God's long-time plan for mankind, and Christ is "True" because He is the truth (John 14:6). He is the only one you and I can trust. The Apostle Peter wrote: "In the last days scoffers will come … They will say, 'Where is this coming he promised?'" (2 Peter 3:3 – 4). Here Christ will make good on His promise. He is faithful. He has come, as our text reveals, to "judge and make war," not to die again on a cross.

19:12 – 13: "His eyes are like blazing fire" is the same description John gave back in chapter 1 (v.14) when he saw the glorified Christ. Just as back then, these eyes speak of the judgment to come upon the earth as He tramples all unrighteousness. He is the righteous King for "on his head are many crowns." Crowns are a symbol of authority, and this means He will come with absolute authority. When Christ comes, all power and authority will be His as the absolute and supreme King and Judge of the earth.

"He has a name written on him that no one knows but he himself." This phrase would suggest that either some aspects of Christ's divine nature are incomprehensible to us, or that Christ has not yet chosen to reveal them to us. Do you really know Jesus? I would say that no one really knows the Son except the Father; but learning to know Him, is one of the things that will make heaven special. He is so wonderful, that it is going to take all of eternity to really know Him.

The phrases, "He is dressed in a robe dipped in blood" and "He treads the winepress of the fury of the wrath of God Almighty" coincide with the prophecy of Isaiah (63:1 – 6) we read earlier. "And his name is the Word of God," reminds us of the words of the apostle: "In the beginning was the Word, and the Word was with God, and the Word was God … The Word became flesh and made his dwelling among us. We have seen his glory, the glory of the One and only, who came from the Father, full of grace and truth" (John 1:1 – 2, 14). If we want to know God, we need only study about His Son Jesus Christ for He "has made him known" (John 1:18).

19:14: The "armies of heaven" were following Christ upon His return to earth. Who are these "armies of heaven" following behind our Lord? "Armies" refer to those who go to fight in wars, such as we saw back in chapter 12 (v.7) with Michael and his angels as they fought against the dragon (Satan) and his demons. Therefore, these armies must include the multitudes of angelic legions faithful to our Lord (5:11). However, I believe this phrase, "armies of heaven," encompasses much more, and our clue was mentioned earlier in chapter 17 (v.14). There the final war between the beast and the Lamb was briefly fore-mentioned and those returning with Jesus were referred to as His "called, chosen, and faithful followers." All three of these terms represent believers – the raptured church that has now become the bride of Christ. Recall from verse 4, that the word *church* is translated from the Greek word meaning "called out." Additionally, the Patriarch Enoch prophesied the following: "The Lord is coming with thousands upon thousands of his holy ones to judge everyone and to convict all the ungodly ..." (Jude 14 – 15). That would certainly substantiate the words of the Apostle Paul: "Do you not know that the saints will judge the world?" (1 Corinthians 6:2). Once joined together in "marriage," it is difficult to imagine Christ being anywhere without His bride. The significance here is that these armies of heaven are all "dressed in fine linen, white and clean." I believe no member of the armies of Christ returning with Him at His glorious appearing will do battle. Not one of them will lift a finger, for the battle will be won by the spoken Word of our Lord.

Recall also from chapter 14 (v.14 – 19), we were given a fore-glimpse of the scene where the angels (here referred to as the armies of heaven) returning with Christ would be used in the great harvest of both the elect (believers) and the wicked (unbelievers) upon His return to earth. This is the final judgment of those surviving the Tribulation Period following Christ's victory over the nations of Antichrist (Matthew 13:36 – 43, 24:30 – 31).

19:15 – 16: The "sharp sword" that comes out of Christ's mouth is used symbolically to represent a sharp instrument of war with which He will destroy the armies of the nations of Antichrist and establish His absolute rule. Christ's sword will be His spoken Word. The Word that called the world into creation will ultimately call the kings and armies of the world into judgment and destruction. The expression "rule them with an iron scepter" fulfills the prophecy of Psalm 2 (v.6 – 9) and represents absolute, unyielding government under which all men are required to conform to the righteous standards of God.

Instead of a sword on His thigh (as with most warriors going into battle) there will be His name:

KING OF KINGS AND LORD OF LORDS

Then will the words of the Prophet Isaiah be truly fulfilled: "For to us a child is born, to us a Son is given, and the government will be on his shoulders. And he will be called Wonderful Counselor, Mighty God, Everlasting Father, Prince of Peace" (Isaiah 9:6).

The Battle on the Great Day of God Almighty

19:17 – 21: These verses primarily deal with Christ as the righteous Warrior, for we see Him coming to do battle with the armies of Antichrist in what is often called "the Battle of Armageddon," but which in truth is a war or campaign. The Battle of Armageddon is a misleading expression because Armageddon refers to the beautiful valley to the east of Mount Megiddo, and the word *battle* here literally means "campaign" or "war." This conflict takes place in a single day, and the Battle of Armageddon will be just one of the battles of this war. Actually, this war will encompass more than just the Valley of Megiddo; as we will see, it covers practically all of the land of Palestine. This conflict, when Christ defeats the armies of Antichrist, will be a series of at least four "campaigns." Therefore, this battle is more properly named "the battle on the great day of God Almighty" as referred to back in chapter 16 (v.14).

The first battle occurs immediately following the destruction of commercial Babylon. I believe the Lord proceeds directly to Edom (present-day Jordan) and bloodies His robe in battle. He will rescue the remnant of Israel who has fled Jerusalem and persecution by Antichrist and his forces (Isaiah 63:1 – 6).

From Edom, Christ will go to the Valley of Megiddo for the second battle. There the great armies of the world will be gathered in opposition to Him (v.19). This conflict can literally be called the Battle of Armageddon as mentioned earlier in chapter 16. In these verses we find that when Christ meets the armies of Antichrist in the Valley of Megiddo, it will be all nations of the earth united together. He will then destroy them with "the sword that comes out of His mouth." All that will be left of these armies is little more than a gigantic feast for birds of prey and other scavengers and is referred to as "the great supper of God" (v.17). God included this scene at the end of His Word to remind us of how revolting the deeds of the flesh are to Him. Men who have lived in the flesh will have their flesh destroyed, or "gorged" upon as our text states. The Prophet Ezekiel gave a similar description of the massacre following God's judgment and destruction of the forces of Gog in their future invasion of Israel (Ezekiel 39:17 – 22). However, this scene will be merely a fore-shadow of the devastation our Lord Jesus Christ will inflict upon the global forces of Antichrist.

The third battle is "the Battle of the Valley of Jehoshaphat." This valley is part of the Kidron Valley between the temple and the Mount of Olives. The name *Jehoshaphat* means, "Jehovah is Judge." This battle is described by the Prophet Joel (3:1 – 3, 9 – 17), and the "multitudes" he mentions are more of the armies of the nations who will be brought into war by the lying spirits. In these verses we also see the prophecy concerning the harvest and judgment of the wicked described earlier in chapter 14 (v.17 – 20).

The fourth and final battle in the war of the great day of God Almighty will be the Battle of Jerusalem. Antichrist and what is left of his forces will storm Jerusalem. This last conflict between Antichrist (Satan incarnate) and Jesus Christ, until after the Millennium, will find Satan making one last fiendish effort to destroy the Son of God, the promised seed of David. Antichrist will order his forces to destroy the entire city of Jerusalem, but Christ will come to her deliverance. The prophet wrote: "On that day when all the nations of the earth are gathered against her, I will make Jerusalem an immovable rock for all the nations … I will set out to destroy all the nations that attack Jerusalem" (Zechariah 12:3 – 9).

Ronald A. Clower

Satan's two pawns, Antichrist and his false prophet, will defy God right up to the very end. Nevertheless, they have the distinction of being the first two of all mankind to be cast into the eternal hell, for our passage reads: "The two of them were thrown alive into the fiery lake of burning sulfur" (v.20). The rest of the unrighteous remain in Hades until they are resurrected to stand in judgment before Christ at the Great White Throne (20:11 – 15).

Jesus Christ the Victor

This is the most dramatic and thrilling moment in world history! After sweeping four successive (or concurrent – God is omnipresent) battles, Christ will set His feet on the Mount of Olives. "Then the Lord will go out and fight against those nations, as he fights in the day of battle. On that day his feet will stand on the Mount of Olives, east of Jerusalem, and the Mount of Olives will be split in two from east to west, forming a great valley, with half of the mountain moving north and half moving south," (Zechariah 14:3 – 4).

When Christ conquers all before Him through judgments of earthquakes, fire, hailstorms, and the sword that proceeds out of His mouth, not only will Jerusalem lay in ruin, but the entire Holy Land as well will be literally bathed in the blood of all the God-opposing and unrepentant of mankind. Not one person will escape the warrior Christ in this great battle at the end of the age. Those who oppose Him during the Tribulation Period will be slain by Him at the revelation and His glorious appearing. The "sword" that comes from the mouth of our Lord Jesus Christ is His spoken Word. This symbolism is clearly explained in both the Old Testament and our New Testament (Isaiah 11:4; Ephesians 6:17; Hebrews 4:12). Unlike you and me, Christ does not have to use His hands or a weapon to strike His foe. Christ speaks, and His will is accomplished. It was His Word that created this universe, and it will be His Word that will bring an everlasting end to all wickedness and rebellion to God. It is the Word of God that will save you.

"As surely as I live, declares the Sovereign Lord,
I take no pleasure in the death of the wicked,
but rather that they turn from their ways and live.
Turn! Turn from your evil ways!
(Ezekiel 33:11)

Review Questions

1) The rejoicing in heaven that opens this chapter is a result of the completion of _____ _____.

2) The wedding of the Lamb is a beautiful description of _____ _____.

3) This wedding of the Lamb takes place where and when? _____ _____ _____.

4) The wedding supper of the Lamb takes place where and when? _____ _____.

5) The most exciting event that every Christian awaits is _____ _____.

6) The "sharp sword" that comes out of the mouth of Christ is used to symbolically represent a sharp instrument of war, but in reality, it refers to _____.

7) Antichrist and his false prophet have the distinction of being the first two of all mankind to be _____.

Up For Discussion

"And behold a white horse, and he that sat upon him was called Faithful and True."
(Revelation 19:11 KJV)

Read through the related lesson entitled "The Judgment Seat of Christ." The five crowns mentioned in Scripture and in the lesson may be just a few of many that will be rewarded by our Lord Jesus Christ when we appear before His judgment seat in heaven. Does this lesson assist you in understanding the believer's judgment; and if so, in what way?

When we join the church, we are asked to support it with our prayers, our presence, our gifts, and our service. Does this lesson cause you to re-evaluate your commitment to your home church? Of the four areas mentioned above, can you increase your commitment to one or more?

The Judgment Seat of Christ

Our Bible speaks of three events whereby every individual will be resurrected at some future time and stand before Jesus Christ for judgment.

The first event or judgment is referred to by the Apostle Paul as the Judgment Seat of Christ. The apostle wrote to the church in Rome: "For we will all stand before God's judgment seat. It is written: As surely as I live, says the Lord, every knee will bow before me, every tongue will confess to God. So then, each of us will give an account of himself to God" (Romans 14:10 – 12).

This judgment is often called the bema. *Bema* is the Greek translation of "judgment seat." This is the believer's (the church) judgment. This judgment will commence just after the rapture when all Christians, dead and living, from the day of Pentecost to the present, will be resurrected into our new glorified bodies to meet our Lord Jesus Christ in the clouds (1 Thessalonians 4:13 – 18; 1 Corinthians 15:51 – 53). We will then return with Christ to heaven and the home He has prepared for us (John 14:2). The question many believers have is: "Will we have to account for our sins? Will Christ bring our sins before us at judgment?"

Many people say yes and quote the following from the Apostle Paul: "For we must all appear before the Judgment Seat of Christ, that each one may receive what is due him for the things done while in the body, whether good or bad" (2 Corinthians 5:10). A closer look at this passage reveals that the phrase "things done while in the body" refers to "works" done for the kingdom of God after being saved and becoming a member of the body of Christ. The body of Christ on earth is the church, having Jesus as its head. The Apostle Paul reinforces this analogy: "And he [Jesus] is the head of the body, the church; he is the beginning and the firstborn from among the dead" (Colossians 1:18). Therefore, what Paul is talking about here are our Christian works, not secular works or worldly sins.

Paul illustrates this idea as follows: "For no one can lay any foundation other than the one already laid, which is Jesus Christ. If any man builds on this foundation using gold, silver, costly stones, wood, hay, or straw, his work will be shown for what it is, because the Day will bring it to light. It will be revealed with fire, and the fire will test the quality of each man's work. If what he has built survives, he will receive his rewards. If it is burned up, he will suffer loss; he himself will be saved, but only as one escaping through the flames" (1 Corinthians 3:11 – 15).

Our "good" or "bad" works are determined by how fruitful we were for God's kingdom here on earth; in other words, how productive we were in bringing others to Christ. The Apostle Paul again explains: "And we pray this in order that you may live a life worthy of the Lord and may please him in every way: bearing fruit in every good work, growing in the knowledge of God" (Colossians 1:10). "Bearing fruit," in the biblical sense, is simply bringing people to Christ! It means to bring others into the knowledge of salvation offered by the grace of our Father God through faith in His Son Jesus Christ.

You see, "good works" are much fruit produced for God's kingdom and "bad works" are little fruit produced for God's kingdom – not our sins. Either way we are all saved by our faith in Jesus Christ and will enjoy eternity with our Lord and Savior, regardless if our fruit was much or little. This is not to say that some might receive a rebuke from Christ for missed opportunities to witness or minister; however, I believe the rebuke will be minor in Christ's eternal plan for us and result only in loss of some heavenly reward or opportunity.

Our Lord illustrated judgment and rewards in His parable of talents found in Matthew 25 (v.14 – 30). In this parable the master is Christ, the three servants represent alleged believers, and the talents of money represent the time, talents, and gifts that Christ gives to each of us. In the parable, two of the servants were faithful (fruitful) with what the master gave them. In other words, they used their God-given talents to advance God's kingdom on earth. However, one was unfaithful (unfruitful) because he hid his talent and kept it to himself. When the master returned and called his servants before him, the two faithful servants were rewarded with more and "given charge over many things." However, the unfaithful servant loss what he had and was cast "outside, into the darkness, where there was weeping and gnashing of teeth." Now this darkness, weeping, and gnashing of teeth are extreme opposite characteristics of what we know to be heaven. Consequently, the unfaithful servant, with no fruit, is cast into hell, where he will suffer eternal punishment and separation from God.

Let's compare this unfaithful servant to the five unprepared virgins in Christ's parable of the ten virgins (Matthew 25:1 – 13). These five virgins had no oil for their lamps when the bridegroom came; as a result, they were shut out of the wedding banquet (Christ's earthly kingdom). The oil is symbolic of the Holy Spirit and the lamps represent the Word of God. Without the Holy Spirit working in you, you have no light. You are unprepared to bring the Light of God – that is the Word of God and the gospel of Jesus Christ, to others. This brings us to the words found in James (2:26): "For as the body without the spirit is dead, so faith without works is dead also." So you see, it is the faith that produces the works. You serve Christ out of your love for Christ.

Thus, there is a distinction between little works and no works. Little works will get you saved, but no works means you probably were not saved in the first place. Only God knows a person's true heart.

Our Lord Jesus Christ died on a Roman cross for the sins of all mankind. He paid our sin debt once and for all. When you accept Jesus Christ as your Lord and Savior and confess your sins, then those sins are forever forgiven and forgotten. The Apostle John tells us, "The blood of Jesus, his Son, purifies us from all sins" (1 John 1:7). Purifies means removes – our sins are removed. The Apostle Paul reminds us: "Therefore, there is now no condemnation for those who are in Christ Jesus, because through Christ Jesus the law of the Spirit of life set me free from the law of sin and death" (Romans 8:1). This should give us all comfort and confidence on that glorious day when we come into the presence of our Lord and Savior Jesus Christ.

Another way to look at it is: If our earthly sins were paraded before us at judgment, how would that make us feel? Would that bring us joy or sorrow?

The Prophet Isaiah wrote the following regarding the future kingdom of God: "On this mountain the Lord Almighty … will swallow up death forever. The Sovereign Lord will wipe away the tears from all the faces; he will remove the disgrace of his people from all the earth. The Lord has spoken" (Isaiah 25:6 – 8).

In the Revelation, the Apostle John wrote likewise regarding the New Jerusalem and the Eternal Order: "He will wipe away every tear from their eyes. There will be no more death or mourning or crying or pain, for the old order of things has passed away" (Revelation 21:4). My friend, we are able to start over!

So let me say it again, I believe that our worldly sins are washed clean by the blood of the Lamb – past, present, and future, and they will not be part of the believer's judgment. In the words of the prophet

Micah, they are hurled "into the depths of the sea" (Micah 7:19), and in the words of the Psalmist, "as far as the east is from the west, so far has he removed our transgressions from us" (Psalm 103:12).

In early times, the city of Corinth was famous for its festival of athletic events similar to our Olympic Games. At the end of the contests the athletes would appear before a large decorated platform called a bema. Here the emperor sat on the judgment seat and handed out rewards to the victorious athletes for their years of dedicated training, perseverance, and endurance in the heat of competition.

Likewise, the Judgment Seat of Christ will also include rewards, as alluded to in our discussion above. Christ will reward crowns to all believers for their years of dedication to God's Word, perseverance in the face of trials, and endurance through the heat of a corrupt and fallen world. The New Testament speaks of five different crowns:

1) Incorruptible Crown or the Victor's Crown (1 Corinthians 9:25; Revelation 3:11).
2) Crown of Life or Martyr's Crown (Revelation 2:10).
3) Crown of Glory or the Elder's Crown (1 Peter 5:2 – 4).
4) Crown of Righteousness, for those who longed for his appearing (2 Timothy 4:8).
5) Crown of Rejoicing or Soul Winner's Crown (1 Thessalonians 2:19 – 20).

So what will we do with these crowns? The Apostle John answered that question in chapter 4 of the Revelation (v.10 – 11). We will do just as the twenty-four elders in heaven do; we will we fall down and cast our crowns before the throne of God and of the Lamb and sing eternal praises to our Creator, Lord, and God.

The second judgment event is the judgment of "the sheep and the goats" found in chapter 25 of Matthew (v.31 – 46). This judgment occurs when Christ returns to earth at the end of the Tribulation Period. This has also been referred to as "the judgment of the nations," whereby the surviving remnant of the nation of Israel and of the Gentile nations will be judged to determine who enters the Millennial Kingdom to eternal life as "sheep," and who are turned away to eternal punishment as "goats." At that time the Old Testament Saints, along with the slain Tribulation Saints will be resurrected and also allowed entrance into Christ's earthly Millennial Kingdom. The first two judgments make up the "first resurrection" with Jesus Christ as the firstfruit.

The third judgment event and final resurrection is that of the Great White Throne found in chapter 20 of Revelation (v.11 – 15). This judgment occurs at the end of the Millennium. Scripture refers to this as the "second resurrection," at which time unbelievers of all ages will be resurrected and summoned to give an account of their lives. This judgment is one of works alone; however, we are not saved by our works, but only through faith in Jesus Christ. Consequently, none of their names are found in the "book of life," and all are thrown into the "lake of fire."

In the last chapter of the Book of Revelation, our Lord gives us the following words of encouragement: "Behold, I am coming soon! My reward is with me, and I will give to everyone according to what he has done" (Revelation 22:12). Are you ready to stand before the bema seat of Christ? Out of our love for Jesus Christ and in appreciation for His gift of salvation, we should serve God faithfully now; and we will be rewarded later. Being awarded any one of these crowns or given an opportunity to reign alongside Christ would be an honor beyond anything we can imagine.

Chapter 20

This chapter introduces the long awaited reign of our Lord Jesus Christ on earth – the Millennial Kingdom. In the first seven verses we see the phrase "thousand years" six times. It must be important for John to have placed so much emphasis on it; therefore, we will take this period of time as literal. This period of a thousand years is God's answer to the prayer our Lord taught us: "Thy kingdom come, thy will be done, on earth as it is in heaven ..." (Matthew 6:10). This coming kingdom age will be an age of righteousness. There can be no doubt as to the scriptural evidence for this coming kingdom of Christ on earth. There are literally hundreds of passages in our Bible that predict an earthly kingdom of God, ruled by the Lord God Almighty and superseding all the kingdoms of the world. All the prophets, both major and minor, spoke of this kingdom – not one of them missed it. They often held it out as a source of encouragement to the children of Israel during times of distress. Read at your convenience what some of the prophets foretold: Psalm 2:5 – 12, Isaiah 2:1 – 5 and 65:17 – 25, Jeremiah 23:3 – 8, Ezekiel chapters 40 – 48, Daniel 2:44 – 45, Micah 4:1 – 8, and Zechariah 14:6 – 11 and 16 – 21.

Satan Bound for A Thousand Years

20:1 – 3: History testifies that the only way to establish a righteous era is for Satan to be taken out of the world. As I stated earlier in our study, this "angel coming down out of heaven having the key to the Abyss," is likely the same angel as the "star" we discussed in chapter 9 (v.1). He is given the great responsibility of controlling access into and out of the Abyss. This is yet another illustration of the ministry of angels in accomplishing God propose on earth. Remember we have already seen the four angels that control the winds (7:1), the angel in charge of the fire from the altar in heaven (8:3 – 5; 14:17), and the angel in charge of the waters (16:5).

According to our passage, the angel "seized the dragon ... and bound him" with a great chain. What a remarkable feat! Think about it; either this angel is the most powerful angel we have seen thus far, or upon His return, our Lord Jesus Christ rendered Satan completely defenseless against him. Nevertheless, Satan, our greatest adversary, is apprehended and imprisoned. Equally amazing are these "great chains" that bind Satan. Whatever supernatural properties they possess, evidently they again render that ancient serpent, the devil, completely inactive and powerless, and for "a thousand years."

Satan's goal has always been to deceive, divide, and destroy mankind, thus separating mankind from God. The binding of Satan will restrict him from doing the thing he does best, for God's purpose in binding him is to "keep him from deceiving the nations anymore until the thousand years were ended." The Millennium cannot begin until Satan is removed from the earth. Subsequently, with Satan unable to tempt or influence mankind, God is going to use the Millennium as a final testing of mankind under ideal conditions. Though the curse (temptation) of sin is lifted, man's heart will still be human and capable of rebellion and rejection. Multitudes of both Jews and Gentiles will enter the kingdom in natural bodies, having survived the Tribulation Period. These are the ones, together with those who are born during the Millennium, who will be tested during this thousand-year period.

Think of rebellion (to God) as a three-armed beast. Satan is but one arm that attacks us. The other two are the world and the flesh. These two represent greed and lust – the carnal tendencies of man's self-indulgent nature that pull him away from a righteous relationship with God. Despite Christ's absolute rule as King during the Millennium, both of these influences will still be present to lead men away from God and into sin.

In writing about the future kingdom of God, the Prophet Isaiah gives us some interesting insight as follows: "He who dies at a hundred will be thought a mere youth; he who fails to reach a hundred will be considered accursed" (Isaiah 65:20). This suggests that the children of the Millennium will be given a hundred years to make a decision to accept Jesus Christ as Lord and enjoy fellowship with Him for eternity, or to reject Him and die. Regardless, here in verse 3 John tells us that Satan will be released at the end of this period for one last time of deception.

The Believers' Resurrection

20:4 – 6: "I saw thrones on which were seated those who had been given authority to judge." This is another statement where there is disagreement amongst biblical scholars. Who are the ones seated on these thrones? There are two responses to this question to be found in Scripture that we should consider. First, and foremost are the words of our Lord Jesus Christ to his disciples: "I tell you the truth, at the renewal of all things, when the Son of Man sits on His glorious throne, you who have followed me will also sit on twelve thrones, judging the twelve tribes of Israel" (Matthew 19:28). This same discourse was likewise recorded in the gospel of Luke (Luke 22:28 – 30). Apparently, Christ will give all judgment authority for the nation of Israel over to the twelve apostles as they reign alongside Christ during the Millennium.

The second response would be the church age saints, now called the bride of Christ. Since our Scripture reference comes to us from the Apostle Paul, the apostle to the Gentiles, Christ, in like manner as above, will give all judgment authority for the Gentile nations over to the saints, again as they reign alongside Christ. In writing to the early church, the apostle explained: "Do you not know that the saints will judge the world?" (1 Corinthians 6:2). In our context, I believe both responses are appropriate in order to guarantee a righteous government for both the Jewish and Gentile branches during Christ's millennial reign (see end-of-chapter illustration: The Government of the Messianic Kingdom).

The next sentence starts with, "And I saw," indicating a different group from those in the first sentence. "Those who have been beheaded because of their testimony for Jesus," is an obvious reference to the "slain" Tribulation Saints because the passage further states, "They had not worshiped the beast or his image."

"Blessed and holy are those who have part in the first resurrection." The first resurrection is made up of believers throughout all history. The Greek word for *resurrection* is *anastasis* which means "a standing up again; a resurrection from death." There are four phases to the first resurrection with Jesus Christ as the Firstfruit:

1) Church Age Saints: As we have already studied, this first phase of the believers' resurrection is outlined in 1 Thessalonians (4:13 – 18) and describes the rapture of the church. This occurs prior to the Tribulation Period when all Christians, dead and living, are "caught up" to meet the Lord in the clouds and taken to heaven. The church becomes the bride of Christ and will reside in the New Jerusalem where she will reign alongside Christ from that exalted place.

2) The two witnesses: Recall from chapter 11 these two supernatural witnesses will prophesy during the first half of the Tribulation Period but are killed at the mid-point by Antichrist. After three and a half days they are resurrected and raptured up to heaven to be with the Lord.

3) Old Testament Saints: The Prophet Daniel suggests that deliverance is promised to these patriarchs at the close of the Great Tribulation (Daniel 12:1 – 2). We saw in chapter 19 that these Old Testament Saints will be in attendance at the wedding supper of the Lamb, which makes up the Millennium. These Old Testament Saints, with David as their prince will reign from the earthly Jerusalem alongside Christ. This is the kingdom that God promised to David (Ezekiel 34:22 – 24 and 37:20 – 28; Psalm 89:34 – 37).

4) The martyred Tribulation Saints: In chapter 6 (v.9 – 11) we saw that these saints are waiting for their resurrection, but "they were told to wait a little longer, until the number of their fellow servants and brothers ... was complete." This refers again to the end of the Tribulation Period; at which time, when Christ returns in glory, these "slain" Tribulation Saints will be resurrected, and together with the Old Testament Saints mentioned above, "will be priests of God and of Christ and will reign with Him for a thousand years" (v.6).

Over whom will they reign? In our related lesson at the end of chapter 19 entitled "The Judgment Seat of Christ," we discussed the second judgment event as illustrated in the parable of "the sheep and the goats" (Matthew 25:31 – 46). This judgment, we said, occurs at the end of the Tribulation Period when Christ returns to earth. This is also referred to as "the judgment of the nations," whereby the surviving remnant of the nation of Israel and the Gentile nations will be judged to determine who will enter the Millennial Kingdom. With Satan out of the world and the curse of sin restrained – so also will disease, famine, violence, and murder be absent during the Millennium – resulting in a population explosion the likes of which we have never seen. These are the children of the Millennium. The prophet tells us: "Never again will there be in it an infant who lives but a few days, or an old man who does not live out his years ..." (Isaiah 65:20).

All who are resurrected in the first or believers' resurrection will be resurrected holy, in other words, "incorruptible" and "immortal" (1 Corinthians 15:53 KJV), meaning incapable of sin. As a result of their faith and the blessings of a loving and merciful God, these believers will hold positions of honor in the government of the Messianic Kingdom. Additionally, the Book of Revelation clarifies that no Christian should ever fear death. Recall from chapter 1 (v.18) that our Lord and Savior Jesus Christ holds the keys to death and Hades, and thus "the second death [the lake of fire] has no power over them" (v.14).

"The rest of the dead," mentioned (v.5) are unbelievers of all ages. In the parable of the "rich man and Lazarus" (Luke 16:19 – 31), our Lord illustrated that after death the spirits of the wicked go to hell (Hades), a place of torment (see Hades Illustration, end of chapter 9) to await their judgment. These unbelievers will make up the final resurrection that occurs at the end of the Millennium. We will see shortly that these unbelievers will not be resurrected to life but to death, a state of separation from God referred to here as the "second death."

The Renewal of the Earth by Fire

Three destructions of the earth are described in the Bible, one past and two yet to come. The first destruction came when the flood covered the earth in the days of Noah (Genesis 6 – 8). In the prophet's description of the Millennium, Isaiah mentions the second destruction of the earth as occurring before the kingdom is established: "Behold, I will create new heavens and a new earth ..." (Isaiah 65:17 – 25). This means God will create a new atmospheric heaven around the earth and re-establish a far better earth. A thorough look suggests that since death appears in this passage, Isaiah was obviously not talking about the eternal order, but the Millennium. I believe this same period of time is referred to by the Apostle Peter (2 Peter 3:10 – 13). In his letter, the apostle predicts that the Day of the Lord will usher in a time of cataclysmic change on the earth. This will commence with the destruction of the old earth and the renewal of its surface (as described earlier at the end of chapter 16), on which Christ will establish His kingdom of righteousness. The third destruction and renewal of the earth is described in the opening verses of chapter 21.

Scripture also speaks of three heavens:

1) The "third heaven" is the throne of God as described by the Apostle Paul in 2 Corinthians (12:2).
2) The stellar heaven is that which contains the great galaxies. These are referred to in Ephesians (4:10) and Hebrews (4:14).
3) The atmospheric heaven is that which surrounds the earth. It is the atmospheric heaven, along with the earth, that are polluted and corrupted by Satan; and therefore will necessitate being created a new, as the Prophet Isaiah suggests.

Satan's Release after the Millennium

20:7 – 9: Here is the last rebellion of Satan and man against God. At the beginning of the Millennium Satan was bound in the Abyss by a great angel. As a result, mankind would not be tempted by Satan for a thousand years. After being "released" from his thousand-year imprisonment, Satan will immediately proceed to do what he has done for centuries, "deceive the nations." According to the above mentioned prophecy of Isaiah (65:17 – 25), if a person reaches a hundred years old and has not accepted Jesus Christ as Lord, then he or she will be "accursed," or in other words, will die. The question begs, whom will Satan deceive? Our passage reads, their numbers "like the sands on the seashore," reinforces our belief in a great population explosion that will occur during the Millennium. Even though Satan is imprisoned during this time, the human heart remains unchanged and opened to worldly allures. Apparently, there will be a great many born during the last century who will turn their backs on God and be deceived into following Satan upon his release. It may be that God, in his omniscience, saved Satan from the first judgment so that He might also give to the last generation, those born during the last hundred years of the Millennium, the free will to make their own choice – Jesus Christ or self-reliance. Sadly for them, this is the end of men's rebellion and disobedience to God. All that remains is the final judgment.

Imagine the scene: Hordes of armies from all around the world, referred to here as "Gog and Magog" (Old Testament symbolism taken from Ezekiel), led by Satan gather around Jerusalem to challenge our Lord Jesus Christ. One moment Satan is surrounded by the multitudes of his global military forces and war machines all pointed at Jerusalem and the next, he is standing there alone, surrounded by nothing but smoldering ashes. All that is left for Satan is to bow on his knees and confess, "Jesus is Lord!" The Apostle Paul echoes the words of the Prophet Isaiah: "That at the name of Jesus every knee should bow, in heaven and on earth and under the earth, and every tongue confess that Jesus Christ is Lord, to the glory of God the Father" (Philippians 2:10 – 11).

20:10: The enemy of God and His children is once and for all brought to eternal justice. Satan is "thrown into the lake of burning sulfur" and suffers the same fate as that of "the beast and the false prophet." Eternal hell is described as a lake of burning sulfur. Our Lord Jesus is the One who gave this most solemn description of hell: "But the subjects of the kingdom will be thrown outside, into the darkness, where there will be weeping and gnashing of teeth" (Matthew 8:12). Jesus further warned: "Then he will say to those on his left, 'Depart from me, you who are cursed, into the eternal fire prepared for the devil and his angels" (Matthew 25:41). Hell is darkness, hell is fire, and hell is a literal place. The Word of God tells us here: "They will be tormented day and night for ever and ever."

The Great White Throne

20:11: This ultimate judgment of the Great White Throne is for unbelievers only – the lost of all ages. This occurs at the conclusion of the Millennium, for the passage begins with, "Then I saw." This is the final resurrection when the lost are raised to stand in judgment of their works for salvation. However, at this judgment no one will be saved, because you cannot be saved by your works. The late J. Vernon McGee explained: "When you stand in the white light of the righteous presence of God, your little works will seem so puny that they won't amount to anything at all." The one seated on the throne is the Lord Jesus Christ, for it is written: "Moreover, the Father judges no one, but has entrusted all judgment to the Son," (John 5:22). The fact that "earth and sky fled from his presence" illustrates the holiness of this throne and represents a prelude to the third and final destruction of the earth and the heavens that were again polluted by Satan's final rebellion.

20:12 – 13: The "dead, great and small" refers to the fact that they are dead and lost in their sins because of their rejection of the Lord Jesus Christ. They never turned to God for salvation. The "books were opened," are the books that record the deeds of all individuals – these are the books of works. This multitude wanted to be judged by their works. However, we have already said that no one is saved by works, but only through faith in Jesus Christ as Lord and Savior. Subsequently, none of their names are found in the "book of life."

"The sea gave up the dead that were in it, and death and Hades gave up the dead that were in them." The sea will give up all those who were drowned or buried at sea, never having accepted Jesus Christ.

"Death" represents the grave where the body lies, and "Hades" the place of torment where the spirits of the unsaved have gone. These verses teach us that there will be a physical resurrection reuniting the bodies of the dead with their souls/spirits. They will be resurrected in order to stand before Jesus at the Great White Throne. Twice in our New Testament, the Apostle Paul quotes the words of the Prophet Isaiah (Romans 14:11 and Philippians 2:10 – 11), and it is appropriate that I mention them here once more: "That at the name of Jesus every knee should bow, in heaven and on earth and under the earth, and every tongue confess that Jesus Christ is Lord, to the glory of God the Father."

20:14 – 15: "Death" the great enemy of man is finally eliminated. The Apostle Paul writes: "The last enemy to be destroyed is death … Where, O death is your victory? Where, O death is your sting?" (1 Corinthians 15:26, 55). "Hades" the prison of lost souls is "thrown into the lake of fire" as well. Finally, the lost no longer exist in Hades, but are also "thrown into the lake of fire" – the eternal hell.

As we have already studied (3:5 and 13:8), the "book of life" contains the names of all humanity. Unfortunately for many, their names will be blotted out because they rejected God and refused to accept His gift of salvation and eternal life through the sacrificial death and resurrection of His Son Jesus Christ. If a man will not accept the life of God, then he must accept the only alternative – to abide eternally with Satan in the lake of fire. God did not create mankind to suffer an eternity in hell, but there is no other place for those who have chosen to reject His grace in favor of self-reliance. Dr. Charles Stanley stated in one of his sermons: "God is a God of grace! You have to absolutely run over God to go to hell." The "second death" means absolute and eternal separation from God.

When we accept Jesus as our Lord and Savior, our name is added to the Lamb's book of life, where it is impossible to be removed. Scripture emphasizes one consistent principle and that is there are only two kinds of people: The righteous and the unrighteous, the believing and the unbelieving, the saved and the unsaved. Our Lord teaches: "He that is not with me is against me; and he who does not gather with me scatters" (Matthew 12:30).

Is your name written in the Lamb's book of life?

Review Questions

1) The only way to establish a righteous era is _____.

2) In the absence of Satan (and temptation), God is going to use the Millennium as _____
_____.

3) The first resurrection occurs in four phases and is made up of _____
_____.

4) When Satan is released after the thousand years, he immediately proceeds to do what? _____
_____.

5) Satan's final fate is _____.

6) The judgment of the Great White Throne is for _____.

7) The Lamb's book of life lists only the names of those who have _____
_____.

Up For Discussion

"For unto us a child is born, unto us a son is given:
and the government will be upon His shoulders:
and his name shall be called Wonderful, Counsellor,
the Mighty God, the Everlasting Father, the Prince of Peace."
(Isaiah 9:6 KJV)

The Apostle Paul informs us: "Everyone must submit himself to the governing authorities, for there is no authority except that which God has established. The authorities that exist have been established by God" (Romans 13:1). Therefore, as with all preceding governments, so also the government of the Messianic Kingdom will have its chain of authority.

Review the flowchart entitled, "The Government of the Messianic Kingdom." Start at the top with Jesus Christ as King and the church as His Bride reigning from the heavenly New Jerusalem, and follow it downwards to those judging, reigning, and residing on earth. Discuss each block and read the Bible references associated with each group. Keep in mind that our King and Lord Jesus Christ is God, and that God is omnipresent.

Ronald A. Clower

Review the illustration entitled, "The Third Heaven." Read from left to right on your own or discuss, as a class, the various events of the timeline. Notice that some of the blocks relate back to our "Hades Illustration" from chapter 9.

Read on your own or as a class the FAQ: Satan's Final Assault.

Review and discuss the illustration entitled, "Time Intervals in the Latter Days Timeline" that follows as class time permits.

THE GOVERNMENT OF THE MESSIANIC KINGDOM

"For unto us a child is born, unto us a son is given: and the government will be upon his shoulders" (Isaiah 9:6a)

JESUS CHRIST– The King **The CHURCH– His Bride**	To Reign from the Heavenly New Jerusalem

Gentile Nations   **Jewish Nation**

Church Saints 1 Corinthians 6:2 Revelation 20:4a	To Judge the Nations	**The Twelve Apostles** Matthew 19:28 Luke 22:28-30
The "Slain" Tribulation Saints Revelation 20:4b-6	To Reign from the Earthly Jerusalem	**David** Jeremiah 30:9 Ezekiel 34:23-24 Ezekiel 37:24-25
Kings Psalm 72:10-11 Isaiah 60:11 Revelation 21:24-26		**Princes** Isaiah 32:1; Ezekiel 45:8
		Judges & Counselors Isaiah 1:26
Gentile Nations Matthew 25:31-46		**Israel** The Redeemed Remnant

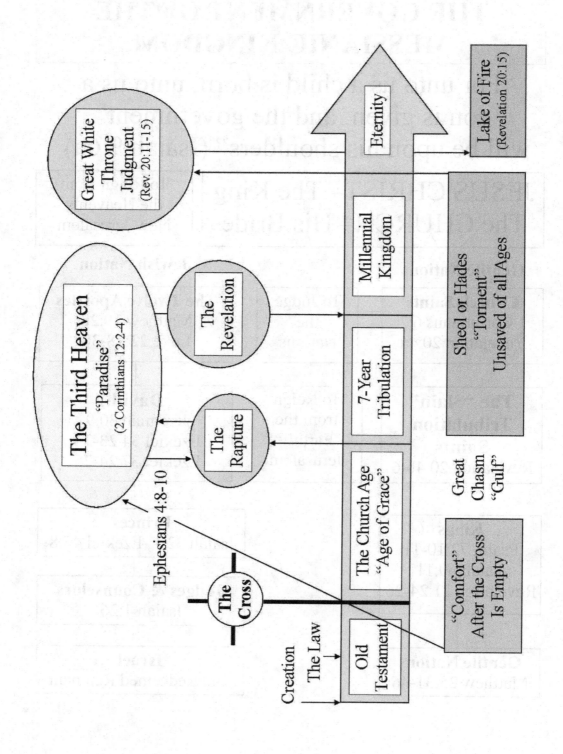

FAQ: Satan's Final Assault

Question: How could Satan amass such an enormous army from all corners of the earth to come against Christ during a time when Christ Himself reigns as King over all the earth?

We learned from chapter 20 (v.7 – 8) that upon the release of Satan from his imprisonment in the Abyss at the end of the Millennium that he "will deceive the nations in the four corners of the earth … to gather them for battle." The "four corners of the earth" is a reference to the entire earth, and Gog and Magog is an Old Testament reference to the enemies of Israel.

Who are those that Satan will deceive and how will he have time enough to amass such a great army? With Satan imprisoned, as we discussed, he would be unable to tempt mankind; thus God intends to use the Millennium as a testing of man under ideal conditions. Though Satan and the curse (temptation of man) are restrained, man's heart will still be human and capable of rebellion during the Millennium. We also predicted a great population explosion. However, we learned from the words of the Prophet Isaiah (65:20) that if anyone born during this time failed to receive Jesus Christ as Lord by age one hundred then that person would be "accursed," or in other words, they will die.

Because of carnal man's fallen nature and God-given freewill, apparently there will be many children born during every generation of the Millennium that will choose self-reliance over following God's law. They may likely form an underground movement – an alternative "Way" per se – which Christ may likewise tolerate for a time. Though they die at age one hundred, they may naively look with anticipation to Satan's release, his victory over Christ, and thus their resurrection to serve him. As the followers of this cult grow in numbers, influence, and resources with each passing century, it is not difficult to imagine after 900 plus years of peace, that the earth would be comprised of literally millions born during the last century who would reach the end of the Millennium at various ages (but not yet one hundred) in complete rebellion and opposition to God in favor of self-reliance. These are the ones who will follow Satan in his final rebellion against God.

The gradual amassing of resources (military or otherwise) over the course of the Millennium might help with our question of time. Jesus may well allow this in order to make one final point for eternity – He is omnipotent! Christ is the Creator, Satan and men are merely His creations.

There is a presumed period of time between the rapture of the church and the beginning of the Tribulation Period. During this time, the world will be in a state of chaos following the rapture (disappearance) of all Christians from the earth. Antichrist will come onto the scene as a great diplomat and sign a covenant of peace with the nation of Israel, thus triggering the beginning of the Tribulation Period. However, the length of this time interval is uncertain. There is also a period of time between the end of the Tribulation Period and the beginning of the Millennium. According to the Prophet Daniel, there is a seventy-five day interval between the return of Christ and the beginning of the "blessed" kingdom (See the following illustration: "Time Intervals in the Latter Days Timeline").

Considering the above, there may likely be a time interval as well between the end of the Millennium and the beginning of Eternity. During this time, Satan will be released to "deceive the nations" and do battle with Christ one last time. As our Lord Jesus Christ stands at the top of the temple stairs looking out over the plains surrounding Jerusalem, these rebellious youth of the Millennium with their military might, led by Satan, will gather in opposition to the King of Kings. Finally, just as the Lord God Almighty spoke to Moses from the burning bush, so too will the Lord Jesus Christ proclaim, "I AM WHO I AM" (Exodus 3:14).

Afterwards, the great deceiver of mankind will be left standing alone surrounded by nothing but smoldering ashes. All that is left is for Satan to bow down on both knees and confess, "Jesus is Lord!"

How long this act takes to accomplish, again is uncertain; however, in God's perfect plan, it will seem quite insignificant.

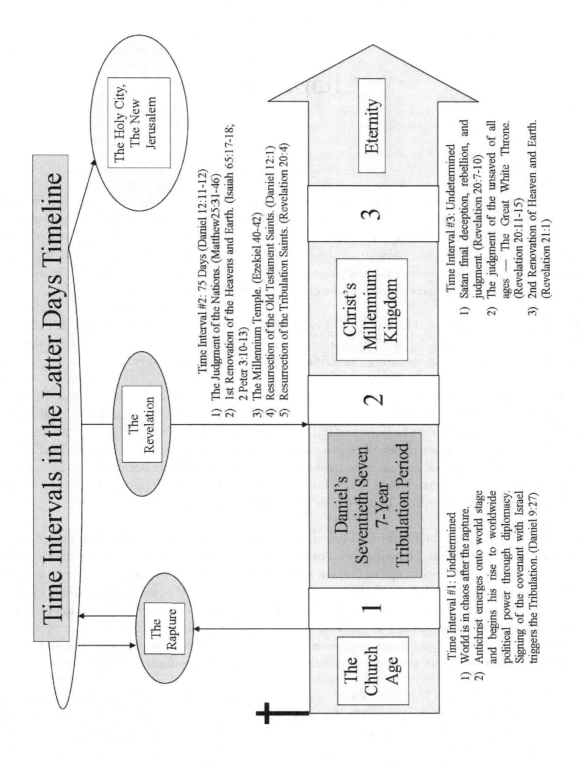

Time Intervals in the Latter Days Timeline

The Holy City, The New Jerusalem

The Revelation

The Rapture

The Church Age

Daniel's Seventieth Seven 7-Year Tribulation Period

Christ's Millennium Kingdom

Eternity

1   2   3

Time Interval #1: Undetermined
1) World is in chaos after the rapture.
2) Antichrist emerges onto world stage and begins his rise to worldwide political power through diplomacy. Signing of the covenant with Israel triggers the Tribulation. (Daniel 9:27)

Time Interval #2: 75 Days (Daniel 12:11-12)
1) The Judgment of the Nations. (Matthew 25:31-46)
2) 1st Renovation of the Heavens and Earth. (Isaiah 65:17-18; 2 Peter 3:10-13)
3) The Millennium Temple. (Ezekiel 40-42)
4) Resurrection of the Old Testament Saints. (Daniel 12:1)
5) Resurrection of the Tribulation Saints. (Revelation 20:4)

Time Interval #3: Undetermined
1) Satan final deception, rebellion, and judgment. (Revelation 20:7-10)
2) The judgment of the unsaved of all ages — The Great White Throne. (Revelation 20:11-15)
3) 2nd Renovation of Heaven and Earth. (Revelation 21:1)

Chapter 21

In the previous chapter, we saw the ultimate judgment and fate of the unbeliever. In contrast, chapter 21 gives us an amazing glimpse of eternity for the believer in Christ beginning with a new heaven, a new earth, a New Jerusalem, and a new age. No two chapters of New Testament Scripture provide a more profound side-by-side contrast of the eternal destiny for the lost and the saved. With the exception of the first few verses, this chapter primarily reveals the wondrous details of the Holy City, the New Jerusalem – the eternal home of the church, the bride of the Lamb, Jesus Christ.

21:1: "Then I saw" is repeated here again by John. This would indicate that the events of this chapter follow in sequence those of the previous chapter. It also serves to remind us that John is the first-hand witness to all the revelation including these final scenes that usher in eternity.

In this opening verse, we find the third and final destruction and renewal of the heaven and the earth as described in Scripture. In chapter 20 (v.7 – 10), we discussed the last insurrection and final defeat of Satan, resulting again in the heavens and the earth being polluted by his rebellion. Therefore, God will again destroy and renew the earth because it had once again become cursed by Satan's evil. God will include the atmospheric heaven to guarantee that all traces of evil have been cleansed completely and permanently. Finally, the words of our Lord, "Heaven and earth will pass away, but my words will never pass away," (Matthew 24:35) will be fulfilled with this prophecy.

Because it is God's plan for the faithful Jewish and Gentile nations to inhabit the earth forever in fulfillment of His promises, He will create a new heaven and a new earth, better than anything this world has ever known – including the Garden of Eden. Many changes will be made as we see again in this opening verse: "There was no longer any sea." The absence of oceans will naturally change earth's climate and atmosphere as we know it. In addition, without the sea, the population on earth can multiply itself many times over because of the increase in land surface. More importantly, this reference may also imply unhindered movement around the globe among brethren in Christ, including travel to and from the earthly Jerusalem to worship and commune with Christ.

21:2: The "Holy City, the New Jerusalem," is the eternal home of the church, the bride of Christ, prepared by our Lord as He promised His disciples: "I am going there to prepare a place for you. And if I go and prepare a place for you, I will come back and take you to be with me that you also may be where I am" (John 14:2 – 3). This New Jerusalem should not be identified with the old Jerusalem, which is the earthly Jerusalem. The New Jerusalem reveals God's ultimate purpose for the church which, according to the writer of Hebrews, is "in bringing many sons unto glory," (Hebrews 2:10 KJV). I cannot think of a more beautiful description than what John gives us here: "Prepared as a bride beautifully dressed for her husband." The marriage took place in heaven before the Millennium, and the Millennium was a long honeymoon. The marriage relationship is the most beautiful, delightful, and intimate of all the relationships instituted by God, and it is the oldest ceremony established for mankind. We are going to celebrate throughout eternity that we are with Christ and that we have been joined in a wonderful marriage relationship to our Lord and Savior.

A New Age

21:3 – 4: The "loud voice from the throne," as with each time before is the voice of our Lord Jesus Christ. The apostle wrote: "The Word became flesh and made his dwelling among us" (John 1:14). That flesh was crucified on a cross, and He was raised with a glorified body and ascended into heaven to sit at the right hand of God the Father. We, who have put our faith and trust in Jesus Christ, will also be given glorified bodies. We will abide with the Father and the Son, for They will no longer dwell in the "third heaven," some far off place in space or another dimension where we cannot see them. As we will see in the next chapter, their thrones will be in the New Jerusalem.

"He will wipe every tear from their eyes." The wiping away of all tears means the normal reaction to present life, sadness and loneliness, will be eliminated. This would also suggest that God in His great mercy will erase all memory of the unsaved from the minds of His children (Psalm 34:16). "There will be no more death or mourning or crying or pain." Since sin produces all of these, a sinless eternity will not allow these miseries. Just imagine – no more cemeteries, hospitals, clinics, or nursing homes – for the Lord tells us, "the old order of things has passed away."

21:5: "He who was seated on the throne said, 'I am making everything new!'" In this life, none of us have been completely satisfied with ourselves. We have all experienced frustration and failures. We have all, at times, made bad or unhealthy decisions resulting in negative consequences both in our lives and in the lives of those we love. We see here the glorious prospect of all things made new. We can start over, and there will never be an end to our growth. Recall the words of the Prophet Isaiah: "Of the increase of his government and peace there will be no end" (9:7).

21:6 – 7: "It is done. I am the Alpha and the Omega, the Beginning and the End," identifies the speaker as our Lord Jesus Christ, just as it did back in chapter 1; and it echoes the message from the throne we heard in chapter 16 (v.17) that proclaimed the completion of God's wrath – all these things have now come to pass.

"I will give to drink without cost from the spring of the water of life" fulfills the promises our Lord gave us throughout the gospels. In His sermon on the mount, our Lord said, "Blessed are those who hunger and thirst for righteousness, for they will be filled" (Matthew 5:6). The Lord proclaimed to the people of His day: "If anyone is thirsty, let him come to me and drink. Whoever believes in me, as the Scripture has said, streams of living water will flow from within him" (John 7:37 – 38). To the woman at the well, Jesus explained, "Whoever drinks the water I give him will never thirst. Indeed the water I give him will become in him a spring of water welling up to eternal life" (John 4:14). We will all thirst after God and the things of God, and we will be satisfied.

"He who overcomes" simply means all believers are overcomers (of the world) because of our faith. We will "inherit all this," because it was promised to God's children. The Apostle Paul likewise wrote: "The Spirit himself testifies with our spirit that we are God's children. Now if we are children, then we are heirs – heirs of God and co-heirs with Christ, if indeed we share in his sufferings in order that we may also share in his glory" (Romans 8:16 – 17). The phrase, "He will be my son" describes a special relationship God has with His children, and one that is incomprehensible to most of us today. In John's first epistle, the apostle wrote: "Dear friends, now we are children of God, and what we will be has not yet been made known. But we know that when he appears, we shall be like him, for we shall see him as he is" (1 John 3:2).

21:8: Verses 7 and 8 together confirm the consistent message throughout Scripture that God sees only two kinds of people, believers (righteous) and unbelievers (godless). Either they are overcomers who have their part with God eternally or unbelievers who have their part in the "fiery lake of burning sulfur." Notice the creation of the new heaven and earth did not affect the status of the lake of fire and those in it. The lake of fire, the "second death," also goes into eternity; and it represents absolute and eternal separation from God. I cannot think of anything more fearful or frightening.

The New Jerusalem

21:9 – 10: The magnificent glory of the New Jerusalem "coming down out of heaven from God" is beyond all comprehension. It is pictured beautifully in the remainder of this chapter, and the next, as the ultimate preparation of God for His children. Inviting John to a high mountain, the angel shows him the "bride, the wife of the Lamb," described as "the Holy City, Jerusalem." The New Jerusalem that John sees is the eternal home of the church, the bride of Christ. The Holy Spirit is going to describe to John that very city our Lord promised His disciples when He told them, "I go to prepare a place for you" (John 14:2). The earthly Jerusalem does not pass away, but it takes second place in eternity. The late commentator J. Vernon McGee stated, "Righteousness *reigns* in Jerusalem; it will *dwell* in the New Jerusalem."

The redeemed have previously received glorified bodies like Christ. The wedding of the Lamb took place in heaven before the Millennium, and the Millennium is over. Our Lord now tells us: "I am making everything new!" (v.5). A new universe suggests new methods and approaches to life. New laws will regulate God's new universe. Let's look at the possibilities as we also include elements from chapter 22.

There will be a total absence of the curse of sin, temptation, and testing of man's heart in the new creation. This alone makes a radical difference. We have already seen (v.4) that, "He will wipe every tear from their eyes. There will be no more death or mourning or crying or pain, for the old order of things has passed away."

Way back in chapter 3 (v.12), and in verses 2 and 10 here, John describes the New Jerusalem as "coming down out of heaven from God." Although it is stated three times that the city comes down out of heaven, there is no suggestion that it comes down to earth. These passages of Scripture leave the city hanging in midair. The logical conclusion is the New Jerusalem will become the new center of God's universe, and the New Earth and all other activity will revolve around it. In chapter 22 (v.3) we read: "The throne of God and of the Lamb will be in the city, and his servants will serve him."

God will be there, it will be His dwelling, and His universe is God-centered. The New Jerusalem is therefore worthy to merit such an important position for eternity.

21:11: The New Jerusalem "shone with the glory of God." The word *shone* speaks of light. Skipping to verse 23, we read the following: "The city does not need the sun or the moon to shine on it, for the glory of God gives it light, and the Lamb is its lamp." In chapter 22 (v.5) John tells us: "They will not need the light of a lamp or the light of the sun, for the Lord God will give them light." The Bible teaches us that "God is light; in him there is no darkness at all" (1 John 1:5). Therefore, the sun and moon will no longer be needed in the eternal order. In that city which Christ has prepared for His bride there will be no created light, simply because Christ Himself, who is "the light of the world" (John 8:12), will be there. You see God wants us to know that the Holy City is a light giver. It does not reflect light as does the moon, nor does it generate light like the sun. It originates light and is the source of light. God will provide sufficient light for His new universe by His very presence.

If the New Jerusalem is indeed the new center of God's universe, then the law of gravity, as we know it, will be radically altered. There will likely be travel between the New Jerusalem and the New Earth. Imagine if you may, just as Jesus walked with His disciples after His resurrection in His glorified body and then ascended into heaven, so too will the bride of Christ (residing in the New Jerusalem) in their glorified bodies along with the children of God's eternal order (residing on the New Earth) in their glorified bodies travel back and forth between the New Jerusalem and the New Earth. When confronted by the Sadducees regarding the resurrection, our Lord replied: "When the dead rise, they will neither marry nor be given in marriage: they will be like the angels in heaven" (Mark 12:25).

In verses 24 – 26, John writes: "The nations will walk by its light, and the kings of the earth will bring their splendor into it. On no day will its gate ever be shut, for there will be no night there. The glory and honor of the nations will be brought into it." Not only will Israel come up to worship, but all the Gentile nations and kings of the earth as well. I believe those of us who make up the church, the bride of Christ, will be the priests at that time. The Apostle Peter tells us that we are "a priesthood" of believers – he says, "you also, like living stones, are being built into a spiritual house to be a holy priesthood" (1 Peter 2:5). Moreover, there will be "no night." Night would imply darkness, and we know, according to John's first epistle: "God is light; in him there is no darkness at all (1 John 1:5). Apparently, with new glorified bodies, we will have no need of rest. I cannot wait for that!

To emphasize the glory of God, the New Jerusalem is pictured as a "precious jewel, like jasper, clear as crystal." This stone transparent and gleaming, in comparison here, is most likely the diamond. We are further told (v.21): "The great street of the city was of pure gold." Notice the analogy; the New Jerusalem is a diamond in a gold setting – the wedding ring, which symbolizes the wedding of the church to Christ.

21:12 – 13: The gates of the Holy City:

The Holy City, the New Jerusalem had "twelve gates," and on the gates were "written the names of the twelve tribes of Israel," and there were "three gates" on each side. This immediately suggests the order in which the children of Israel camped around the tabernacle in the wilderness described in the Old Testament Book of Numbers (2:1 – 31). The tribe of Levi was the priesthood and served in the tabernacle. The New Jerusalem, in a sense, is representative of a temple or tabernacle since God is there dwelling with man. The bride of Christ, like the Levites of the Old Testament, makes up the priesthood who serve Him. The New Jerusalem will be a tabernacle to Israel and to all the nations of the New Earth.

The nation of Israel on earth, along with the other nations of the world, will come into this city to worship throughout eternity. They will not dwell in the city anymore than they dwelt in the tabernacle of old. The bride of Christ now occupies the closest place to God in eternity.

There are "twelve angels," one at each gate, representing the relationship and role of angels even in the eternal order.

21:14: The foundations of the Holy City:

The city is built on "twelve foundations, and on them were the names of the twelve apostles of the Lamb." According to the Apostle Paul, who many consider the twelfth apostle, the church is "built on the foundation of the apostles and prophets, with Christ Jesus himself, as the chief cornerstone" (Ephesians 2:20). To these apostles were committed all the writings of the church. These men preached the first sermons, organized the first churches, and were among the first martyrs. The Lord Jesus Christ is the chief cornerstone, and His church is built upon the foundations the apostles laid.

21:15 – 16: The size and shape of the Holy City:

The size of the New Jerusalem is tremendous: 1,380 miles (12,000 stadia) by 1,380 miles by 1,380 miles. The Lord Jesus Christ, Carpenter of Nazareth, is the One who built this city. When you consider all His hands have made – beautiful mountain ranges, lush forests, enormous oceans, and vast galaxies – there is no wonder this city also bears the trademark of its Maker. Biblical scholars do not agree as to whether this will be a cube, pyramid, or sphere-shaped city. Based on our discussion thus far, and suggesting that the New Jerusalem will be the new center of God's universe, I lean toward the latter, that of a sphere. Our Lord originally created the law of gravity to hold us onto the earth; otherwise we would fly out into space. We walk on the outside of the earth, but I agree with those who suggest we will walk on the inside of the New Jerusalem. Its great size will afford sufficient space for inhabitation of the saints of all ages. If you were to enclose a cube measuring 1,380 miles on each side into a "clear as crystal" sphere, you would come up with the diameter of the New Jerusalem to be about 2,390 miles, somewhat larger than our moon, which is about 2,160 miles in comparison.

21:17 – 18: The wall of the Holy City:

Throughout history, the wall of a city was for protection. A walled city ensured safety and peace. The name Jerusalem originally came from the Hebrew *Shalem*, meaning "city of peace." The wall of the New Jerusalem symbolizes absolute and eternal peace. However, despite its great thickness of "144 cubits" (216 feet), it is beauty, not protection that is the intention of its design. The "wall was made of jasper" which we suggested earlier may be the diamond, along with the "city of pure gold" as a setting, is a beautiful symbol of a wedding ring – the gift that Christ bestows to His bride, the church.

21:19 – 20: The stones in the foundation of the Holy City:

The twelve foundations of the city not only have the names of the twelve apostles but were also "decorated with every kind of precious stone." These stones express in human terms the magnificence of the New Jerusalem. These stones, with their varied hues and tints, form a beautiful array of rainbow colors. Let us look at each:

1) Jasper: It is commonly defined as an opaque variety of quartz, but here it is clear, and as mentioned before is more likely the diamond. It is crystal clear, a reflector of light and color.
2) Sapphire: Its color is blue. This stone occurs in Exodus (24:10) as the "pavement under the feet of God" and "clear as the sky itself" (paraphrased).
3) Chalcedony: Its color is greenish, possibly the green silicate of copper from the mines of Chalcedon in Asia Minor.
4) Emerald: Its color is green, brilliant, and transparent.
5) Sardonyx: Its color is red, white with parallel layers of red.
6) Carnelian: Its color is fiery red. It is one of the gems found most frequently in Palestinian excavations.
7) Chrysolite: Its color is golden yellow. It was valued for its hardness and transparency.
8) Beryl: Its color is green, closer to aquamarine or sea green.
9) Topaz: Its color is greenish yellow. These were said to have come from the islands of the Red Sea.
10) Chrysoprase: Its color is golden green, a "green apple" variety occurring in slabs large enough to make counter tops.
11) Jacinth: Its color is violet, the color of the hyacinth.
12) Amethyst: Its color is purple, a clear purple variety of quartz crystal. Although abundantly found in Egypt, the finest amethyst came from India and Ceylon.

The foundations of the New Jerusalem are constructed of the flashing brilliance of rich and costly gems. It will be a most breathtaking sight. The New Jerusalem is a city of light and a city of color. God is light, and He is there. The light shining from within through the jasper stone, acting like a prism, will produce every color of the rainbow, and probably even some you and I cannot even begin to imagine. A rainbow, as we know it, will likely seem faint in comparison to the beauty emanating from our future heavenly home.

21:21: The city gates and the street of gold of the Holy City:

"The twelve gates were twelve pearls." Pearls have always been prized for their beauty, rarity, warmth of color and symmetry. This reminds us of the parable of the pearl found in Matthew (13:45 – 46). In this parable, the merchant who bought the pearl was the Lord Jesus Christ, and the pearl is His bride. The Lord paid a great price to buy this pearl. We are told here that each gate will be made of a single pearl, obviously large enough for people to pass through. We are later told (v.25) that, "on no day will its gate ever be shut." They will stand open for eternity, as a beautiful reminder to God's children on earth to come and worship and enjoy complete and uninterrupted access to the throne of God the Father and the Son.

In addition, John says the street of the city will be "pure gold, like transparent glass." We were told earlier that the Holy City was "clear as crystal" (v.11) and made of "pure gold, as pure as glass." All of these descriptions imply transparency throughout. This is why I believe what we are looking at is the inside of a globe. The fact the street is transparent gold means that light will shine out. Not even the street will hinder the light.

21:22 – 23: "I did not see a temple in the city, because the Lord God Almighty and the Lamb are its temple." From the very beginning of creation, God has chosen to fellowship with man. However, once sin entered into the old creation, God withdrew His presence. Thereafter He used His created lights – the sun, moon, and stars – to illuminate His universe. Today, in a spiritual sense, the Lord Jesus Christ is "the light of the world" (John 8:12). In His new creation, the "Lord God Almighty and the Lamb" will be both physical and spiritual lights, for here we are told, "The glory of God gives it light, and the Lamb is its lamp." In the earthly tabernacle the golden lampstand was symbolic of Christ, but in the New Jerusalem Christ is the golden lampstand. Though the city may be thought of as a temple, the actual presence of God with the redeemed eliminates the need for a temple. The nations of the New Earth, including Israel, will come to the New Jerusalem as did the high priest of the Old Testament entering the Holy of Holies, to worship in the very presence of God Himself. The New Jerusalem will be independent of the sun and moon for light and life, for the One who is light will be there and His glory will be unhindered. It is more likely the sun and moon will be dependent on the New Jerusalem for its power to transmit light.

21:24 – 26: "The nations will walk by its light" does not mean that the nations will live there, but that the New Jerusalem will give light unto the earth. "The kings of the earth will bring their splendor into it," as I mentioned earlier, is one reason I believe there will be travel between the New Jerusalem and the New Earth. All nations of the earth will travel back and forth to worship God the Father and the Son.

All who dwell in the New Jerusalem and on the New Earth are not only redeemed from sin but have also lost all allure to it. They come through the gates that are never closed. In John's day, just as in ours, a walled city or fenced in property has gates for the purpose of protection and keeping an intruder out. However, there is no longer an enemy outside; and so the procession through these gates will be continuous. Lastly, there will "be no night." God is the source of all light, and as mentioned earlier, "in him there is no darkness." God's children will no longer have need for rest in His eternal order.

21:27: The Scriptures do not tell us the location of the lake of fire, only that those committed there will be "tormented day and night for ever and ever" as we discussed back in chapter 20. One thing is for certain; it is somewhere outside the gates of the New Jerusalem. There will yet remain a great gulf between the saved and the unsaved. Here we see God's last reiteration to all people who are "shameful or deceitful"; those who reject His Son will not be admitted into His city. We have already confirmed that "their place will be in the fiery lake of burning sulfur" (v.8).

The greatest joy imaginable in the hearts of the redeemed will be that of abiding in the presence of our Lord and Savior Jesus Christ for eternity. "That you also may be where I am," is what our Lord told His disciples (John 14:3). Heaven is to be with Christ. Revelation is all about Jesus Christ – He is the centerpiece of God's universe.

> With the wondrous glories presented here that God has in store for His children in His new creation, every individual should be inspired to receive Jesus Christ as Lord and Savior and thus have their names recorded in the Lamb's book of life.

Review Questions

1) Why does God destroy and renew the heaven and earth? _____
   _____.

2) The Holy City, the New Jerusalem, is the eternal home of _____
   _____.

3) "The Alpha and the Omega, the Beginning and the End," identifies the speaker as _____
   _____.

4) The New Jerusalem becomes the new _____.

5) The twelve gates of the Holy City were twelve pearls, and written on them were _____
   _____.

6) The Holy City was built on twelve foundations, decorated with every kind of precious stone, and
   on the foundations were written _____.

7) With its walls of clear crystal (diamond), and the city and street of pure gold, the New Jerusalem
   is a beautiful symbol of a _____, the gift that Christ bestows to His bride, the church.

Up For Discussion

"And I heard a great voice out of heaven saying, Behold, the tabernacle of God is with men,
and he will dwell with them, and they shall be his people, and God
himself shall be with them, and be their God."
(Revelation 21:3 KJV)

View the illustration: "The New Jerusalem." As mentioned, the New Jerusalem is a city of light and of color. Take a moment and imagine the sight, as the redeemed of the New Earth look up at the New Jerusalem. With the light of the glory of God within shining through the crystal stones, acting like a prism, the appearance will be eternally breathtaking! What are your thoughts and feelings?

Consider for a moment that among the foundations of the New Jerusalem, the Apostle John saw his own name. Keep in mind John survived his stay on the Isle of Patmos. Writings of the early church fathers indicate that he returned to Ephesus after his exile. Now try to imagine how the remainder of John's life and ministry was impacted by all he saw in the Revelation. As he recalled over and over again in his memory the vision of that wall and its foundations – can you imagine how he was both overcome and humbled that God honored him so?

In further discussion, review the illustration entitled, "Millennium to Eternity." Do the illustrations help reinforce your overall understanding of the message?

The New Jerusalem

1,380 miles

Diameter: 2,390 miles

1,380 miles

Circumference: 7,505 miles

Our Lord Jesus Christ is its Creator

"For by Him all things were created ..." (Col. 1:16).

"In my Father's house are many rooms; if it were not so, I would have told you. I am going there to prepare a place for you. And if I go and prepare a place for you, I will come back and take you to be with me that you also may be where I am" (John 14:2-3).

The diameter is about 2,390 miles, somewhat larger than our moon, which is about 2,160 miles.

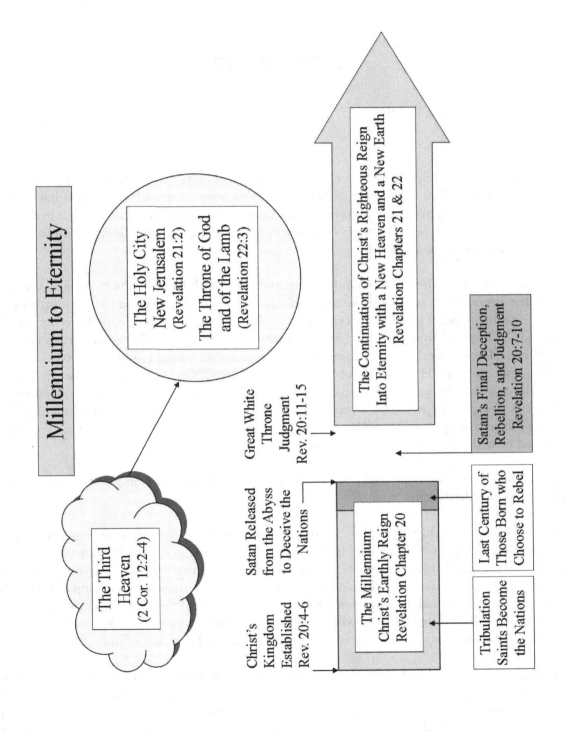

Millennium to Eternity

The Third Heaven
(2 Cor. 12:2-4)

The Holy City
New Jerusalem
(Revelation 21:2)

The Throne of God
and of the Lamb
(Revelation 22:3)

Christ's Kingdom Established Rev. 20:4-6

Satan Released from the Abyss to Deceive the Nations

Great White Throne Judgment Rev. 20:11-15

The Continuation of Christ's Righteous Reign Into Eternity with a New Heaven and a New Earth Revelation Chapters 21 & 22

Satan's Final Deception, Rebellion, and Judgment Revelation 20:7-10

The Millennium Christ's Earthly Reign Revelation Chapter 20

Last Century of Those Born who Choose to Rebel

Tribulation Saints Become the Nations

Chapter 22

This chapter not only brings us to the end of the greatest of all books on prophecy but also to the end of the Word of God. God gives us His final words here; therefore, these words have greater significance. In this life many questions remain unanswered and problems unsolved; but in this final chapter of God's Word, mankind enters eternity in fellowship again with God, and all things will be revealed and made "new" (21:5).

Our Holy Scriptures – the Word of God – opens and closes with basically the same type of setting. In the first two chapters of Genesis we see God's description of creation and the paradise on earth prepared for mankind. These last two chapters of John's Revelation describe the heavenly paradise that God will re-establish for His children, those who, through the ages, have placed their faith and trust in Him. Remember that God is sovereign; He has brought mankind through the ages according to His master plan, and He has always been in absolute control. God paid a great price. He sent His Son to die on a cross because He loves us so much. The victory and the glory belong to God and He is satisfied. The prophet wrote these touching words so many years ago: "After the suffering of his soul, he will see the light of life and be satisfied; by his knowledge my righteous servant will justify many and he will bear their iniquities" (Isaiah 53:11).

The opening five verses give us additional details of our eternal heavenly home that we have come to know as the New Jerusalem.

22:1 – 2a: "The river of the water of life" is a description reminiscent of the river of "water coming out from under the threshold of the temple" in the Prophet Ezekiel's vision (ch.47). We cannot live without water in this life; likewise, in our eternal life, we will apparently thirst as well. However, our thirst for this water will not necessarily be life-sustaining, but rather life-nourishing. As a living fountain, this endless supply will proceed directly from the "throne of God and of the Lamb," indicating that God the Father and His Son Jesus Christ will be the source of this sweet and wholesome water. Notice again that the description of the water is "as clear as crystal" – the essence of purity.

22:2b – 2c: "The tree of life, bearing twelve crops of fruit yielding its fruit every month." Way back in Genesis (3:22), the writer tells us that after Adam and Eve had sinned, God forbid Adam to "reach out his hand and take also from the tree of life and eat, and live forever." Here at last, eternity reveals that man will finally be allowed to eat of the tree of life, thus testifying to our blessed future state. In the New Jerusalem, these trees on "each side of the river" will continually bring forth "crops of fruit" each month; therefore, we will be able to eat and drink without fear or consequence in our new heavenly home.

"The leaves of the tree are for the healing of the nations." This phrase does not indicate that anyone will be sick. Instead, the nations which have fought throughout their known history will be healed in their relationships and live in perfect harmony for eternity. The Prophet Ezekiel had a similar description in his vision of the river flowing from the throne of the millennial temple (mentioned above); he wrote: "Fruit trees of all kinds will grow on both banks of the river. Their leaves will not wither, nor will their fruit fail. Every month they will bear, because the water from the sanctuary flows to them. Their fruit will serve for food and their leaves for healing" (Ezekiel 47:12). In a spiritual sense, the tree of life could symbolically represent the New Earth and the leaves symbolic of the nations of the earth. The tree with its leaves is nourished by the water of the river from God – God dwelling with man. Therefore, the tree and its leaves (the New Earth and its nations) remain together as one in perfect unity for eternity, never again to fall away and perish from the face of the earth.

22:3: The phrase, "No longer will there be any curse" means that God's new creation will never be marred by sin. Man's unlimited potential will be realized for the first time. Temptation and sin will be removed forever. The very presence of God and the Lamb will be adequate to prevent it. God will again commune with man just as He did with Adam and Eve before the fall.

"The throne of God and of the Lamb" is in the New Jerusalem. In my research, I have found that some biblical commentators note the absence of any reference to the Holy Spirit in the New Jerusalem and eternity. These scholars agree that in the first creation the Holy Spirit came to renew and renovate the earth (Genesis 1:2) and that today the Holy Spirit acts to renew the hearts and lives of sinners. However, in the new creation when God will again dwell with men, these same scholars suggest that there will be no need for the work of the Holy Spirit and that the silence of Scripture at this point is appropriate. I agree with their assessment regarding the work of the Holy Spirit in past ages, as well as today; however, I disagree with their suggestion that the Holy Spirit does not continue into eternity. My conviction rests in my faith in the Trinity. I am convinced that the Holy Spirit will continue as always to dwell in the hearts of God's children even into eternity. The Spirit is the cement that bonds us into a perfect and intimate relationship with the Father and with the Son. For that reason, the Trinity, including the Holy Spirit, always was, remains today, and will continue on into eternity as we have always known it – God in three Persons.

"His servants will serve him" simply means the New Jerusalem and the New Earth will not be a place of unoccupied idleness but a place of ceaseless activity. We will all perform some service to God throughout eternity, including governmental and priestly duties (20:4 – 6 and 21:24 – 26). Furthermore, we read earlier (21:25) that there will be "no night"; and as such, presumably there will be no need for rest. Mankind will at last achieve its full God-given potential on the New Earth.

22:4: "They will see his face" is the most wonderful, the most glorious statement of this final chapter of Scripture. We know, according to Scripture, that no man has ever seen God (Exodus 33:20; John 1:18); however, in the New Jerusalem man will at last see His face. This was the ultimate desire expressed by Moses and David in the Old Testament and Philip in the New Testament. It is our highest objective for living. We will know the Lord God to the fullest extent possible, for the Apostle Paul wrote: "Now we see but a poor reflection as in a mirror; then we shall see face to face" (1 Corinthians 13:12). The fact that "his name will be on their foreheads" illustrates again that all believers are the blood-bought children of God and stands in stark contrast to the mark of the beast that will identify those who chose to worship Antichrist in rebellion to God. This fulfills the promise our Lord Jesus made to the church earlier in chapter 3 (v.12).

22:5: "There will be no more night. They will not need the light … for the Lord God will give them light." As we discussed in chapter 21 (v.11 and 23) and is repeated here, God the Father and the Son – who are light – will illuminate eternity from the New Jerusalem by their very presence. "And they will reign for ever and ever." Just as we will rule alongside Christ during the Millennium, so too will we reign along with Him for eternity.

22:6: The angel is sent by our Lord Jesus Christ to tell the Apostle John that "these words are trustworthy and true." This means the Lord is putting His seal of approval upon this book. Our Lord's endorsement is final, and thus man is not to spiritualize or reduce it to meaningless symbols. Our Lord Jesus Christ is talking about realities yet to come.

22:7: "Behold, I am coming soon" is an expression we find three times in these final verses of John's Revelation. The Lord is not saying this to refer to some appointed time soon to come. Instead, His "coming soon" refers to the time period described in this book; and at that time, the events of the Revelation all take place in a short period of not more than seven years. The reference here is the end of the Tribulation Period, and the encouragement here is the Lord saying it will not be a long period. In fact, our Lord tells us: "If those days had not been cut short, no one would survive, but for the sake of the elect, those days will be shortened" (Matthew 24:22).

"Blessed is he who keeps the words of the prophecy in this book." The Lord Jesus repeats the blessing we read in the beginning of this book (1:3). The Book of Revelation is not only meant to be read but also to be acted upon. What does the study of John's Revelation motivate you to do? Is it to be a better witness, to spend more time studying Scripture, or to become a teacher of God's Word? Dr. Charles Stanley describes the work of the church (all believers) today as evangelism and states: "You cannot invest your life in anything better than sharing and bringing the Gospel of Jesus Christ to someone who does not know." Subsequently, our first and greatest responsibility is to offer the message of grace – that God loves everyone and is willing to save them through faith in His Son Jesus Christ, and our efforts should begin at home with those closest and dearest to us.

22:8 – 9: Here is John's final and often repeated statement that he "heard and saw these things." He is the firsthand witness to all the scenes and visions of the Revelation. Moreover, John again bows before the angel; and as before, he is forbidden to do so, for the consistent message in the Word of God is that we worship God only. Satan's primary objective is to entice us to bow to anything or anyone other than God; but just as before (19:10), the angel commands John: "Do not do it!" It is interesting to note here the humility of this angel. Though angels were created above man (Psalm 8:5), this angel identifies himself as a fellow servant with John and the other prophets. He is merely a messenger. The Lord Jesus Christ is the centerpiece of the Book of Revelation.

22:10 – 11: "Do not seal up the words of the prophecy of this book, because the time is near." Daniel was told to seal up the words of his prophecy because of the long interval of time before its fulfillment. The prophet wrote: "But you, Daniel close up and seal the words of the scroll until the time of the end. Many will go here and there to increase knowledge" (Daniel 12:4). In contrast, John lived on after the time of Christ's resurrection and ascension, the era which began the age of grace – the church age. The prophecy given to John was even then in the process of being fulfilled; and for almost two thousand years, the church has been evolving through the time periods of the seven churches as discussed in chapters 2 and 3.

"Let him who does wrong continue to do wrong; let him who is vile continue to be vile" refers to the sinful condition of the lost. It is permanent and eternal, and this verse suggests that the condition of the lost gets progressively worse. On the other hand, the righteous continues to grow in their righteousness and holiness. What a wonderful prospect for the children of God to know they have all eternity to grow in knowledge.

22:12 – 16: "Behold, I am coming soon! My reward is with me, and I will give to everyone according to what he has done." Our Lord personally promises that He is coming again, and no believer can doubt or deny His promise. He will personally reward each believer individually. Those who make up the church will be rewarded after the rapture, at the judgment seat of Christ (2 Corinthians 5:10). Those who receive Jesus Christ as Lord and Savior during the Tribulation Period, including the remnant of the nation of Israel and those of the Gentile nations, will receive their reward at the time of Christ's return to establish His earthly kingdom just prior to the Millennium (Matthew 25:31 – 46). No wonder Paul could write so passionately about the resurrection (read on your own or as a class: Philippians 3:10 – 14). On the basis of His "reward," all believers will reign alongside Christ for eternity.

Here at the conclusion, just as in the beginning of the Book of Revelation, the Lord Jesus Christ asserts His deity: "I am the Alpha and the Omega, the First and the Last, the Beginning and the End." Only those who have "washed their robes" in the blood (righteousness) of Christ have a "right to the tree of life" and entry into the Holy City. The Apostle Paul wrote concerning the fulfillment of all things brought under Christ (Read Ephesians 1:7 – 10).

In Disney movies, cats are oftentimes portrayed as the bad guys; but in the Scriptures, dogs get the bad rap. Dogs were scavengers in the ancient world and were considered unclean and impure. "Dogs" was also another word for Gentiles (Matthew 15:22 – 28), and Paul used the same word for Judaizers (Philippians 3:2). Here, it simply refers to those who are eternally lost because of their wickedness and rebellion to God and confined to the lake of fire.

"I, Jesus" is the name of our Savior; the name He received when He took on humanity. The "testimony for the churches" is the eternal gospel. Jesus Christ is alive today and is seated in heaven at the right hand of God the Father. He promises that when we accept Him as Lord and Savior, our eternity will be spent with Him and centered on Him.

Jesus is called "the Root and Offspring of David" which connects Him with the Old Testament, but He is the "bright Morning Star" to the church. The bright morning star always appears at the darkest time of the night, and its appearance indicates the sun will be coming up shortly. The Old Testament ends with these words from the prophet: "But unto you that fear my name shall the Sun of righteousness arise with healing in his wings; and ye shall go forth and grow up as calves of the stall" (Malachi 4:2 KJV). This is the Old Testament hope; but to the saints, Jesus Christ is the bright and Morning Star who will come at the very last moment of earth's darkest age to usher in everlasting righteousness and healing to all the nations.

22:17: The "Spirit" is the Holy Spirit that is in the world today convicting and converting the hearts of men. The "bride" is the church. Together they issue a dual invitation – an invitation to Christ to return and an invitation to sinners to come to Christ before He returns. As I mentioned earlier, the mission of the church is to evangelize; we are to sow the seeds of the gospel of the Jesus Christ. The Holy Spirit will water the seeds and do the rest. The words of our Lord tell us: "If anyone is thirsty, let him come to me and drink. Whoever believes in me, as the Scripture has said, streams of living water will flow from within him" (John 7:37 – 38). Jesus Christ is the "water of life," and this invitation goes out still today.

22:18 – 19: Here is one of the most fearful warnings from our Lord against tampering with the Word of God. It is a dreadful thing to disbelieve or worse, to deny God, and it is unbelief that causes someone to twist the Scriptures to fit their own personal agenda. Dr. Charles Stanley has stated many times in his sermons: "The Bible is not a pick and choose book, but a trust and obey book." Although this is not a reference to Bible-believing students of God's Word who mistakenly translate a passage and inadvertently minimize it, it does serve as a soul-stirring challenge to those of us who have taken on the responsibility to write and teach on the Word of God.

22:20 – 21: "Yes, I am coming soon." As mentioned earlier, this refers to the period in time during which the events of the Revelation begin to come to pass.

"Amen. Come, Lord Jesus," is the daily prayer of every true believer.

The Old Testament ends with a curse upon Israel if she does not repent, but the New Testament ends with a benediction of "grace" upon all of "God's people." Grace is offered to all who repent and put their faith in Jesus Christ; it is God's method for saving sinners. This entitles you to entry into the Holy City, the New Jerusalem, access to the living water and the tree of life, and the eternal blessings of a loving God.

The Apostle John lived to be a very old man. Beth Moore, in her book *The Beloved Disciple*, wrote: "His passionate heart continued to beat wildly for the Savior he loved so much … Only disciples who are convinced they are beloved will in turn love beyond themselves." In closing let us read together some of the words obviously written upon this disciple's heart from that last earthly night spent with Jesus:

The words of our Lord Jesus: "My command is this: Love each other as I have loved you. Greater love has no one than this that he lay down his life for his friends. You are my friends if you do what I command. I no longer call you servants, because a servant does not know his master's business. Instead, I have called you friends, for everything that I learned from my Father I have made known to you. You did not choose me, but I chose you and appointed you to go and bear fruit – fruit that will last. Then the Father will give you whatever you ask in my name. This is my command: Love each other" (John 15:12 – 17).

Review Questions

1) The crystal clear river of the waters of life flow from _____.

2) On each bank of the river stood _____.

3) The throne of God and of the Lamb is no longer in heaven, but is now in _____
_____.

4) What two things are mentioned as being absent for eternity? _____
_____.

5) Christ's "coming soon" refers to _____
_____.

6) The angel forbids John from bowing before him because the Word of God tells us to _____
_____.

7) The testimony for the churches is _____.

Up For Discussion

"Blessed is he that keepeth the sayings of the prophecy of this book."
(Revelation 22:7 KJV)

The Lord Jesus repeats the blessing we read back at the beginning in chapter 1. The Book of Revelation is not only meant to be read, but also to be acted upon. What does this study of John's Revelation motivate you to do?

Has it encouraged you to become a better witness in the world?

Has it motivated you to spend more time reading and studying the Scriptures?

Will you volunteer to facilitate a Bible study or even consider becoming a regular teacher of God's Word in your church?

As stated earlier, Dr. Charles Stanley describes the work of the church (all believers) today as evangelism and states: "You cannot invest your life in anything better than sharing and bringing the Gospel of Jesus Christ to someone who does not know." Therefore, our first and greatest responsibility is to offer them the message of grace and that God loves them and is willing to save them.

Amen. Come, Lord Jesus.

CHART OF EVENTS

THE FIRST HALF OF THE TRIBULATION PERIOD

THE SEAL JUDGMENTS – Revelation 6

1) The rider on the white horse: Antichrist and his kingdom.
2) The rider on the red horse: War that follows.
3) The rider on the black horse: Famine that follows war.
4) The rider on the pale horse: Name was "Death" and represents plague and pestilence. Hades follows and 1/4 of the earth's population dies.
5) Vision of the souls under the altar: The Old Testament Saints and the martyred Tribulation Saints awaiting God's final judgment.
6) "The Wrath of the Lamb": Great earthquake, sun turned black, moon turned blood red, and stars (meteorites) fell to earth.
7) Silence in Heaven: This introduces the seven trumpet judgments.

Revelation 7: 144,000 Jewish witnesses are sealed, and the vision of the great multitude standing before the throne of the Lamb.

THE TRUMPET JUDGMENTS – Revelation 8 and 9

1) Hail and fire rained down, and 1/3 of the earth burned up.
2) Something like a huge mountain fell into the sea, and 1/3 of the sea turned to blood, 1/3 of the living creatures died, and 1/3 of the ships are destroyed.
3) A blazing star (meteor) named "Wormwood" fell from the sky and pollutes 1/3 of the earth's water supply.
4) The light from the sun, the moon, and the stars is diminished by 1/3.
5) The "first woe": Demonic locust creatures are released from the Abyss to torment the unsaved for five months.
6) The "second woe": Four evil angels are released along with their demonic army and 1/3 of mankind is killed.
7) Rejoicing in heaven: This brings us to the mid-point of the Tribulation Period and introduces the seven bowl judgments.

Revelation 11: The temple in Jerusalem is rebuilt, and Old Testament worship is reinstated. The two supernatural witnesses prophesy for 1,260 days.

CHART OF EVENTS

MID-POINT OF THE TRIBULATION PERIOD

Revelation 11: The two supernatural witnesses are killed by the beast (Antichrist). After three and a half days they are resurrected and ascend to heaven in a cloud.

Revelation 12: The Woman (nation of Israel) flees into the desert to escape persecution from Antichrist for 1,260 days. God will again care for them as He did during Israel's desert wanderings following the Exodus.

Revelation 12: There is war in heaven, and the dragon (Satan) is hurled to earth. Satan's banishment and confinement to earth during the second half of the Tribulation Period is the "third woe" of the Book of Revelation.

Revelation 13: After the beast (Antichrist) receives a fatal wound, Satan will possess him to produce a counterfeit resurrection. Antichrist becomes Satan incarnate.

Revelation 13 and Daniel 9:27: Antichrist breaks his covenant with Israel, then along with the second beast (the false prophet) desecrates the temple by setting up an image (idol) of the beast (Antichrist). All people are forced to worship the image of the beast and to receive his mark – 666.

Revelation 17 – Destruction of Religious Babylon: A system of false religion that operates during the first half of the Tribulation Period emphasizing idolatry and sexual immorality. Termed "the Great Prostitute," this worldwide religious system will likely be headquartered in present-day Rome and headed up by the second beast, the false prophet. This false church takes over after Christ removes the true church from earth in the rapture. Antichrist will allow this false system of religion to operate during the first half of the Tribulation Period while he gathers power. At the mid-point of the Tribulation Period, Antichrist (along with the ten kings) destroys this false church, sets himself up as world dictator (and God), and relocates his idol worship to the temple in Jerusalem.

CHART OF EVENTS

THE SECOND HALF OF THE TRIBULATION PERIOD

THE BOWL JUDGMENTS – Revelation 16

1) Ugly and painful sores brake out on the people who worship the beast and take his mark. This parallels the 6th plague of Egypt in Exodus.
2) The remainder of the sea turns to blood, and every living thing in it dies.
3) The rivers and springs (the only remaining sources of water) turn to blood. The 2nd and 3rd bowl judgments parallel the 1st plague of Egypt where the Nile River was turned to blood. The passage does not state such; however, this means more human death on an even greater scale because people simply cannot live without water!
4) The sun scorches people with fire. They refuse to repent and glorify God.

Remember, there is no water to quench them.

5) The kingdom and headquarters of the beast is plunged into darkness. This is similar to the darkness of Egypt during the 9th plague. The people still refuse to repent.
6) The Euphrates River is dried up to make way for the kings of the East, and the three evil (deceiving) demonic spirits that looked like frogs. These verses refer to the oriental nations of the world, and Satan's ability to deceive them into uniting with him in his upcoming battle against Christ.
7) A horrendous earthquake shakes the whole earth, and 100-pound hailstones fall upon men.

Revelation 18: "Babylon the Great" is destroyed. The governmental and commercial headquarters and kingdom of Antichrist (most likely the rebuilt city of Babylon in present-day Iraq) is destroyed in one day as a result of the seventh bowl judgment from God.

Revelation 19: The Revelation and glorious appearing of our Lord Jesus Christ as King of Kings and Lord of Lords, and the battle on the great day of God Almighty (Armageddon). Our Lord Jesus Christ returns to earth and defeats the armies of Antichrist, and all who stand in opposition to Him with the sharp sword from out of His mouth – His spoken Word.

The beast (Antichrist) and his false prophet are thrown into the lake of fire.

CHART OF EVENTS

THE MILLENNIAL KINGDOM

THE WEDDING SUPPER OF THE LAMB – Revelation 19:9

This is God's answer to the prayer He taught us: "Thy kingdom come. Thy will be done in earth, as it is in heaven," (Matthew 6:10 KJV).

Revelation 20: The Millennium begins with the binding and the imprisoning of Satan into the Abyss where he will no longer be able to deceive mankind. This is God's final testing of man under ideal conditions. The prophet describes the Millennial Kingdom in Isaiah 65:17 – 25, beginning with the creation of "new heavens and a new earth."

The Wedding Supper of the Lamb
Christ's Millennial Kingdom on Earth

Those invited to attend and enter into Christ's earthly kingdom:

1) The martyred Tribulation Saints: Revelation 20:4b – 6.
2) The Old Testament Saints: Daniel 12:1 – 2, Psalm 50:1 – 5.
3) The redeemed remnant of Israel: Jeremiah 23:3, Romans 11:5.
4) The surviving Tribulation Saints (Gentile nations): Matthew 25:31 – 46.

The Millennium ends with the release of Satan, his last deception of mankind and rebellion against God, and his final defeat by being thrown into the lake of burning sulfur along with Antichrist and the false prophet.

The Great White Throne: The final judgment of the unsaved of all ages. They will be resurrected to stand before Christ in judgment for their works. However, we are not saved by our works, but through faith in Jesus Christ as Savior; consequently, their names are not found in the Lamb's book of life, and they are also thrown into the lake of fire.

ETERNITY

Eternity begins with a new heaven and a new earth. The throne of God and of the Lamb is in the Holy City, the New Jerusalem. God's dwelling is once again with men.

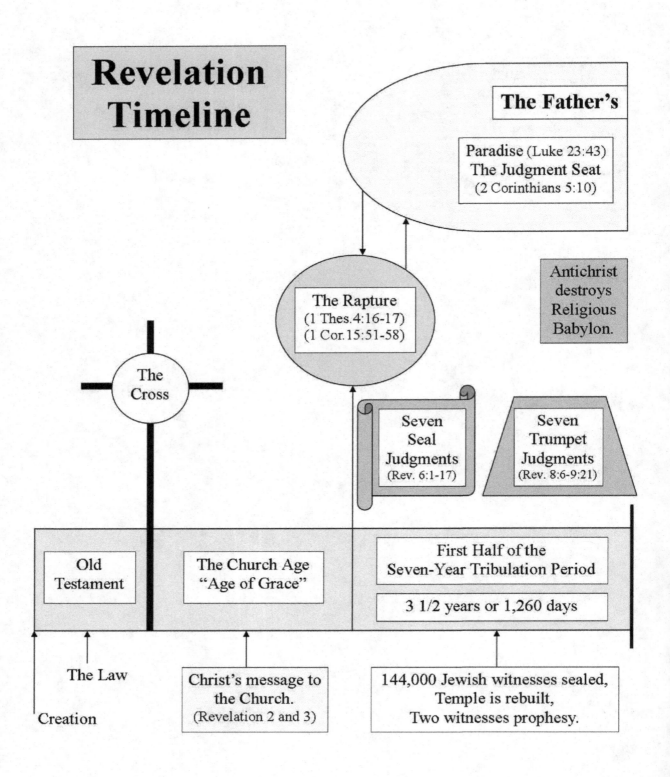

Revelation Timeline

The Father's

Paradise (Luke 23:43)
The Judgment Seat
(2 Corinthians 5:10)

Antichrist
destroys
Religious
Babylon.

The Rapture
(1 Thes.4:16-17)
(1 Cor.15:51-58)

The
Cross

Seven
Seal
Judgments
(Rev. 6:1-17)

Seven
Trumpet
Judgments
(Rev. 8:6-9:21)

First Half of the
Seven-Year Tribulation Period

3 1/2 years or 1,260 days

Old
Testament

The Church Age
"Age of Grace"

The Law

Creation

Christ's message to
the Church.
(Revelation 2 and 3)

144,000 Jewish witnesses sealed,
Temple is rebuilt,
Two witnesses prophesy.

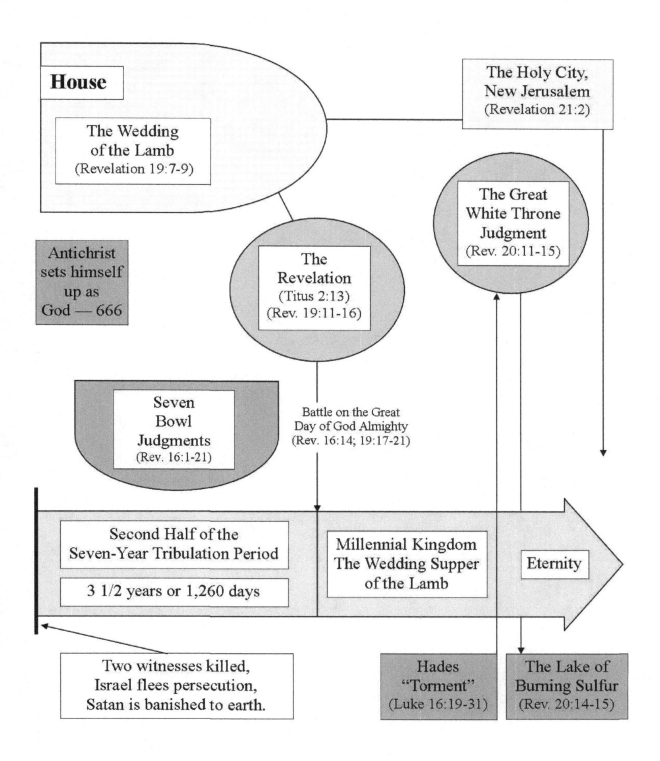

House

The Wedding
of the Lamb
(Revelation 19:7-9)

The Holy City,
New Jerusalem
(Revelation 21:2)

The Great
White Throne
Judgment
(Rev. 20:11-15)

Antichrist
sets himself
up as
God — 666

The
Revelation
(Titus 2:13)
(Rev. 19:11-16)

Seven
Bowl
Judgments
(Rev. 16:1-21)

Battle on the Great
Day of God Almighty
(Rev. 16:14; 19:17-21)

Second Half of the
Seven-Year Tribulation Period

3 1/2 years or 1,260 days

Millennial Kingdom
The Wedding Supper
of the Lamb

Eternity

Two witnesses killed,
Israel flees persecution,
Satan is banished to earth.

Hades
"Torment"
(Luke 16:19-31)

The Lake of
Burning Sulfur
(Rev. 20:14-15)

Answers to Chapter Review Questions

Chapter 1
  1) Appearing; to uncover or unveil.
  2) Perfection or completeness.
  3) The person of Jesus Christ and His return in power and great glory as Judge of all the earth.
  4) The seven churches.
  5) The spiritual leaders or pastors of those seven churches.
  6) He fell at His feet as though dead.
  7) I am the First and the Last, I am the Living One, I am alive for ever and ever, and I hold the keys of death and Hades.

Chapters 2 and 3
  1) The Church is the body of all believers who have put their faith and trust in Jesus Christ as their Lord and Savior. The church is the body of Christ and Jesus is its head.
  2) To worship God, to pray, and to edify fellow believers.
  3) To evangelize the world.
  4) Our Lord Jesus Christ.
  5) The churches at Smyrna and Philadelphia.
  6) The church at Laodicea.
  7) Put their faith, trust, and hope in Jesus Christ.

Chapter 4
  1) The church in heaven with Christ.
  2) The Tribulation Period.
  3) The rapture before the Tribulation Period and the revelation at the end of the Tribulation Period.
  4) Our High Priest, Jesus Christ.
  5) The church in heaven.
  6) Seraphim (angels).
  7) The Lord Jesus Christ on His throne.

Chapter 5
  1) Our Lord Jesus Christ.
  2) Book of Judgement.
  3) A power or authority.
  4) Knowledge and wisdom.

5) The music and praise in heaven.
6) The prayers of the saints.
7) They are power, wealth, wisdom, strength, honor, glory, and blessing.

Chapter 6
1) The seven-year covenant confirmed between Israel and Antichrist.
2) The end-times Antichrist and his kingdom.
3) War.
4) Famine.
5) One-fourth of the world's population dies.
6) The righteousness of Christ through faith.
7) The Wrath of the Lamb.

Chapter 7
1) Tribulation Saints.
2) God's judgment or wrath.
3) Their worship of idols.
4) Protect them from the judgments to come upon the earth.
5) The Holy Spirit.
6) People from all over the world who receive Christ as a result of the ministry of the 144,000 witnesses – Tribulation Saints.
7) The blood of the Lamb.

Chapter 8
1) The Lord Jesus Christ.
2) The prayers of the saints under the altar in heaven.
3) The answer to those prayers in the form of the next set of judgments – the trumpets.
4) It burns up one-third of all the earth's vegetation.
5) It turns one-third of the sea to blood, kills one-third of the living creatures in the sea, and destroys one-third of the ships.
6) The contamination of one-third of the earth's fresh water supply.
7) It diminished the light from the sun, the moon, and the stars by one-third.

Chapter 9
1) A good angel from heaven entrusted with the keys.
2) Hell or Hades; the present abode of all wicked/unsaved spirits.
3) Torment people for five months.
4) Abaddon, or in the Greek, Apollyon.
5) They are evil or fallen angels.
6) Babylon.
7) They killed one-third of mankind.

Chapter 10
1) The Angel of the Lord.
2) The Son of God in all His deity.
3) Service.
4) The voice of God.

5) The salvation of all mankind, Jew and Gentile, through Jesus Christ.
6) Mentally feeding on the Word of God and receiving it with faith.
7) It is sweet to those who hear and accept it, but it is bitter to those who reject it.

Chapter 11
1) The covenant confirmed with Antichrist.
2) The Court of the Gentiles.
3) An individual who brings God's light (truth) to the world.
4) The work of the Holy Spirit through that individual.
5) Prophesying, witnessing, and testifying to the gospel of Jesus Christ.
6) Resurrected and raptured up to heaven in a cloud.
7) Introduces the next set of judgments.

Chapter 12
1) The nation of Israel.
2) The twelve tribes of Israel.
3) The devil – Satan.
4) Christ's rule during the Millennium.
5) To escape persecution from Antichrist.
6) Satan's expulsion from heaven and his confinement to earth during the second half of the Tribulation Period.
7) God will deliver her to safety.

Chapter 13
1) The end-times Antichrist and his kingdom.
2) The nations of the earth.
3) First, one blasphemes by thinking of themselves as equal to God, and secondly, by slandering and taking God's name in vain.
4) Antichrist is one who is against Christ, and Antichrist is one who imitates Christ.
5) Satan enters the dead body of Antichrist resulting in Antichrist becoming the incarnation of Satan.
6) The first beast – Antichrist.
7) Worship Antichrist by demanding everyone to take this mark in order to buy or sell.

Chapter 14
1) The seal of the living God.
2) The eternal gospel of Jesus Christ to all the inhabitants of the earth, and to fear God and give Him glory.
3) Religious Babylon.
4) Worships the beast and receives his mark.
5) The Lord Jesus Christ.
6) Elect or believers – Tribulation Saints.
7) Wicked or unbelievers – those who have rejected Christ and followed Antichrist.

Chapter 15
1) A symbol of revelation.
2) The Word of God.

3) The persecution endured by the saints during the Tribulation Period.
4) God's deliverance, salvation, and faithfulness.
5) Jesus Christ as our Redeemer.
6) God is dealing with the nation of Israel.
7) Complete.

Chapter 16
1) Worshiped the beast and took his mark.
2) The death of all living creatures in the sea.
3) Antichrist had shed the blood of His saints and prophets.
4) The sun scorched people with fire.
5) Antichrist and his kingdom.
6) Euphrates River; our Lord Jesus Christ.
7) A severe earthquake that collapses all the cities around the world, and huge hundred- pound hailstones fell upon men.

Chapter 17
1) Idolatry and immorality.
2) The rapture of the true church.
3) Have never trusted Jesus Christ as Savior.
4) Control the masses as he gains power.
5) At the mid-point of the Tribulation Period.
6) Antichrist and the ten kings, as God purposed.
7) To establish Antichrist as the sole object of worship.

Chapter 18
1) On the rebuilt site of ancient Babylon.
2) To flee before judgment falls.
3) Her pride and arrogance.
4) Revenue and corrupt profits gained through commerce.
5) One day.
6) The seventh bowl judgment.
7) The Great Tribulation.

Chapter 19
1) God's judgments upon the earth.
2) The final and complete union of Jesus Christ and the church.
3) The wedding takes place in heaven and just after the judgment seat of Christ when all believers have been completely cleansed and the church made whole.
4) The wedding supper takes place on earth in Christ's kingdom during His millennial reign.
5) The glorious appearing and second coming of our Lord and Savior Jesus Christ to earth.
6) His Spoken Word.
7) Thrown into the lake of burning sulfur – the eternal hell.

Chapter 20
1) For Satan to be taken out of the world.
2) A final testing of mankind under ideal conditions.

3) Believers throughout all generations.
4) He proceeds to deceive the nations.
5) Being thrown into the lake of burning sulfur.
6) Unbelievers from all ages.
7) Put their faith and trust in Jesus Christ as Lord and Savior.

Chapter 21
1) To completely cleanse them of the pollution caused by Satan and his final rebellion against God.
2) The church – the bride of Christ.
3) Our Lord Jesus Christ.
4) Center of God's universe.
5) The names of the twelve tribes of Israel.
6) The names of the twelve apostles.
7) Wedding ring

Chapter 22
1) The throne of God and of the Lamb.
2) The tree of life.
3) The Holy City of the New Jerusalem.
4) No longer will there be any curse or night.
5) The short period of only seven years after the events of the Revelation begins.
6) Worship God only.
7) The eternal gospel of Jesus Christ.

Bibliography

Barry, Mark. *Map of Ancient Israel and Judah*. Australia: Australian Fellowship of Evangelical Students. 2009.

Jeffrey, Grant R. *Heaven, The Mystery of Angels*. Canada: Harmony Printing Limited, 1996.

LaHaye, Tim. *Revelation Unveiled*. Grand Rapids: Zondervan Publishing House, 1999.

LaHaye, Tim, and Jerry B. Jenkins. *Are We Living in the End Times?* Wheaton: Tyndale House Publishers, Inc. 1999.

LaHaye, Tim. *Prophecy Study Bible*. United States of America: AMG Publishers, 2000.

Lindsey, Hal. *Planet Earth, The Final Chapter*. Beverly Hills: Western Front Ltd, 1998.

McBirnie, Ph.D., William Steuart. *The Search for the Twelve Apostles*. Wheaton: Living Books, Tyndale House Publishers, Inc. 1973.

McFarland, Dan. *Bible Reading Calendar*. Sharpsburg: 2004.

McGee, J. Vernon. *Thru The Bible*. Nashville: Thomas Nelson Publishers, 1983.

Moore, Beth. *The Beloved Disciple*. Nashville: Broadman and Holman Publishers, 2003.

Pfeiffer, Charles F., Vos, Howard F., Rea, John, Editors. *Wycliffe Bible Dictionary*. Peabody, Mass.: Hendrickson Publishers, Inc., 2000.

Radmacher, Earl (General Editor); Allen, Ron (Old Testament Editor); House, H. Wayne (New Testament Editor). *Nelson's Bible Commentary*. Nashville: Thomas Nelson Publisher, 2004.

Stanley, Charles F. *The Revelation*. Atlanta, Georgia: In Touch Ministries, 1994.

Strauss, Lehman. *The Book of Revelation*. Neptune, N.J.: Loizeaux Brothers, 1964.

Strong, James, LL.D., S.T.D. *Strong's Expanded Exhaustive Concordance of the Bible*. Nashville, Tennessee: Thomas Nelson Publishers, 2001.

Swindoll, Charles R. et all. *The Road to Armageddon*. Nashville: Word Publishing, 1999.

The Lost Books of the Bible. The Gospel of Nicodemus. Translated from the original tongues. New York: Gramercy Books, 1979.

Van Impe, Jack. *Revelation Revealed*. Dallas: Word Publishing, 1996.

Printed in the United States
By Bookmasters